IMAGES
of America

LAKE CHAMPLAIN

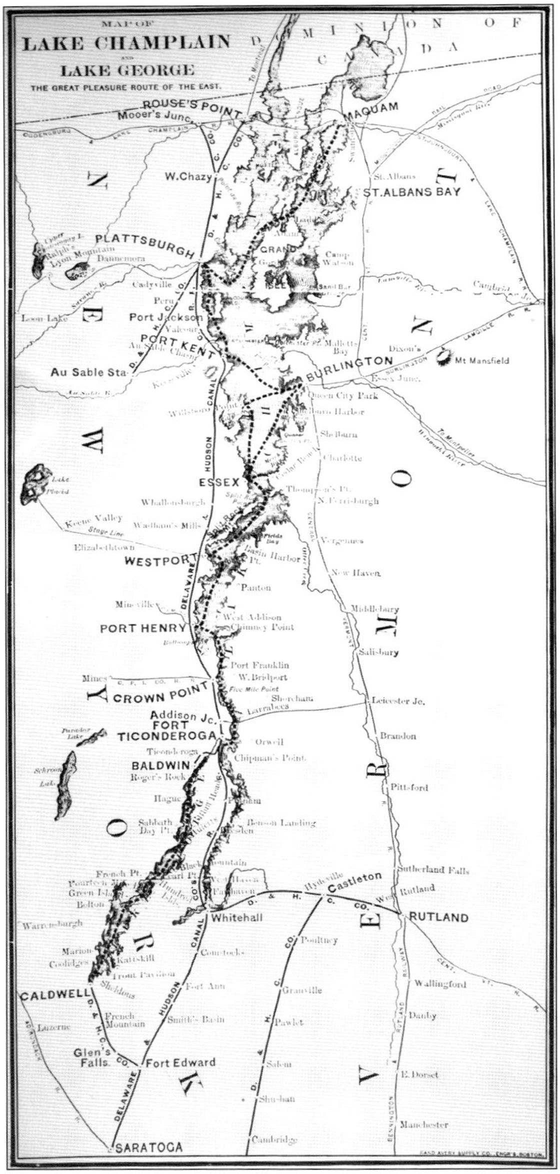

This *Map of Lake Champlain and Lake George: The Great Pleasure Route of the East* was published in 1887 by Rand Avery Supply Company, Boston. Intended for travelers in all modes of transportation, it includes an array of large and small communities, local landmarks, the north-south steamboat route, railroad lines, ferry crossings, and the Colchester Reef Lighthouse. (Courtesy of the Lake Champlain Maritime Museum.)

On the Cover: A crowd of festive, well-dressed people is seen disembarking from the steamer *Chateaugay*, with the steamer *Vermont III* (left) alongside. The presence of Dr. William Seward Webb's steam yacht *Elfrida I* (right) suggests that the location is the dock at Shelburne Harbor, Vermont, and the occasion could be the wedding of Frederica Vanderbilt Webb to Ralph Pulitzer on October 14, 1905, an event attended by some 800 guests. (Courtesy of the Shelburne Museum.)

IMAGES
of America

LAKE CHAMPLAIN

Lake Champlain Maritime Museum

ARCADIA
PUBLISHING

ISBN 978-1-4671-2220-7

Published by Arcadia Publishing
Charleston, South Carolina

Printed in the United States of America

Library of Congress Control Number: 2014931057

For all general information, please contact Arcadia Publishing:
Telephone 843-853-2070
Fax 843-853-0044
E-mail sales@arcadiapublishing.com
For customer service and orders:
Toll-Free 1-888-313-2665

Visit us on the Internet at www.arcadiapublishing.com

Contents

Acknowledgments

In describing the interconnected history of the Lake Champlain region, the Lake Champlain Maritime Museum (LCMM) often refers to "Our Shared Waterways" and "Our Shared Heritage." This is certainly accurate in describing the process of gathering images for inclusion in this volume. LCMM is grateful to the generous and supportive individuals and organizations that shared their beloved photographs with this project.

The images in this volume appear courtesy of Bob and Pennie Beach, fourth-generation hosts of the Basin Harbor Club (BHC); the Bixby Memorial Free Library (BMFL); the Bodette family (BF); Eric A. Bessette (EAB); Darcey and Bruce Hale and the Hale Historical Research Foundation (HHRF); the Isle La Motte Historical Society (ILM); the Lake Champlain Maritime Museum (LCMM); the Shelburne Museum (SM); the Smithsonian Institution (SI); the University of Vermont's Bailey/Howe Library, Special Collections (UVM); the Vermont Historical Society (VHS); the Historical Society of Whitehall (HSW); and the Wiseman family collection (FMW).

Finally, this project would not have been possible without a team of LCMM staff, in particular, cofounder Arthur Cohn, Eloise Beil, and Sarah Tichonuk.

INTRODUCTION

Lake Champlain is one of the most beautiful places on earth. Cradled between the Adirondack and Green Mountains and formed by glaciers, it is often presented as the nation's sixth Great Lake. Smaller than the other Great Lakes, Champlain stretches 120 miles in a north-south orientation and up to 12 miles wide and surely can be counted among our nation's most historic waterways.

More than 12,000 years ago, generations of native peoples inhabited the lakeshore and surrounding forests, traveling upon the lake and its tributaries in dugout and birch bark canoes. They hunted and fished the lake and rivers, raised crops in the fertile soils, and occasionally made war on their neighbors. Long before Europeans arrived in the area, Abenaki people lived on the eastern side of the lake, with villages located near the mouths of Otter Creek and the Winooski, Lamoille, and Missisquoi Rivers, hunting territories that were also defined based on watercourses. Mohawk people have lived for millennia on the western shores of Lake Champlain.

In July 1609, French explorer Samuel de Champlain was guided by native allies from the north to "the large lake filled with beautiful islands and a great deal of beautiful country around it." During times of conflict between tribes to the north and south of the lake, most native inhabitants of the Champlain Valley dispersed to avoid the combatants. Champlain's brief visit of about three weeks culminated in a battle that introduced the region's native people to gunpowder weapons and established the Mohawk–British and Abenaki–French alliances, which determined the course of historical events in the region and, ultimately, changed the world.

For the next two centuries, the French and the English brought their Old World conflicts to a New World stage, with native peoples being drawn into the Europeans' quest for furs, forest products, and territory. French, British, and Americans constructed fortifications along the waterways and built naval ships to control the movement of armies along the north-south axis that separated French and British territories. Lake Champlain's location between the two expanding European colonies and its capacity for large vessel navigation made the waterway a strategic prize. France and England fought for control of the Lake Champlain region for 150 years.

Great Britain's victory over the French in 1760 ushered a new era of relative peace into the Champlain Valley, but this was short-lived. Great Britain's American colonies were moving steadily toward rebellion. In April 1775, hostilities began with the "shots heard 'round the world" from Lexington and Concord. Just three weeks later, offensive actions were taken against the British on Lake Champlain. So began a three-year drama in this northern theater that helped define the outcome of the war. When the Revolutionary War was brought to a close, the United States of America emerged into the world of nations and Lake Champlain became a transportation superhighway.

The same attributes that made the lake so valuable in war now made it a principal artery of peaceful transportation and trade. With few decent roads and a limited number of bridges, water was the highway in all seasons. Soon after peace was declared, former soldiers who had visited the lake in times of war began to migrate to its fertile shores and rich forests filled with valuable timber and abundant game. The best trees were harvested for building homes, barns, and boats, and the remaining trees were burned for potash and charcoal in the process of converting the forest to farmland.

Champlain Valley residents used oars, paddles, and sails to power small boats, and commercial sloops appeared on the scene. Resourceful entrepreneurs assembled huge rafts of pine and oak timbers, some covering several acres of water surface, and followed the flow of water to the north. Most boats terminated their journeys at St. Johns, Québec. Log rafts could be broken down into smaller components, driven through the rapids at Chambly, and then reconstituted for their journey to Québec City, where the timber was sold and shipped to Europe. These timber rafts often carried a cargo of barrels filled with potash, also destined for the markets of Europe, where it was used in the manufacturing of soap, glass, textiles, and gunpowder.

With each new navigation season, the number of vessels involved in transporting people and goods throughout the lake increased. Responding to the needs of the growing population, docks and warehouses were constructed and waterfront communities began to develop along the increasingly busy lake. Ferry crossings were established and began to advertise their services.

The first decade of the 19th century saw a momentous innovation on the lake that was to change the maritime world profoundly: the advent of steam power applied to watercraft. After the appearance of the world's first successful steamboat on the Hudson River in 1807, Lake Champlain's first steamboat was built the following year in the bustling port of Burlington, Vermont. For the next 150 years, steamboats played a starring role in Lake Champlain transportation.

Shortly after the steamboat *Vermont I* began service, increasing tensions between Great Britain and the United States escalated into the War of 1812. On land and water, Lake Champlain was again contested. The American victory on Lake Champlain in 1814 paved the way for the alliance between the United States, Canada, and Great Britain, and the lake entered its commercial heyday.

The potential for a canal system to connect Lake Champlain to the Hudson River and beyond was first recognized in the 1700s. After an initial building attempt begun in 1792 failed, the State of New York started again in 1817. The Northern (Champlain) Canal was completed in 1823, connecting Lake Champlain with the navigable Hudson River. Two years later, when the Erie Canal was finished, a boat loaded with Lake Champlain products or passengers could travel all the way to New York City or to the Great Lakes region and Buffalo, New York. Shipwrights and merchants rose to the opportunity, and canal boats soon dramatically outnumbered every other type of boat on the lake.

The commercial success of the Champlain and Erie Canals exceeded all expectations. Before the canal, much of the Champlain Valley's trade flowed north into Canada. The canal opened a floodgate of trade between the valley and ports along the Hudson River and the Atlantic seaboard. Almost overnight, natural resources too bulky to ship overland became valuable commodities, and boom years began for commercial enterprises served by a rapidly increasing number of vessels. At wharfs all along Lake Champlain and the Champlain Canal, the holds and decks of southbound canal boats were packed with iron and iron ore, marble, lumber, and agricultural products. Northbound canal boats returned with manufactured goods, spirits, coffee, coal, and sugar.

When other states and British Canada added their efforts to the canal mania, the network of navigable commercial routes increased drastically. The Chambly Canal, which bypassed the Richelieu Rapids north of Lake Champlain, opened in 1843, contributing further to the economic boom. Federally funded lighthouses helped boats to navigate around the clock and in all weather conditions. Breakwaters improved harbor safety.

Into this dynamic inland world of wooden ships driven by sail or steam and towed on the canals by horses and mules came the railroads. Steam-powered trains could make connection with all points of the compass and could operate year-round, while the lake fleet was immobilized for three to four months a year by winter ice. Arriving in the Champlain Valley around 1850, railroads were soon outcompeting the lake's commercial fleet. Passengers still liked to travel on ever larger and more elegant steamboats, but, over time, the novelty of steamboat travel succumbed to the scheduling efficiency of the rails.

By the close of the 19th century, Lake Champlain was in the midst of another shift, again spearheaded by a new form of transportation technology. The internal combustion engine was making its appearance. A network of highways linking local roads paved the way for commercial trucking and beckoned vacationers. When the Lake Champlain Bridge opened in 1929, ferries that had operated for decades ceased operations and once-prosperous waterfront communities fell on hard times. Many of the wooden commercial fleet headed to the breaker's yard or retirement. A few wooden canal boats struggled into the 1930s and 1940s, but their time had passed.

As the 20th century approached, smaller and more elegant recreational boats gradually replaced the working watercraft of earlier times. More people came to the lake for relaxation, returning to the days of oar, paddle, and sail. New hotels, camps, and yacht clubs began to appear around the lake as people explored new recreational options. Boats were used to fish, hunt, or just simply enjoy the scenery. Around the lake, the tents of temporary summer camps were converted to permanent summer cabins. Artists painted the sunsets and scenes of history. Steamboats hung on until they could no longer be sustained, and the last of the proud vessels was taken overland to the Shelburne Museum in 1954. While the canals tried to find a viable economic niche shipping petroleum products to lakefront tank farms, many communities turned away from the lake to look inland for prosperity.

Fittingly, the American Revolution bicentennial celebration in 1976 helped to spark a revival of interest in the lake's waterfront heritage. A new generation began to discover and appreciate the lake's history and its extraordinary collection of shipwrecks. In the following decades, archaeologists have discovered and studied more than 300 shipwrecks at the bottom of Lake Champlain, working with the States of New York and Vermont to create a system of Underwater Historic Preserves. Waterfront parks have been restored or created, downtowns revitalized, open lands preserved, and economic strategies adapted, as communities throughout the Champlain Valley act to protect the quality of water, air, and life on Lake Champlain. The glimpses of the past found in this portfolio of photographs can help provide an enriched perspective on the ways each generation contributes to the ongoing story of the vibrant, living waterway at the heart of the Champlain Valley.

One

Recreational Boating

Although sailing ships and steamboats often capture the limelight in historical records and works of art, small watercraft have been an indispensable part of daily life on the shores of Lake Champlain since ancient times. Indigenous people used a variety of wooden and bark canoes. In the 17th and 18th centuries, explorers and traders came to the lake in canoes, bateaux, and whaleboats. The large sailing vessels of the Colonial Wars and the American Revolution were accompanied and aided by smaller auxiliary boats.

By the 19th century, innovations in technology made travel easier and provided more opportunities for leisure pastimes. While relatively few of the small wooden boats of earlier days have survived in private hands, museum collections, or archaeological sites, historical photographs reveal a treasure trove of small pleasure craft in use on Lake Champlain. Boats powered by paddles, oars, and sails are joined by steam launches, naphtha launches, inboard motors, and, finally, outboard motors.

Some of the images speak of the pleasure of a solitary outing; others document family and community gatherings. In many localities, the working waterfront and the facilities for leisure boating are found side by side. The universal appeal of boating is summed up by Kenneth Graeme in the 1908 children's classic *Wind in the Willows*: "There is nothing, absolutely nothing, half so much worth doing as simply messing about in boats."

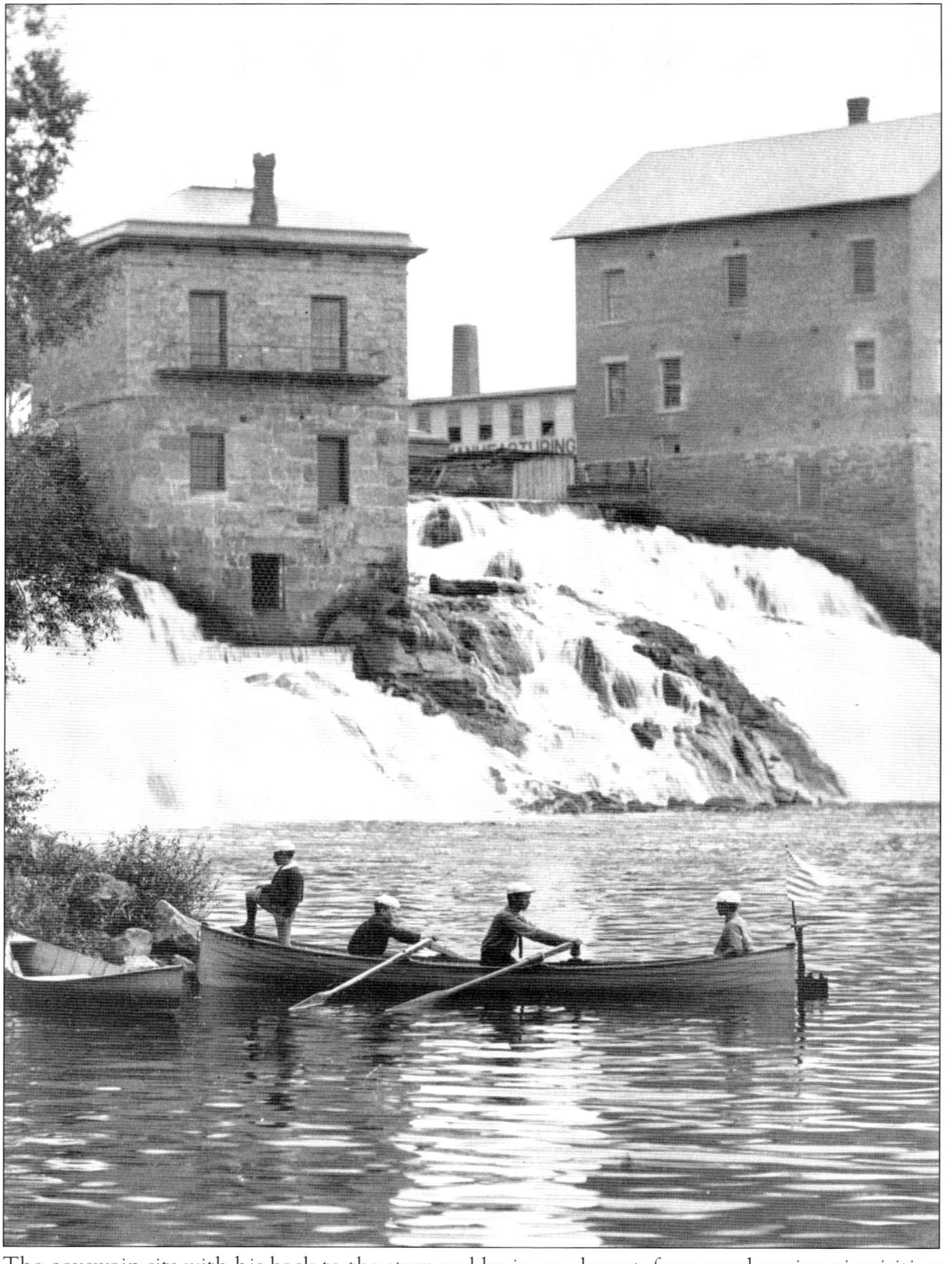

The coxswain sits with his back to the stern rudder in an elegant, four-oared rowing gig visiting the falls on Otter Creek at Vergennes, Vermont, in the early 1900s. The earliest industry at this location was a 1764 sawmill. The 1874 pump house (left) and 1878 gristmill have recently been restored. Today, rowing teams in similar boats built by local students visit a scene that is practically unchanged. (BMFL.)

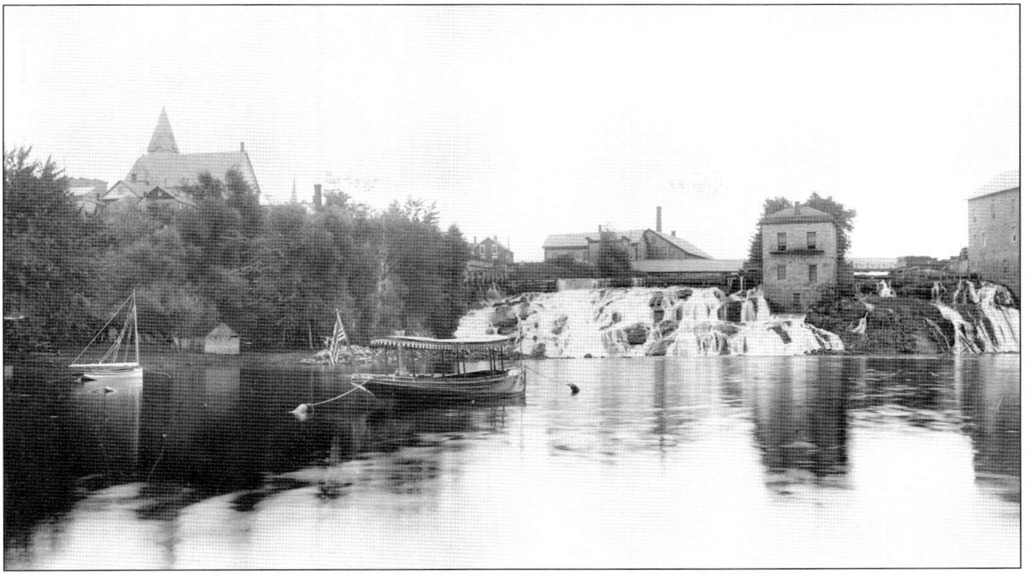

This view of the Vergennes falls is probably the work of Custer Ingham (1863–1931), a Vergennes artist and photographer who lived near Otter Creek most of his life. Ingham's compositions often included small watercraft. This photograph shows a small catboat on the left with a single mast at the bow, as well as an elegant naphtha launch at anchor. Just visible beyond the trees on the left is the Baptist church, which burned in 1934. (BMFL.)

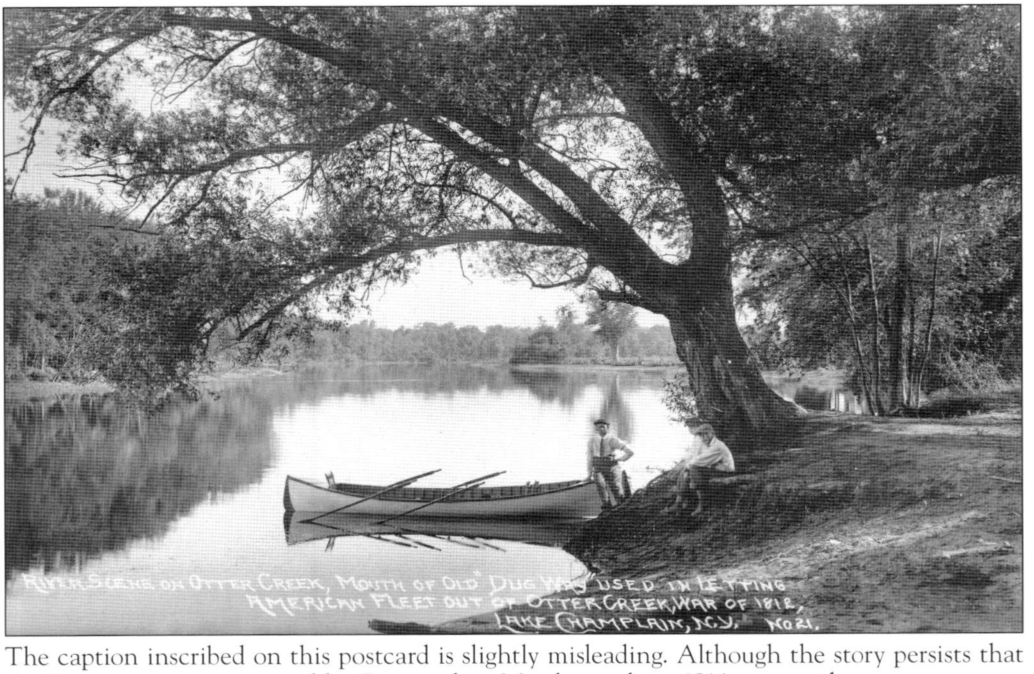

The caption inscribed on this postcard is slightly misleading. Although the story persists that the Dugway was constructed by Commodore Macdonough in 1814 to provide an escape route for the American fleet that was then building at Vergennes should the British attack, it is more likely that the Dugway was built by local people as a shortcut in and out of Otter Creek with their small boats. (LCMM.)

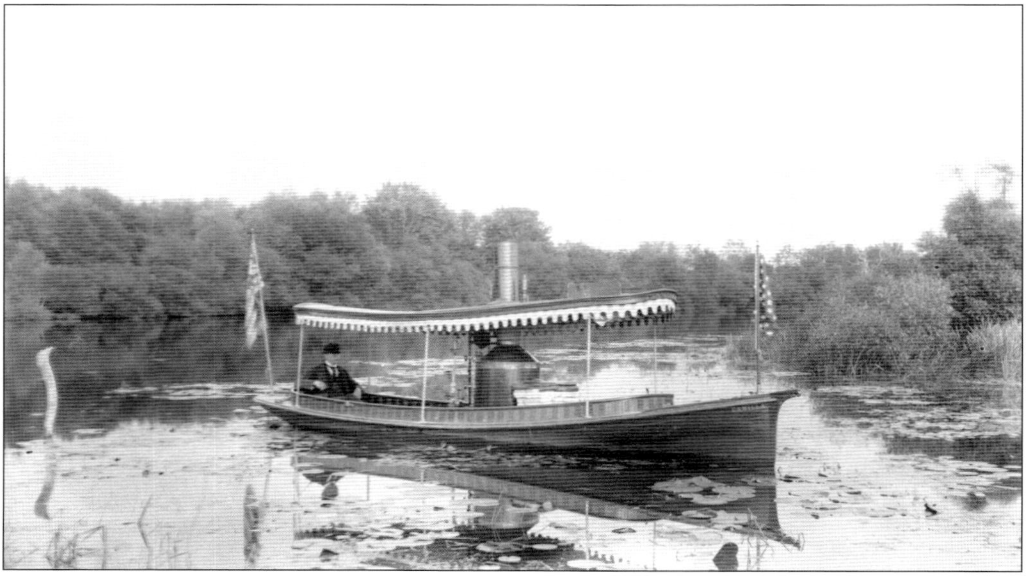

Educator and entrepreneur Leicester Felix "L.F." Benton poses in his steam launch *Camilla* on Otter Creek in this photograph taken by Custer Ingham. In 1906, after fire destroyed a building overlooking Otter Creek, Benton purchased the site and began a business manufacturing spark plugs. Benton's grandson, who operates W.D. Benton, Inc., Appraisers, in the small Italianate office building used by L.F. Benton, who was elected mayor of Vergennes in 2013. (UVM.)

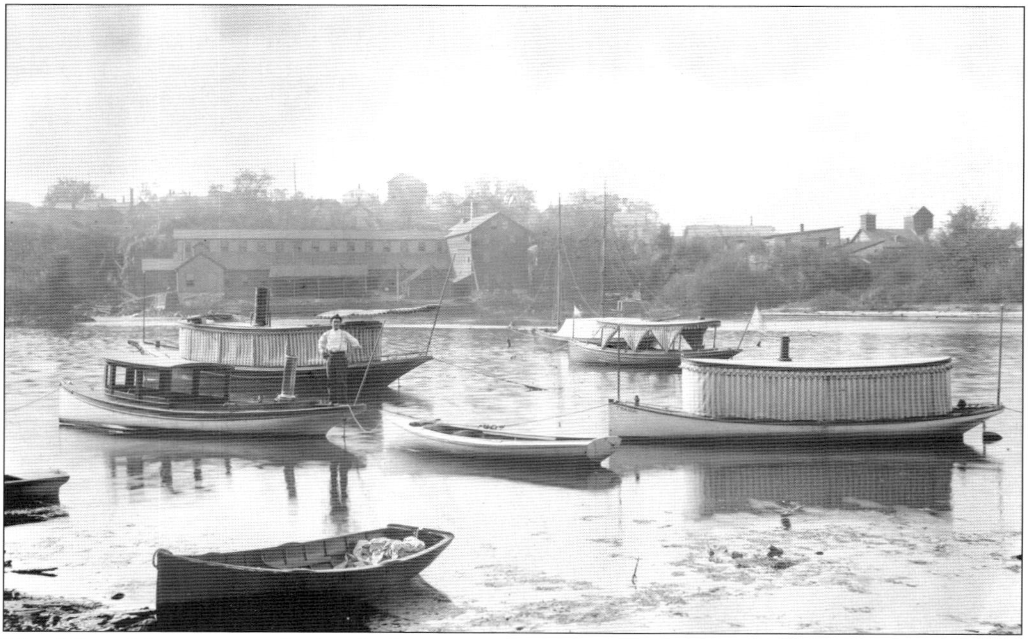

The falls at Vergennes is the head of navigation on Otter Creek. The location's popularity with recreational boaters is evident in this late-19th-century view by Custer Ingham, which includes rowing boats, steam and naphtha launches, and a small schooner. At the time, Lake Champlain had the nation's largest fleet of naphtha launches. The industrial building in the background is believed to be the National Horse Nail Factory. (BMFL.)

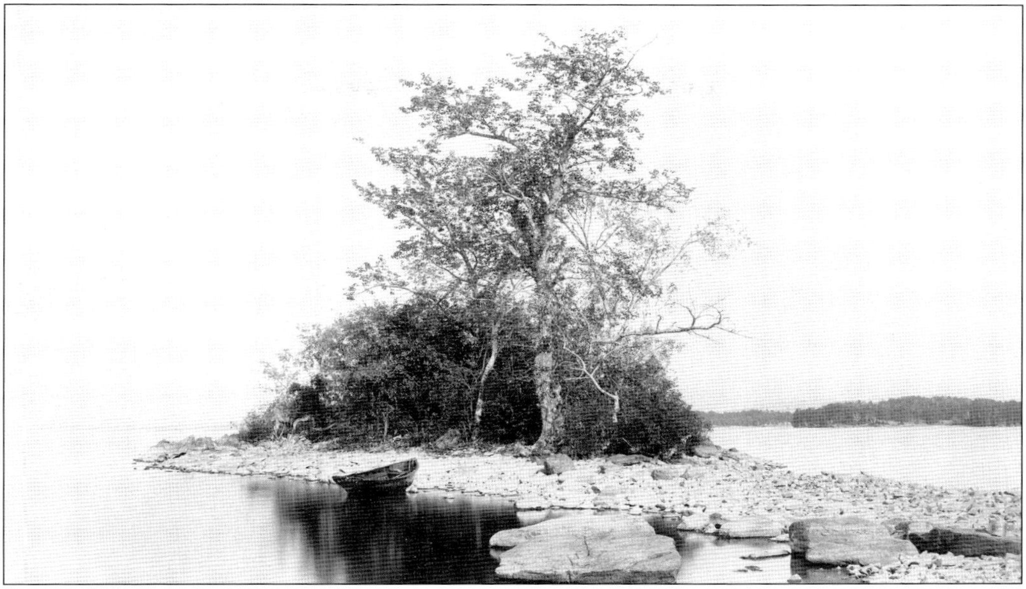

Custer Ingham (1863–1931) was a Vergennes-based artist and photographer whose work most frequently depicted scenes along Otter Creek and nearby parts of Lake Champlain. For the photograph above, Ingham rowed out to Diamond Island, just opposite the mouth of Otter Creek, and took the photograph looking east toward the Vermont shore. The rowboat seen here also appears in several of Ingham's paintings. The impressive vertical rock wall below, known as the Palisades, rises from Lake Champlain at Split Rock Mountain, New York, just opposite historic Basin Harbor, Vermont. The Palisades, seen here in another Ingham photograph, shines in the morning sun and has long been a favorite destination for summer boaters, who enjoy viewing it from the water. Ingham also created paintings from this same vantage point. (Both, UVM.)

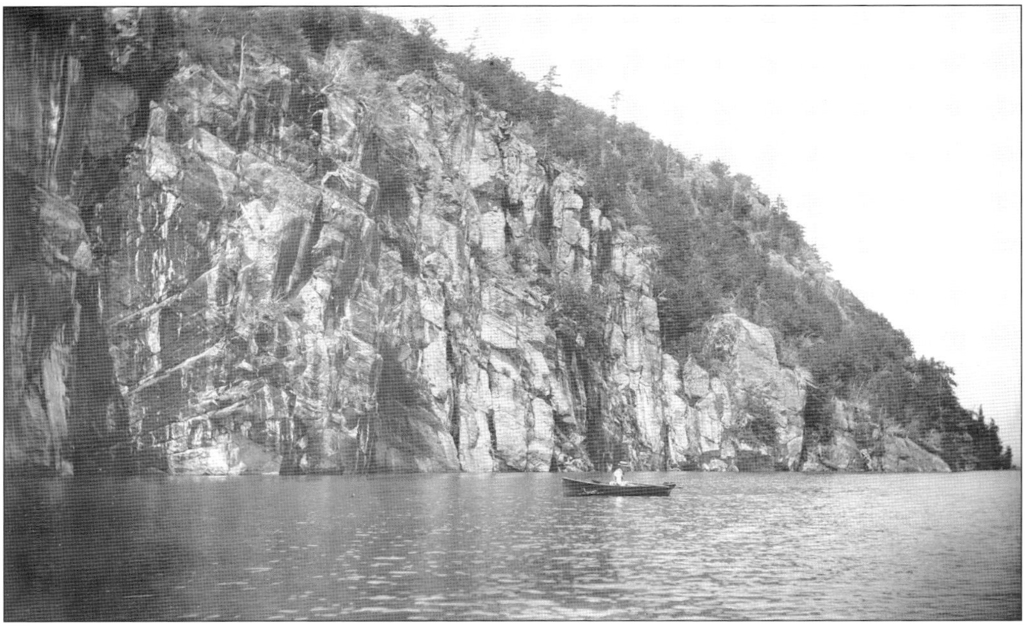

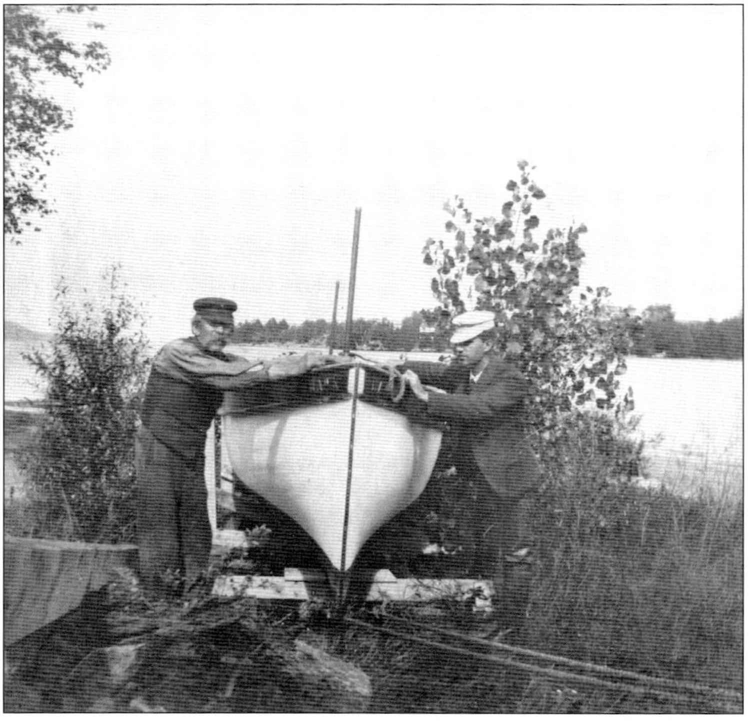

Harvey Hayes (left) and William Menelly pose beside a boat at Mile Point in Ferrisburgh, Vermont. The boat, a power launch, was large enough that a marine railway was used to move it in and out of the water. The railway consisted of a track that extended under the water and had a moving cradle upon which the boat sat for its upward or downward journey. (LCMM.)

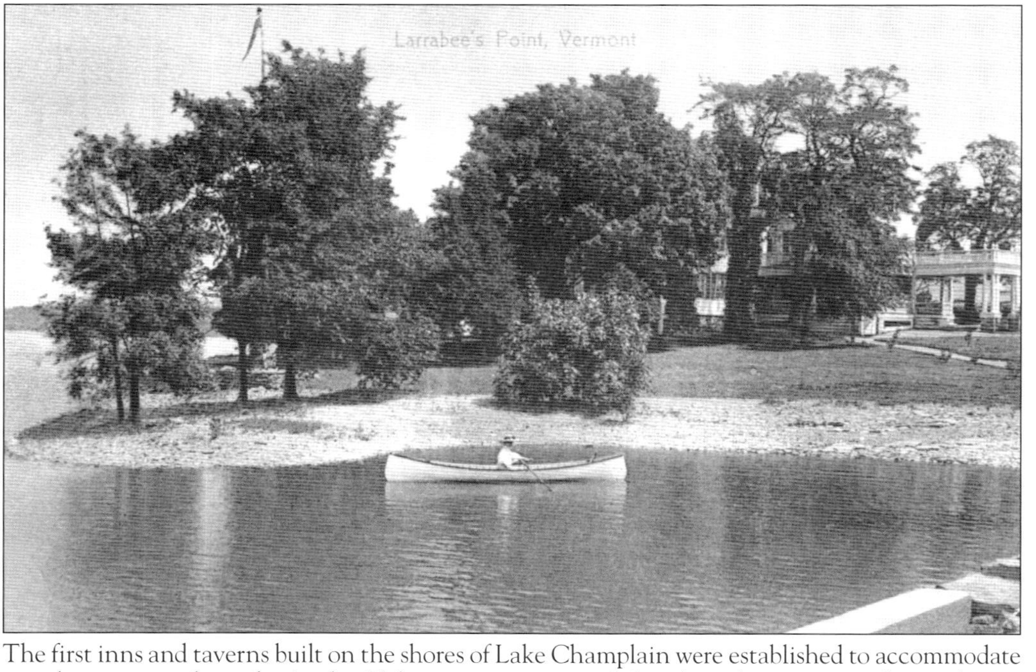

The first inns and taverns built on the shores of Lake Champlain were established to accommodate travelers passing through. As the 19th century progressed, hotels and summer residences began to advertise to people who wished to spend some of their newfound leisure time on beautiful Lake Champlain. The United States Hotel at Larrabee's Point in Shoreham, Vermont, was one of these popular places. (LCMM.)

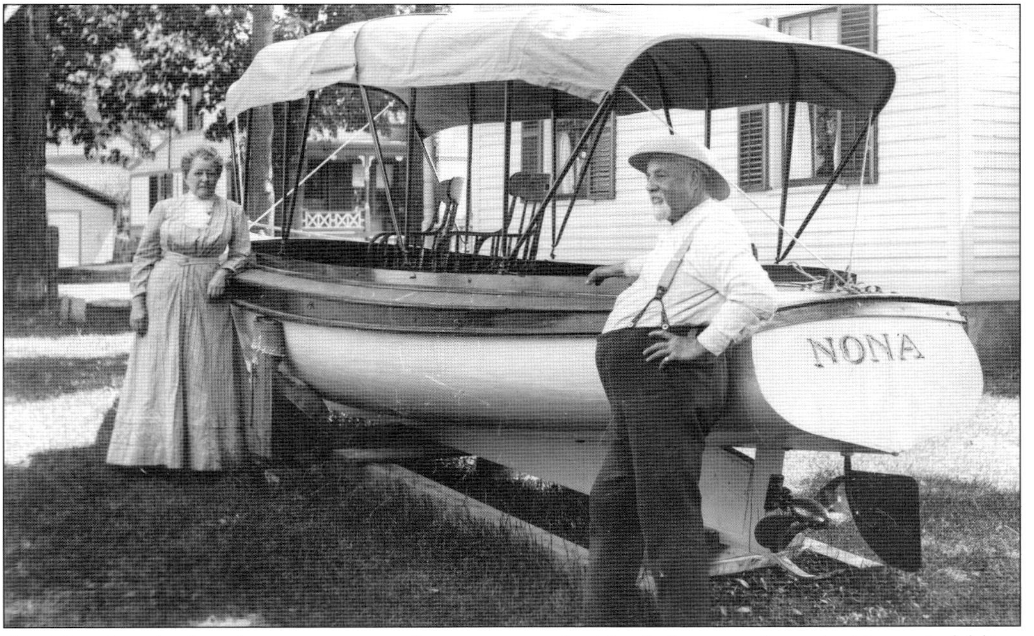

Anticipating the boating season, proud owners pose beside their power launch, *Nona*. A folding canvas canopy with adjustable supports, similar to a buggy top, and a pair of wooden armchairs help ensure that passengers will travel in comfort. Inboard motor boats can be recognized by the position of the propeller. (LCMM.)

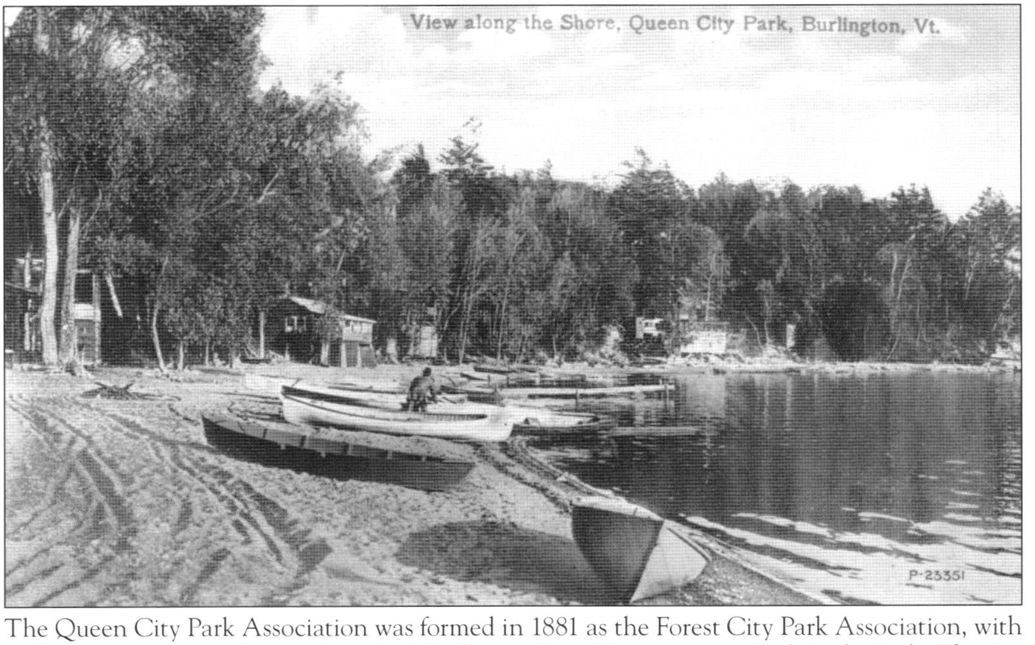

The Queen City Park Association was formed in 1881 as the Forest City Park Association, with a 50-acre property at the north end of Shelburne Bay, Vermont, now Red Rocks Park. The site boasted a stop on the Rutland Railroad line, and was used for spiritualist camp meetings, picnic parties, and as a summer resort. Many seasonal residents kept boats on the beautiful sand beach, which was also used for swimming. (LCMM.)

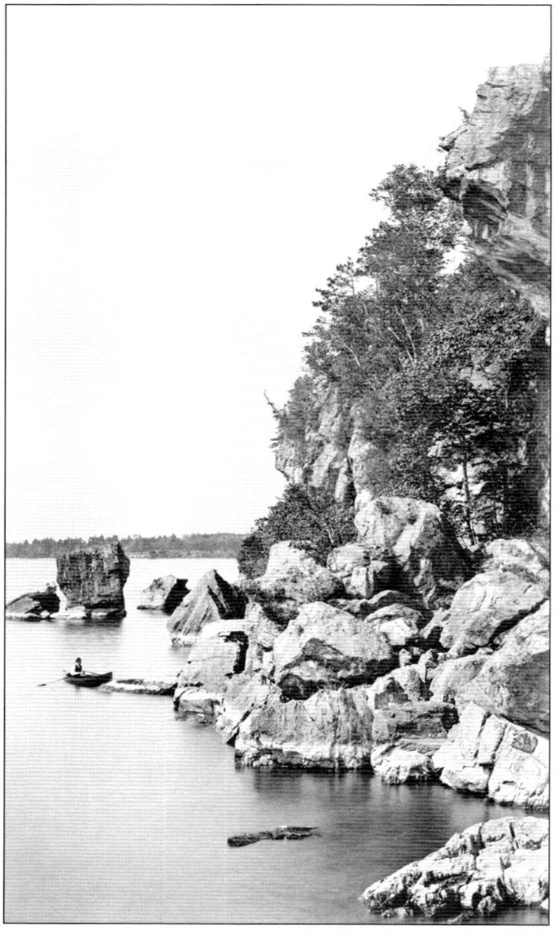

Lone Rock Point, which forms the northern shoreline of Burlington Bay, Vermont, is one of the lake's most distinctive landmarks. The stepped and tumbled layers are known to geologists as the Champlain thrust fault, remarkable for the fact that older rock deposits now rest above younger layers. Trees clinging to the rocky outcroppings are shaped by the wind, creating picturesque effects that were much admired in the 19th century. (UVM.)

The geological formations of Lake Champlain have attracted public and scholarly interest for generations. Charles P. Hibbard (1823–1895), who published a book of scenic photographs of Burlington, Vermont, in the 1880s, captured this view of a white canoe visiting the shoreline at Rock Point, on the north side of Burlington Harbor. By 1890, Hibbard had relocated to Lisbon, New Hampshire, where he produced views of the White Mountains. (UVM.)

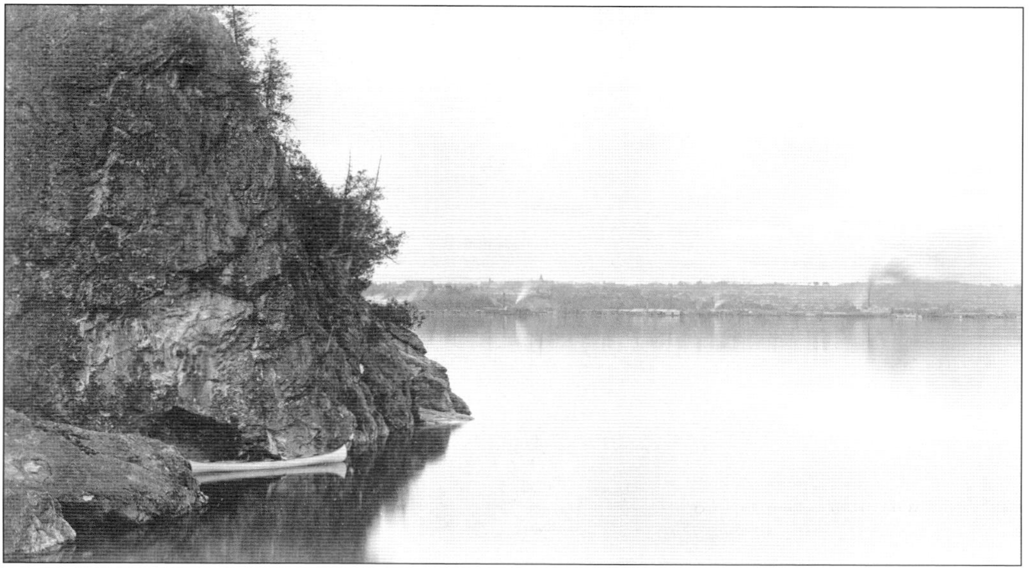

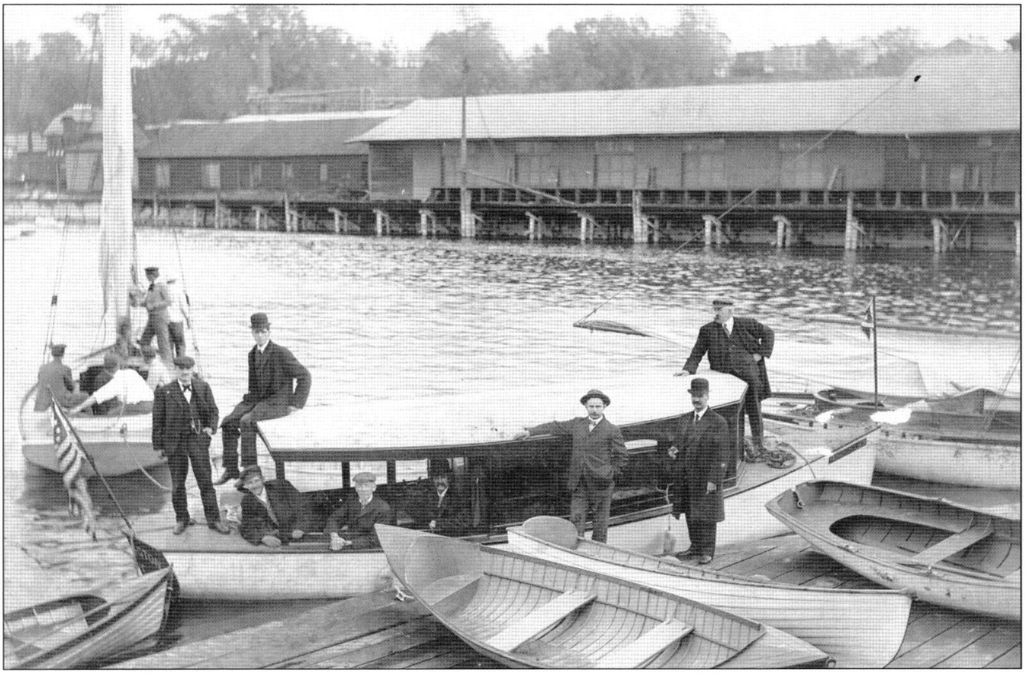

Eight well-attired men stand on the dock north of the Lake Champlain Yacht Club at Burlington Bay, Vermont, ready to board the power launch *Montpelier*. To the left, a small sloop sets sail, and the gaff-rigged sail of a second sloop is visible at the right. In the foreground, an assortment of lapstrake rowing boats is ready for rental or use as tenders to larger vessels. Railroad warehouses can be seen in the background. (LCMM.)

Most large harbors offered boat liveries where the public could rent a boat by the hour, day, or week. Some also offered boats for sale and, later, gasoline for motorboats. Almost every Lake Champlain town had a boatbuilder who could fill the demand for boats for local people. These boats were often designed with features adapted for the part of the lake where the builder worked. (UVM.)

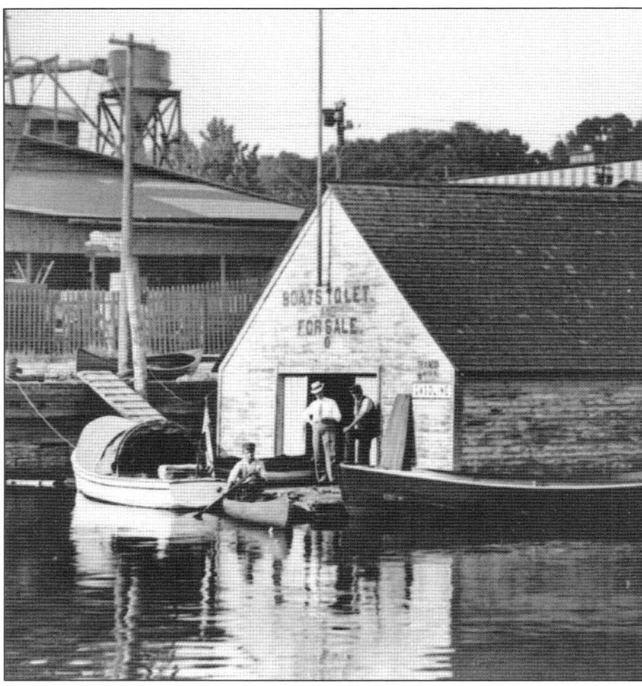

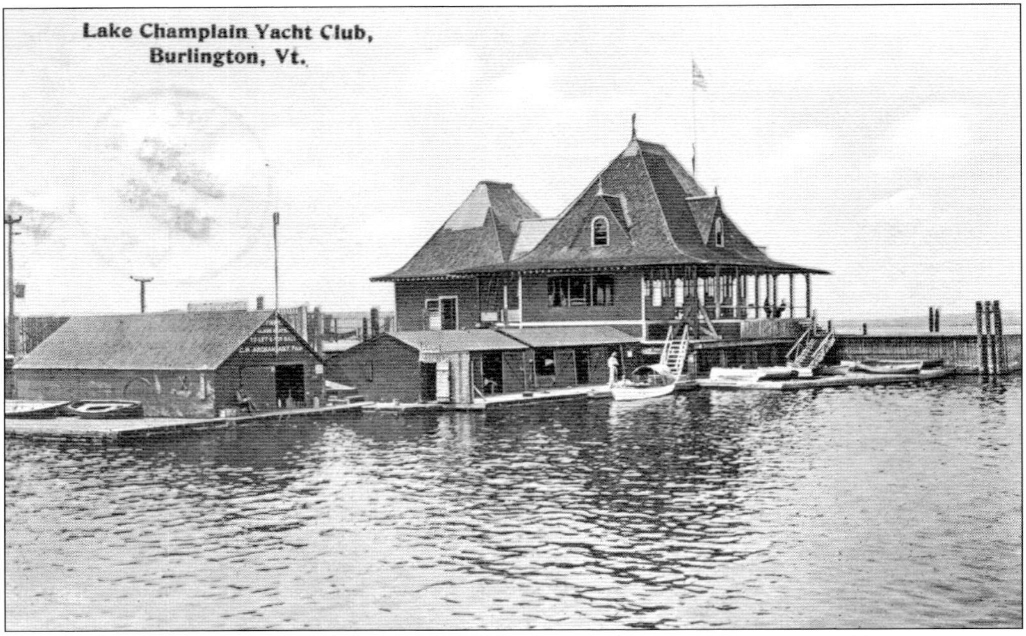

The Lake Champlain Yacht Club was established in Burlington, Vermont, in 1887 to organize regattas and other social events and promote recreational use of the lake. Three different clubhouses were built on the site. This postcard shows the second clubhouse, which was completed in 1902, a year after the first clubhouse, with all its contents, was consumed by fire. The 35 boats located in adjoining boathouses were all saved. (LCMM.)

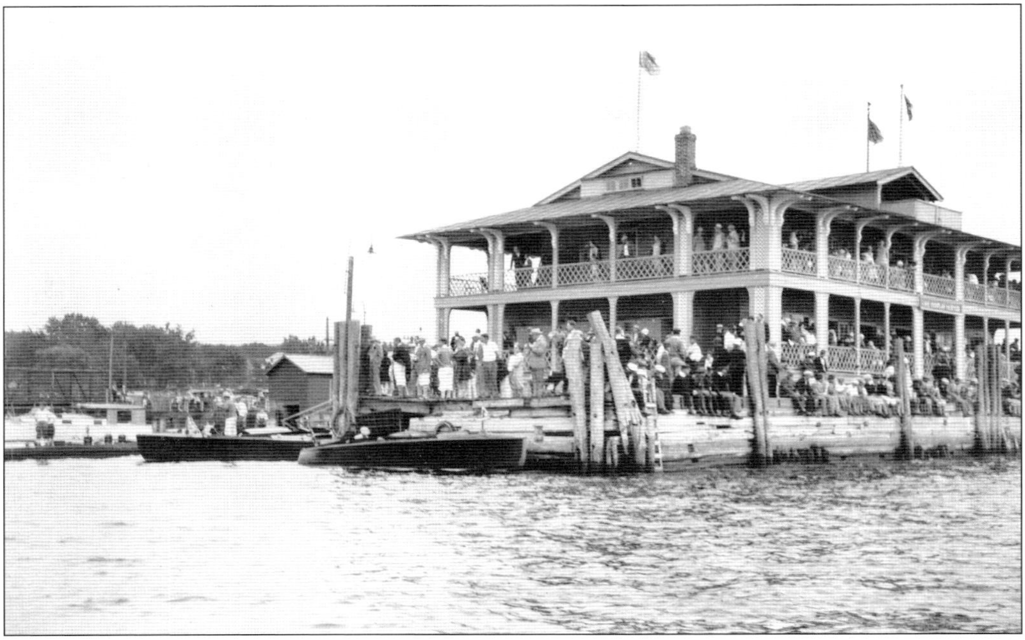

This photograph captures a festive day at the third clubhouse of the Lake Champlain Yacht Club. This clubhouse was built after the second clubhouse burned in 1911. The presence of the speedboat at the side of the dock places the time of the photograph around 1925. (UVM.)

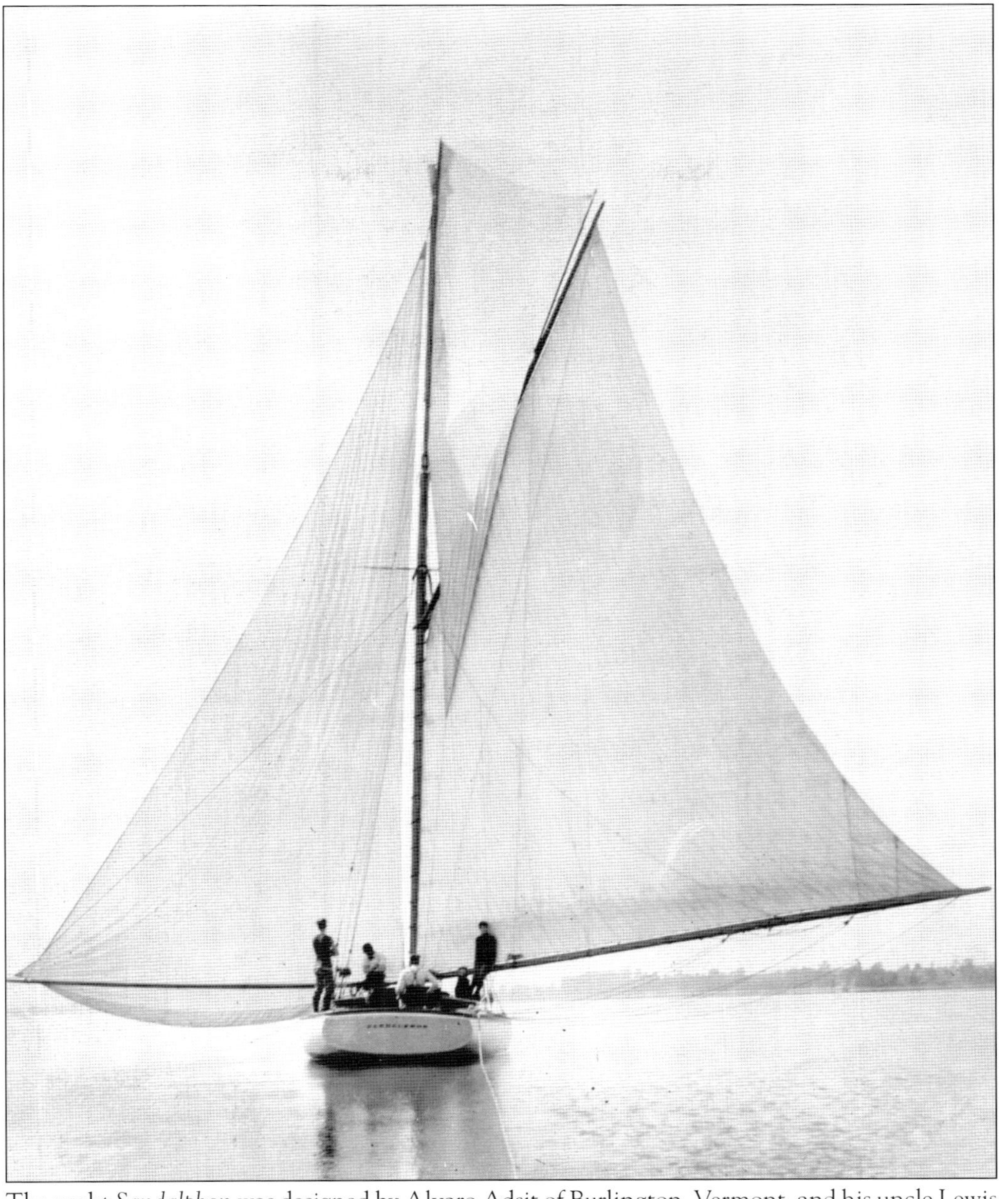

The yacht *Sandalphon* was designed by Alvaro Adsit of Burlington, Vermont, and his uncle Lewis Clark of Ligonier Point, New York, both marine engineers and members of the Lake Champlain Yacht Club. The image of a yacht sailing wing on wing may have been associated by the designers with Henry Wadsworth Longfellow's 1858 poem "Sandalphon," about Sandalphon, the Angel of Glory. (LCMM.)

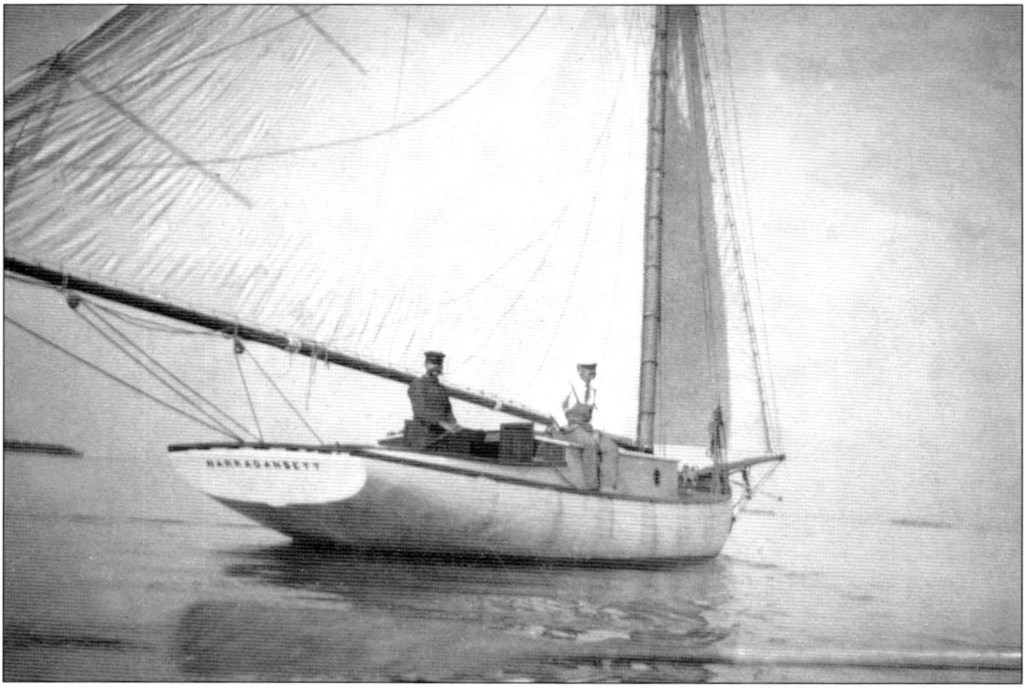

Narragansett, one of the sloops designed and built by Lewis H. Clark (1828–1909) at his shipyard on Ligonier Point, is on the ways in preparation for launching around 1890. Clark, who trained as a marine engineer, worked on Monitor-class vessels at Greenpoint, New York, during the Civil War. (HHRF.)

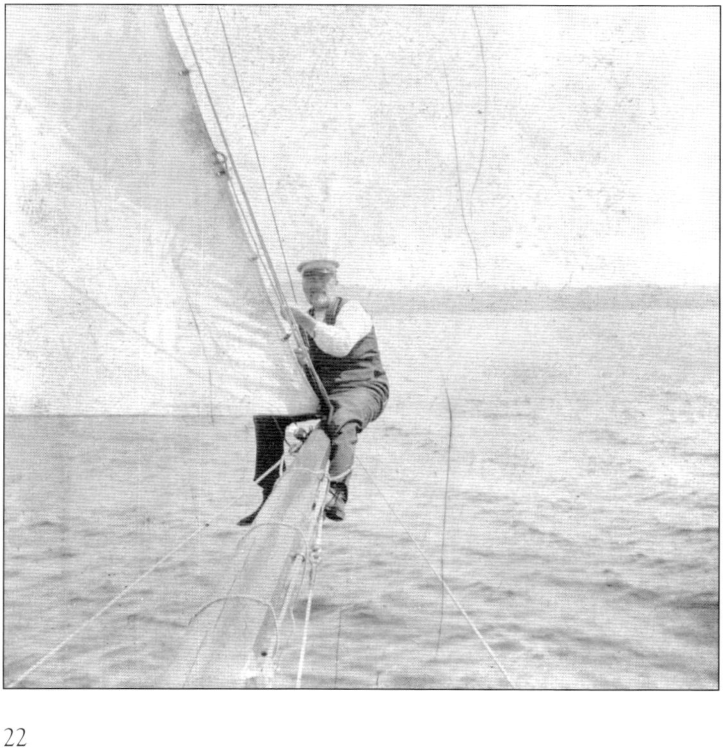

Lewis Clark sits on the bowsprit of *Comet*, the fastest racing sloop on Lake Champlain for a decade. *Comet*, 49 feet long with a 17-foot, 6-inch beam, was built at the Clark shipyard in 1876 and won so many races that she was purchased by a member of the New York Yacht Club. *Comet* established Lewis Clark's reputation as a leading yacht builder in the last quarter of the 19th century. (HHRF.)

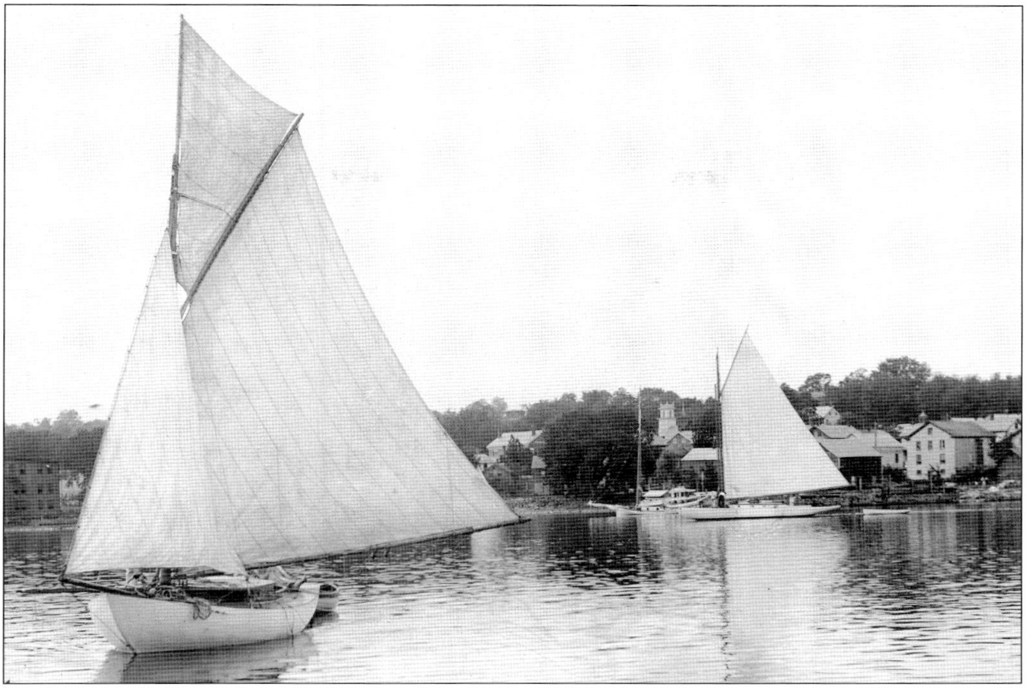

Racing yacht *Sandalphon* is seen above leaving the Essex, New York, harbor under full sail. Professional boatbuilder Joseph Richards constructed the vessel at Alvaro Adsit's Burlington, Vermont, home. The 48-foot racing yacht was launched in May 1898 and immediately began to win most of the races she entered. It is believed that *Sandalphon* was later converted to a powerboat on the Hudson River. The view below of the main cabin of *Sandalphon* shows the mast tabernacle at center, surrounded by elegant furnishings. (Above, LCMM; below, HHRF.)

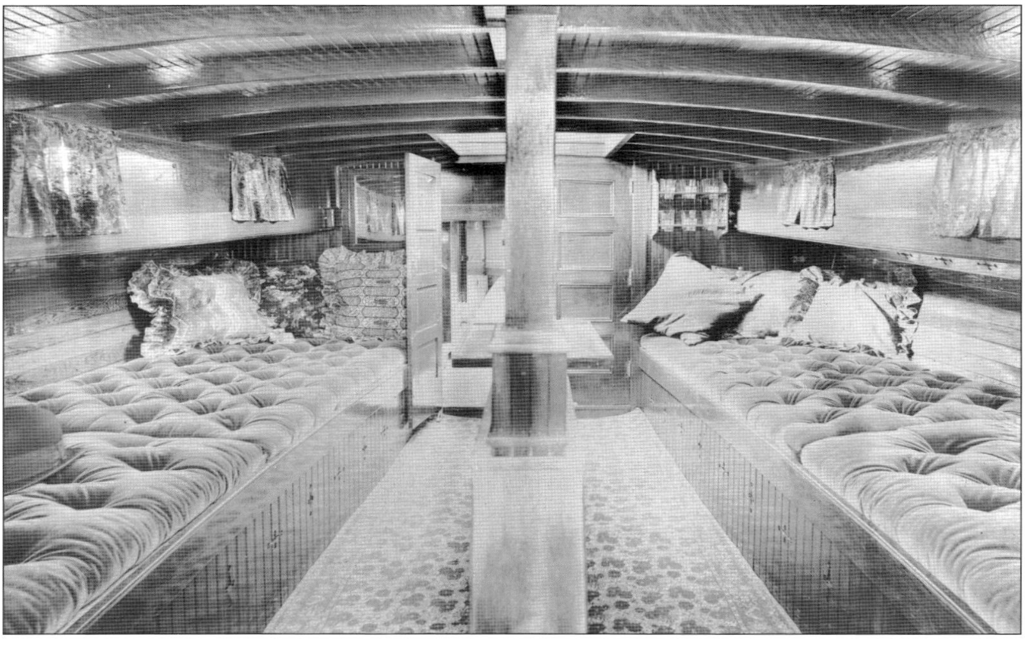

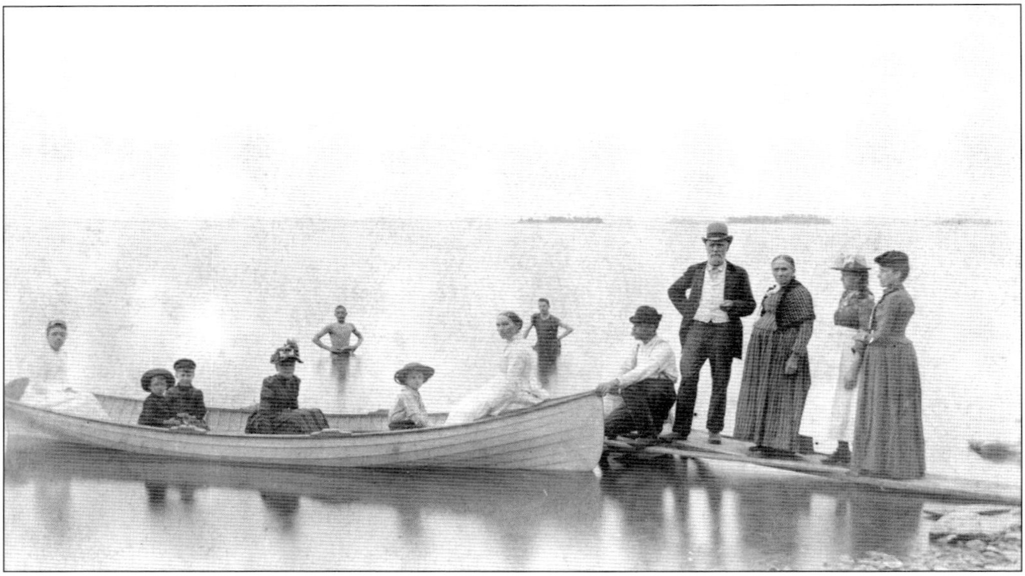

Above, Lewis Clark and his wife, Elizabeth (Adsit) Clark, stand on the dock on Ligonier Point, New York, during a family gathering in the early 1900s. Their niece Luella J. Clark, daughter of Solomon and Rhoda (Adsit) Clark, is in the stern of the large rowing boat. Below, Florence Wood, granddaughter-in-law of Solomon and Rhoda (Adsit) Clark, is fending off a sea monster (her husband, Fiske Wood) as he tries to board her boat. (Both, HHRF.)

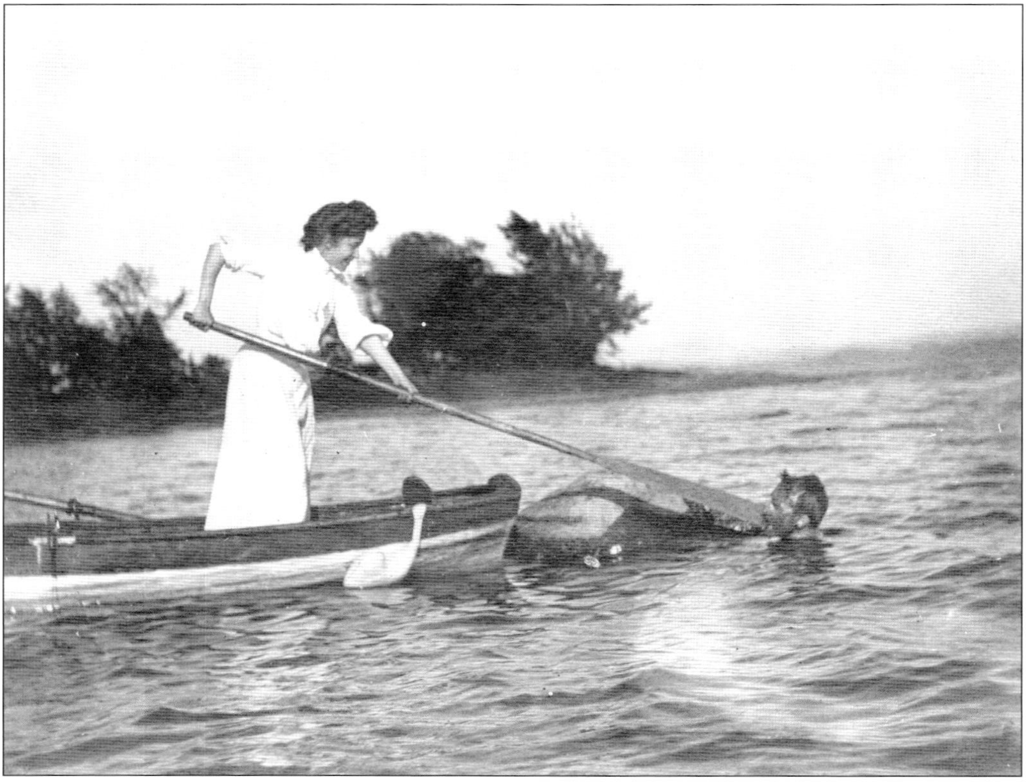

Two

Commerce in the Canal Era

The opening of the Champlain Canal in 1823 marked the end of the Champlain Valley's relative isolation from the outside world and its entry into the national economy. Lake Champlain now had direct shipping to the Hudson River and New York City. The Chambly Canal, completed in 1843, added Canadian ports to the inland waterway system and further transformed the region.

Thousands of wooden canal boats were built in waterfront communities on Lake Champlain. Timber cutting, stone quarrying, and iron mining experienced a surge of activity. Apples, potatoes, grain, butter, cheese, and other semi-perishables could be shipped quickly and inexpensively to urban markets. The Champlain Canal also brought affordable manufactured goods and raw materials to residents of the Champlain Valley.

For several decades, life on and along the canals offered mobility and economic opportunity to families who lived and worked aboard their boats during navigation season and wintered on land. Popular magazines promoted the pleasures of canal boat travel for people with modest incomes and leisure time.

Unfortunately, canal proponents had either not anticipated or had underestimated the competition from railroads, which began in earnest around 1850. By the early 20th century, although canal expansion continued in an effort to hang on, commercial use of canals was becoming more and more limited. Today, the historical New York and Canadian Canal systems provide hydroelectric power and flood control. They also offer an extraordinary recreational and cultural experience, as they continue to connect Lake Champlain to the region's other historical waterways.

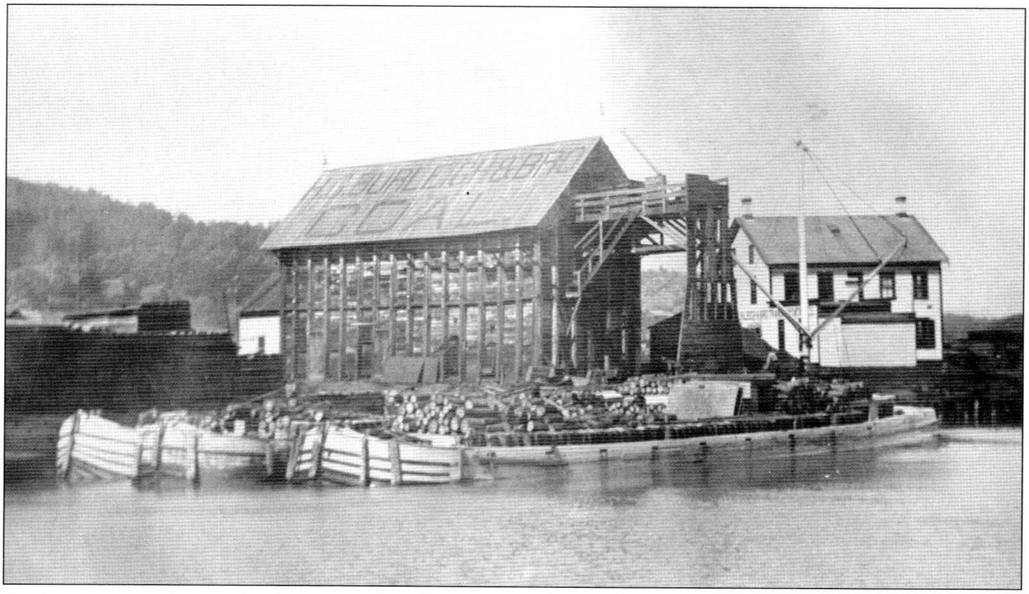

A close look at the roof shingles in the photograph above identifies the coal yard of H.G. Burleigh & Bro. in Whitehall, New York. Henry Gordon Burleigh was a visionary businessman, financier, and statesman. In partnership with his younger brother Brackett Weeks Burleigh, he operated a fleet of 150 canal boats and steamers and developed extensive landholdings and business interests in New York, Vermont, and Canada. Below, the canal boat *Smith M. Weed* passes another Whitehall landmark, the brick headquarters of the Champlain Transportation Company. Tugs with tall smokestacks are seen at the docks in the background, as well as the painted stern boards of canal boats. (Above, HSW; below, LCMM.)

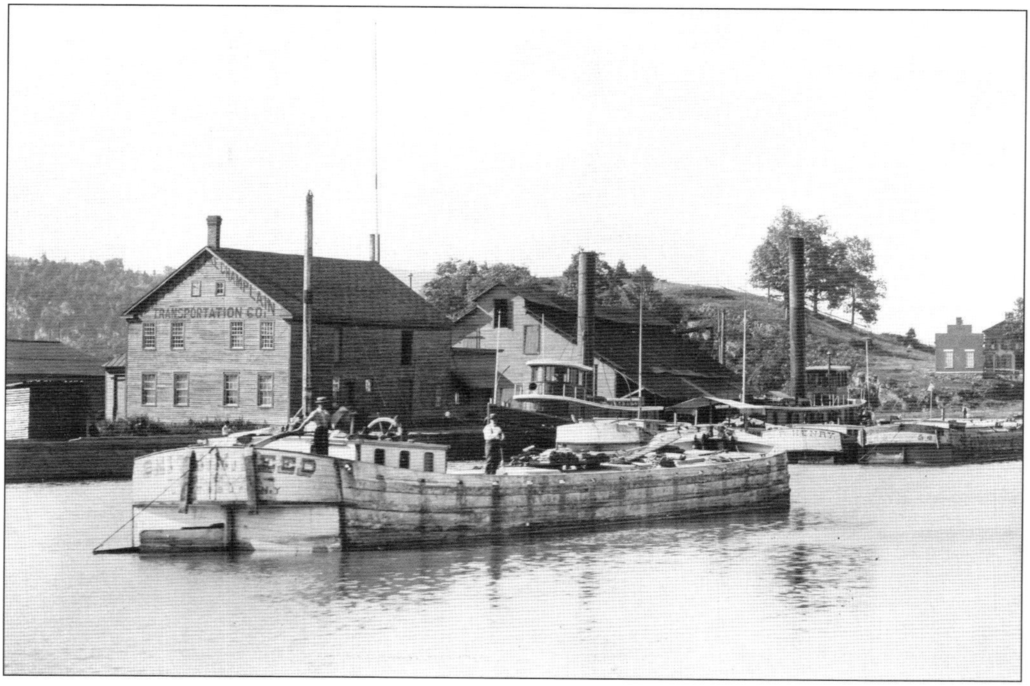

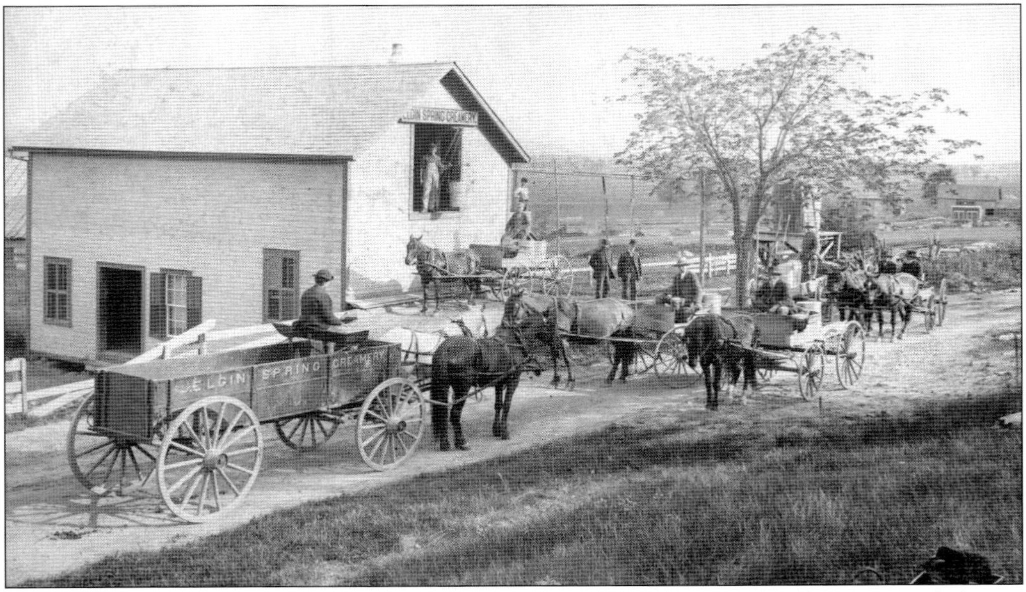

The Elgin Spring Creamery in Panton, Vermont, provided centralized butter and cheese manufacturing for dairy farmers in Addison County in the late 19th century. Railroad lines with ice-cooled cars competed with canal boats for transporting agricultural products. (UVM.)

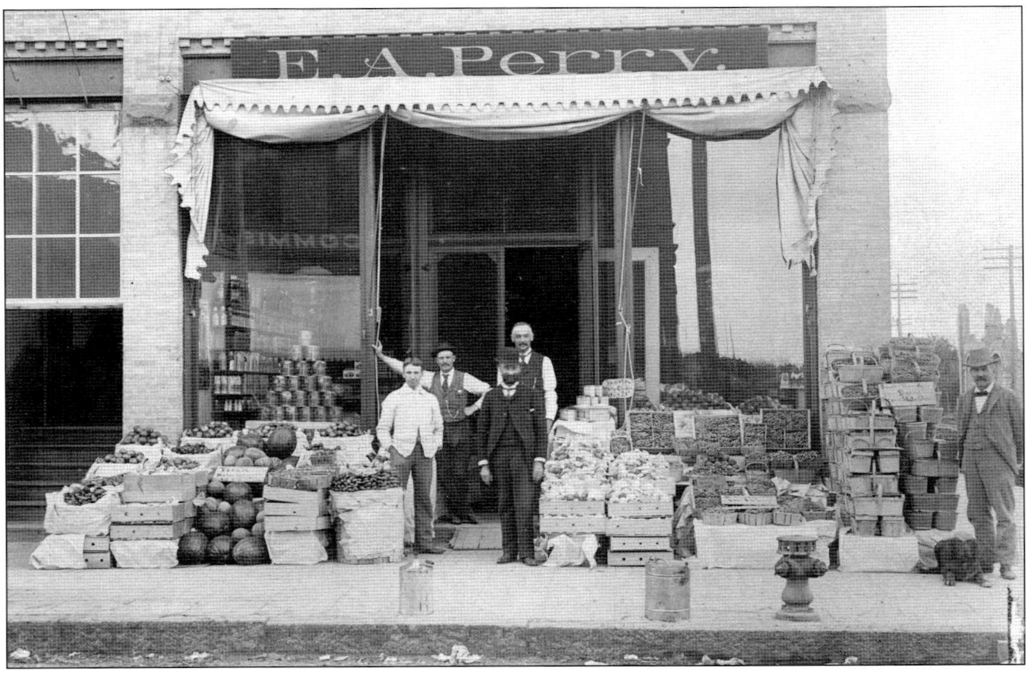

St. Albans, Vermont, grocer E.A. Perry displays some of the abundant produce for which Grand Isle and Franklin Counties were famous. By 1889, the new St. Albans Cold Storage facility boasted 900 tons of ice in a massive warehouse, with separate rooms for dairy products and other produce. (UVM.)

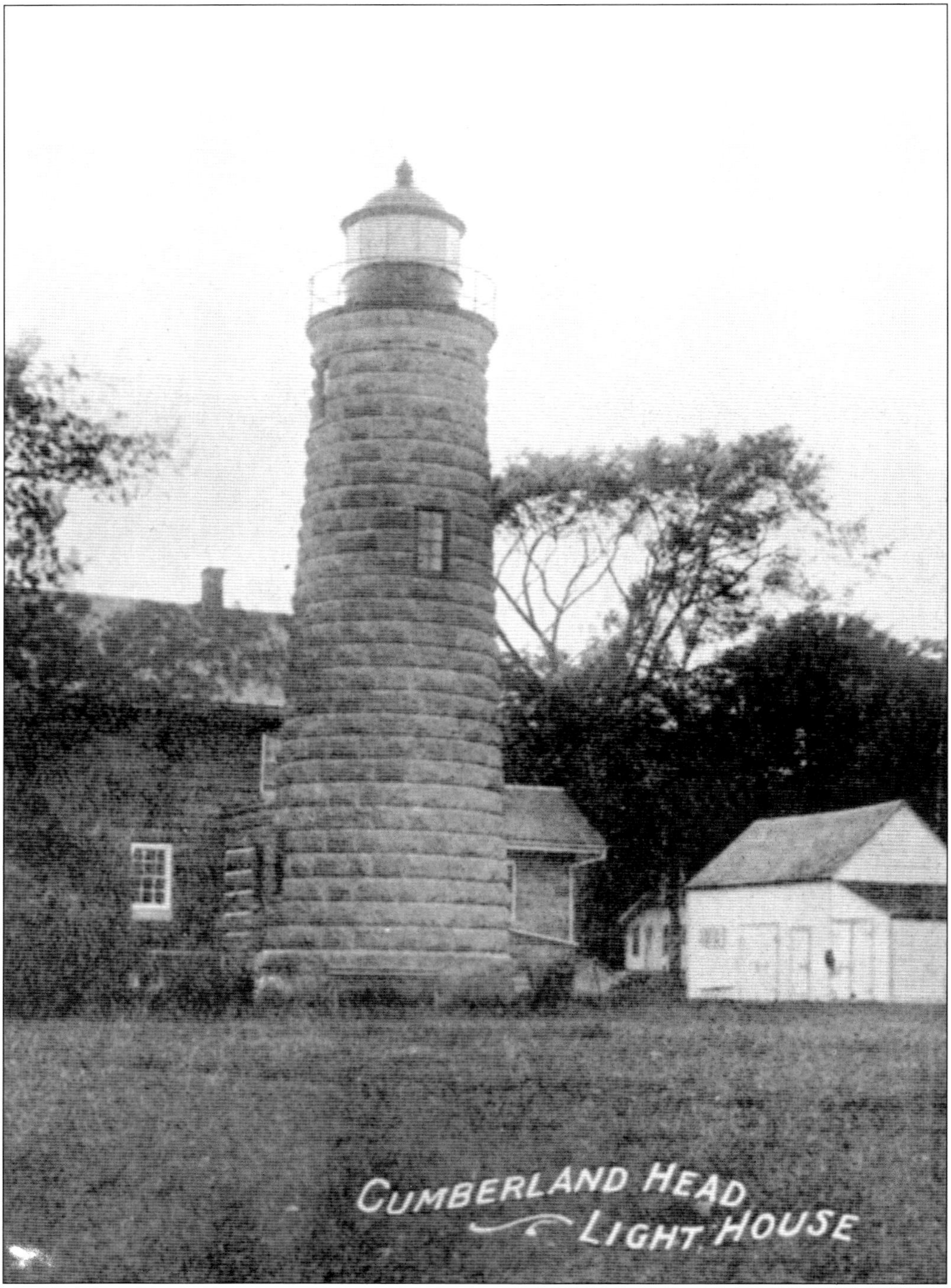

Established in 1838, the Cumberland Head (New York) Light was an essential beacon in the system of lights that guided mariners through the lake at night. This stone tower was constructed in 1867–1868 using blue limestone from S.W. Clark & Company. In 1934, the light was moved into a steel skeleton tower. A replacement tower is still in operation today. (UVM.)

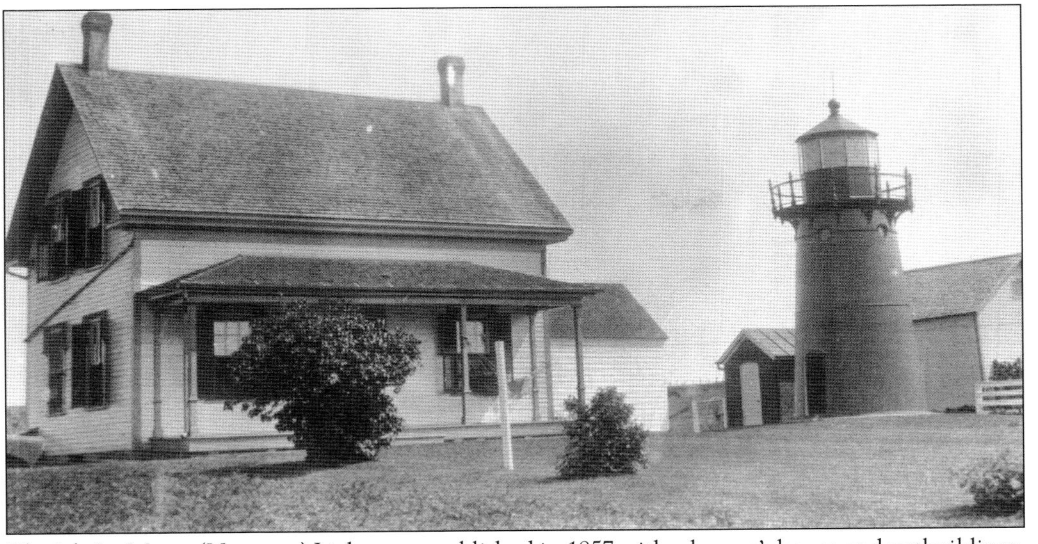

The Isle La Motte (Vermont) Light was established in 1857 with a keeper's house and outbuildings, including the small oil house at right. The federally funded lighthouse service purchased land, constructed facilities, and hired lighthouse keepers, who often lived with their families on the lighthouse property. (LCMM.)

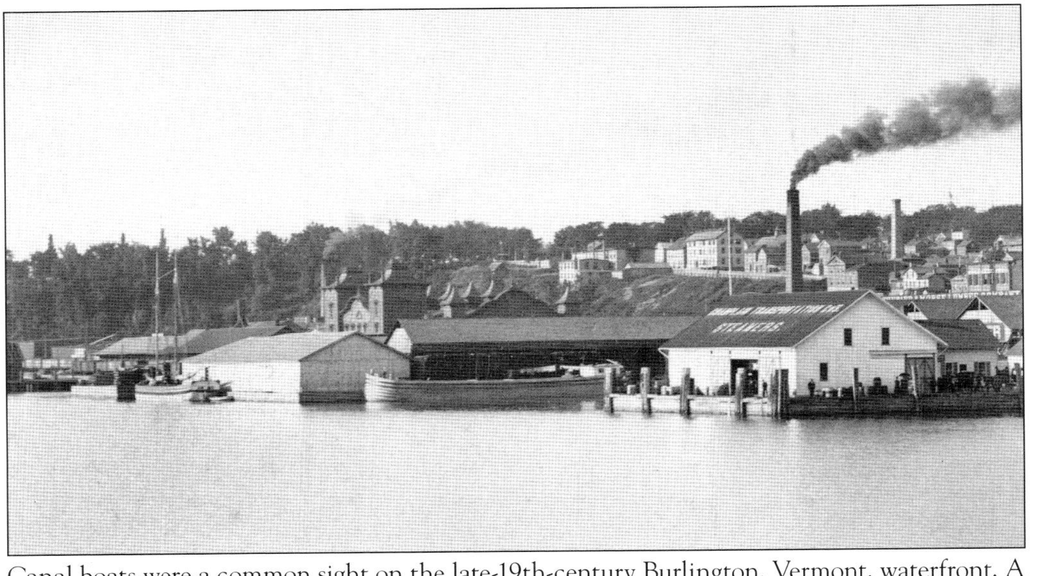

Canal boats were a common sight on the late-19th-century Burlington, Vermont, waterfront. A sailing canal boat (left) is distinguished by the masts, while an empty standard canal boat (center) may be in position to load cargo. At right, passengers await a Champlain Transportation Company steamer. The turreted roof of the railroad station can be seen in the background. (UVM.)

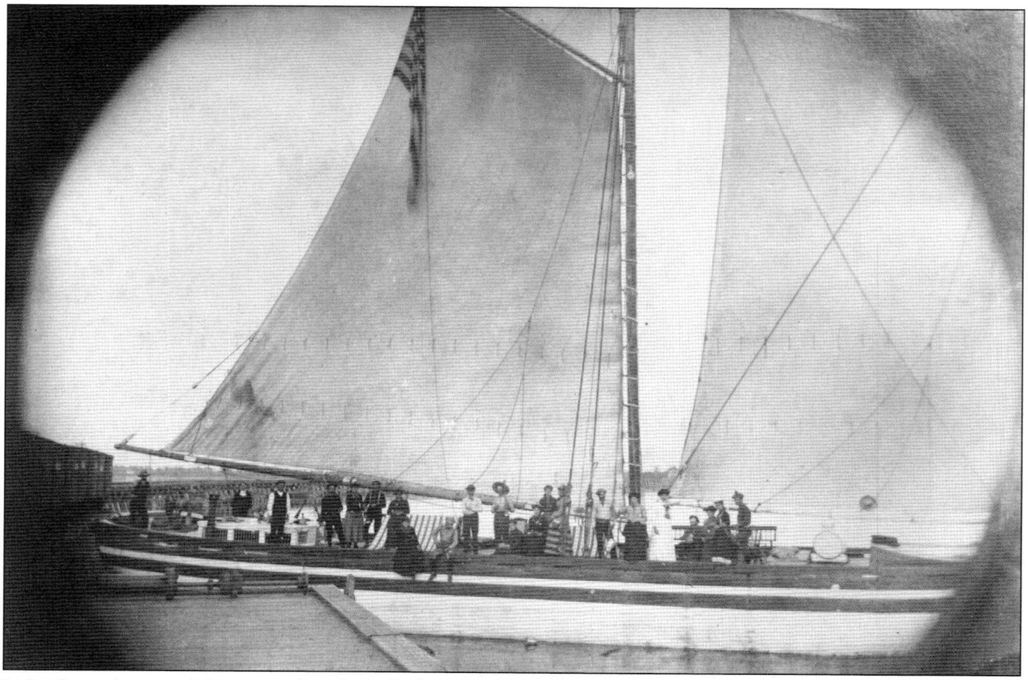

Life aboard a canal boat was hard work, but canalers also found the time to socialize. This group of musicians poses with their instruments aboard a docked sailing canal boat. Although the location cannot be confirmed, the railroad trestle in the background suggests this could be Rouses Point, New York, or one of the other rail crossings across Lake Champlain. (LCMM.)

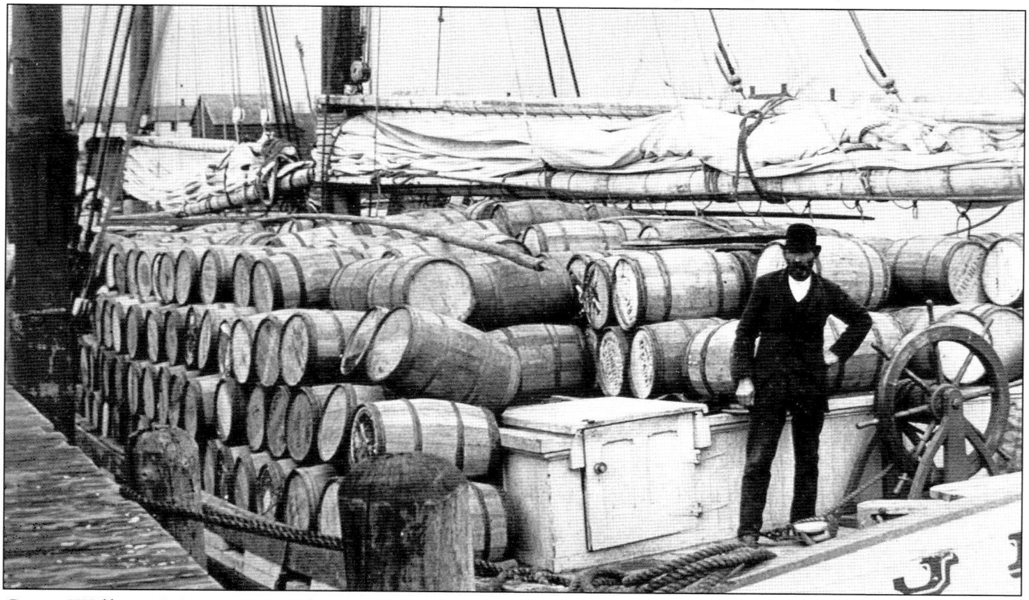

Capt. William Montgomery has just taken on a record load of 2,500 barrels of apples aboard the schooner-rigged scow *J.P. Howard* from Isle La Motte, Vermont. In the 19th century, particularly after the canal was completed, much of the Champlain Valley's farm produce was transported on wooden boats. (ILM.)

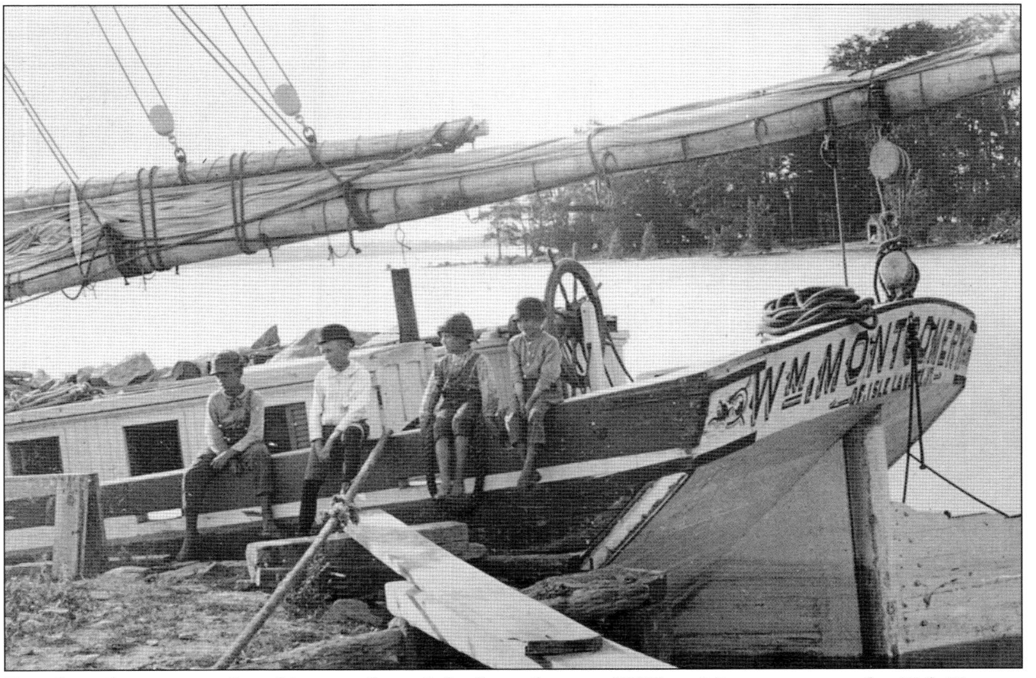

Four boys have a comfortable seat aboard the big schooner *William Montgomery* at the Fisk Quarry landing at Isle La Motte, Vermont. Docks and wharves at key places facilitated the loading and unloading of cargo and passengers onto deeper-draft vessels and helped shelter the boats from wind and waves. (VHS.)

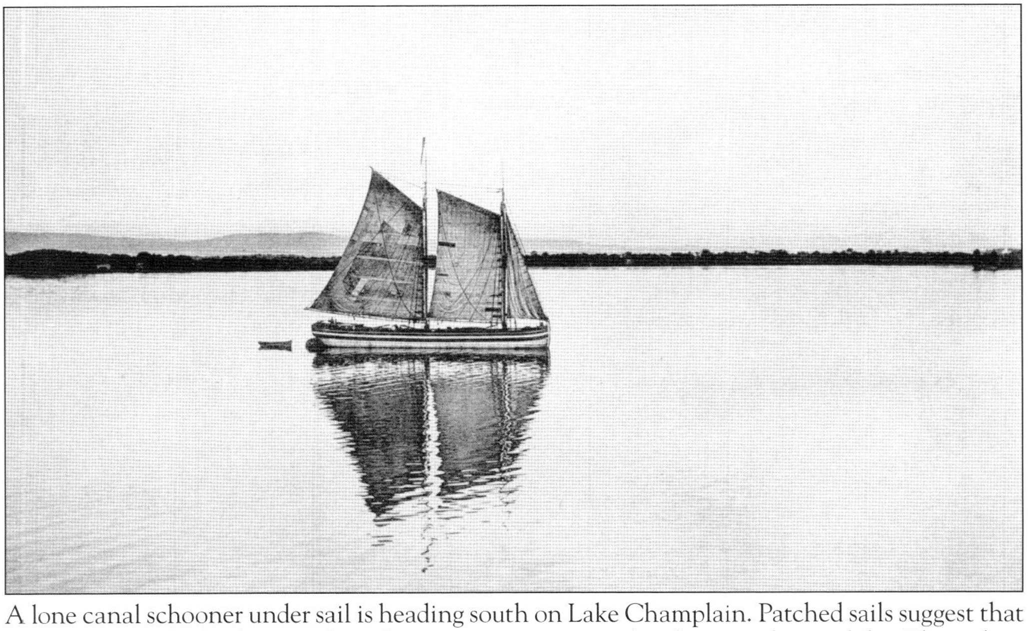

A lone canal schooner under sail is heading south on Lake Champlain. Patched sails suggest that this vessel has had a long and productive career moving freight in and out of the Champlain Valley. The schooner is towing a small rowing boat, which was used when at anchor to get the crew ashore and back aboard. (UVM.)

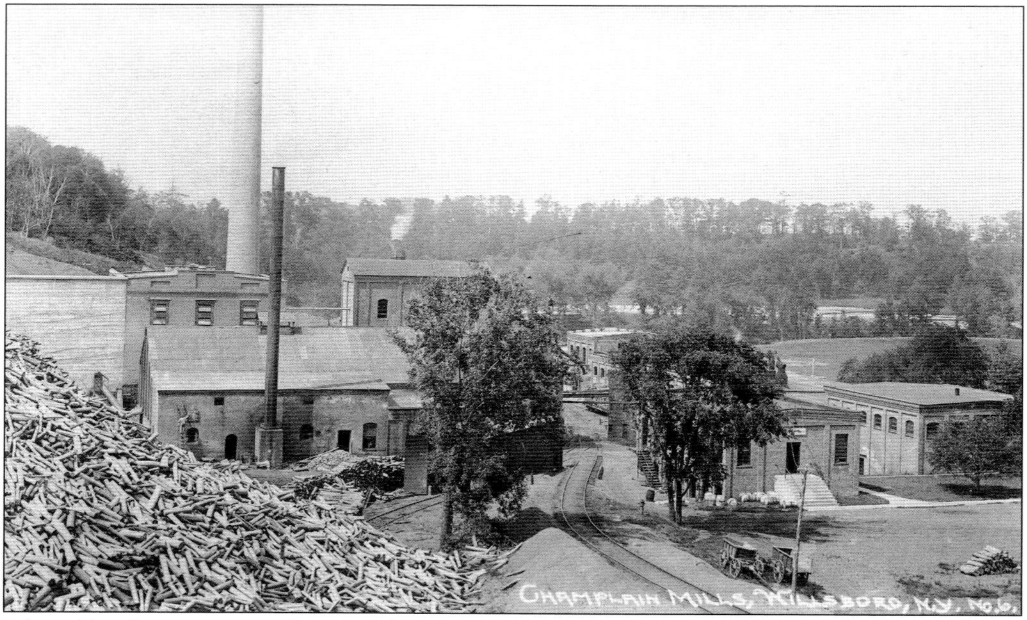

Piles of lumber waiting to be turned into pulp surround the Champlain Mills, which operated at the falls on the Boquet River in Willsboro around 1910. Augustus G. Paine purchased the property from the Champlain Fiber Company in the 1880s. The magazine-quality pulp produced by the plant capitalized on the burgeoning demand for periodicals. It was sent to paper mills in New York and Pennsylvania. (HHRF.)

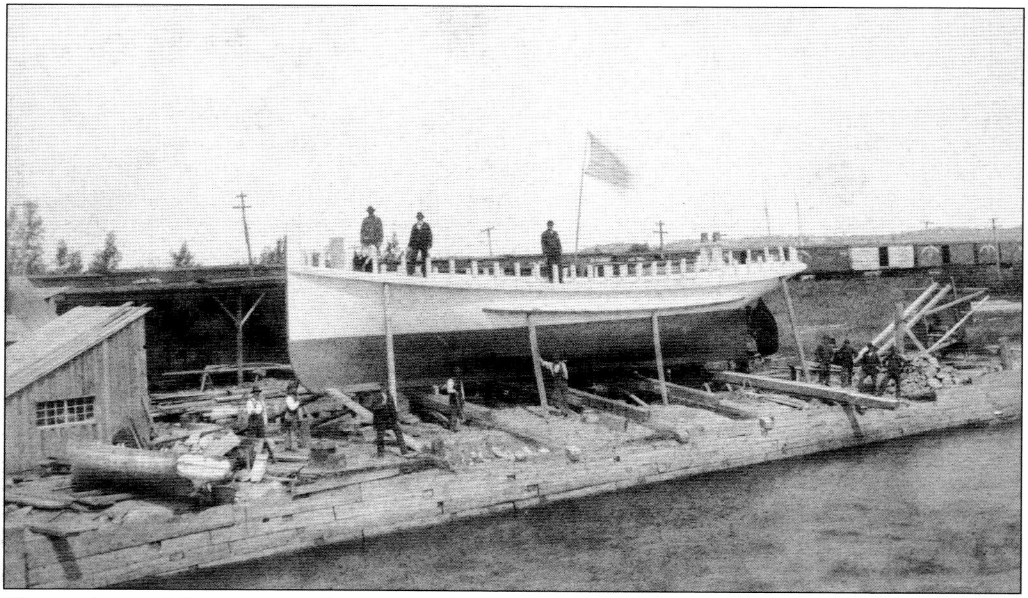

The work vessel *Rescue* is seen here around 1885 at a temporary shipyard in Burlington, Vermont, between the Delaware & Hudson Railroad tracks and the shore. Sixty feet long with a 15-foot beam, *Rescue* was used primarily to tow barges of sand, stone, and other materials for Luther Whitney's marine contract work on breakwaters and seawalls. *Rescue* was captained by George Clark, the youngest son of Solomon and Rhoda Clark. (HHRF.)

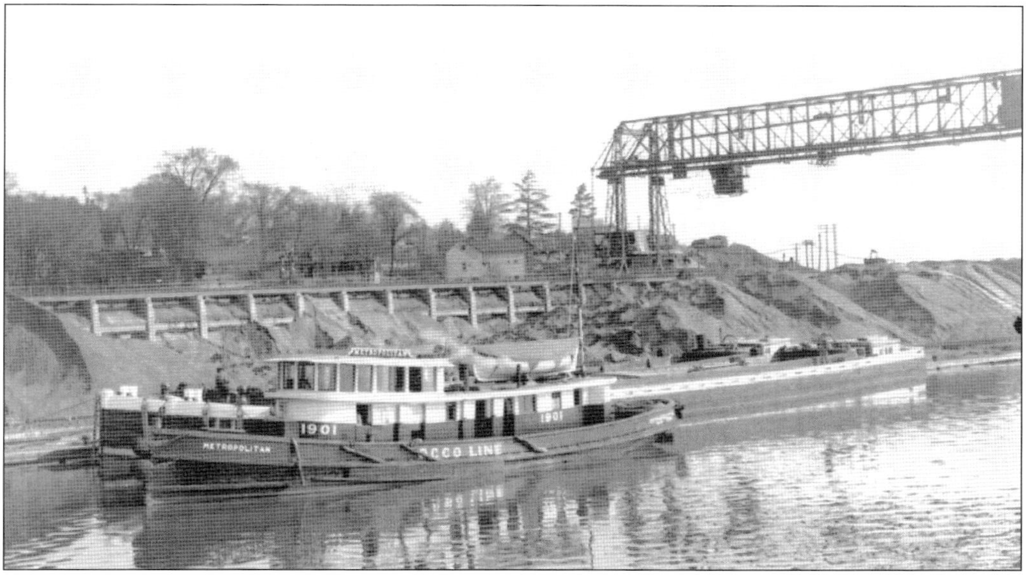

Above, the tug *Metropolitan* sits at the Port Henry, New York, ore dock, powering a canal barge in the final days of waterborne commercial transportation. In an effort to remain competitive, New York's canal system was repeatedly enlarged. Port Henry, also seen below, was a port for the vast iron-mining operations in nearby communities such as Moriah, Ironville, Mineville, and Witherbee. Miners worked as deep as 2,000 feet in the ground, which took them more than an hour to commute to from the surface. The high-grade iron ore was shipped to processing centers by horse-drawn wagons, canal boats, and railroads to be transformed into everything from stoves to ironclads. (Both, BF.)

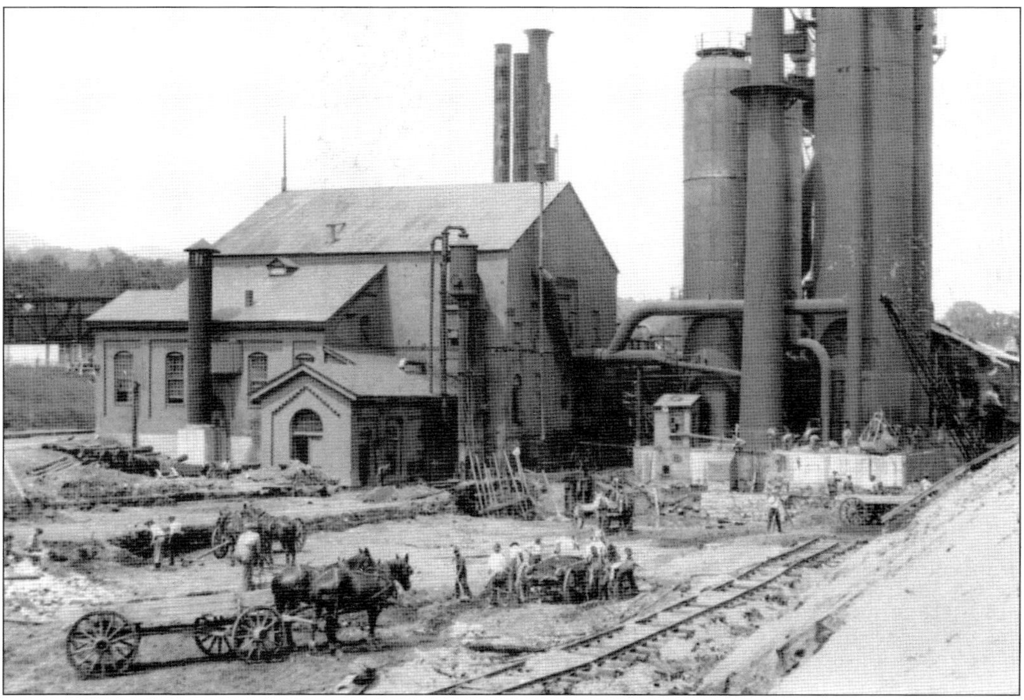

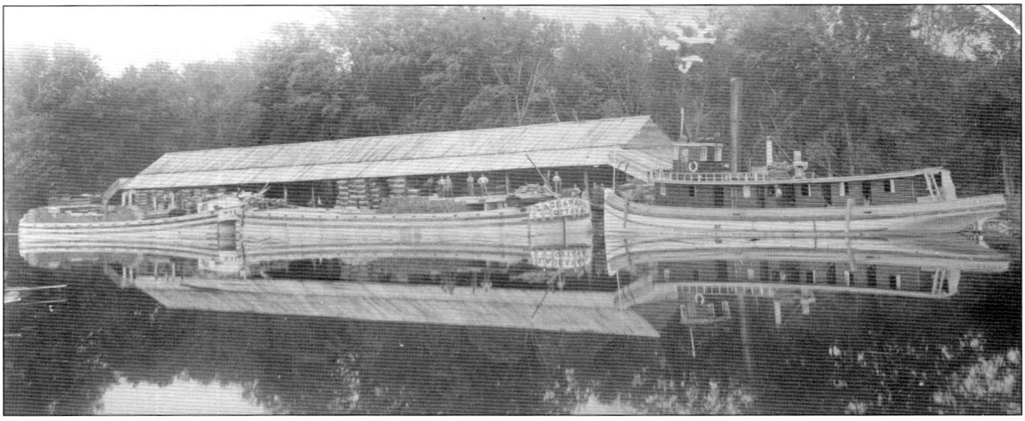

Two canal boats and a companion tugboat from the Ottawa Transportation Company sit at the dock on Otter Creek below Vergennes, Vermont, in this image from 1892. Industry boomed in the late 19th century, particularly shipping connected to the Champlain Canal and wood-finishing related to lumber imported from Canada. As railways supplanted the canal system, manufacturing declined. A railroad spur from Ferrisburgh to the base of the falls at Vergennes proved a failure, as the grades were too steep for practical operations. (UVM.)

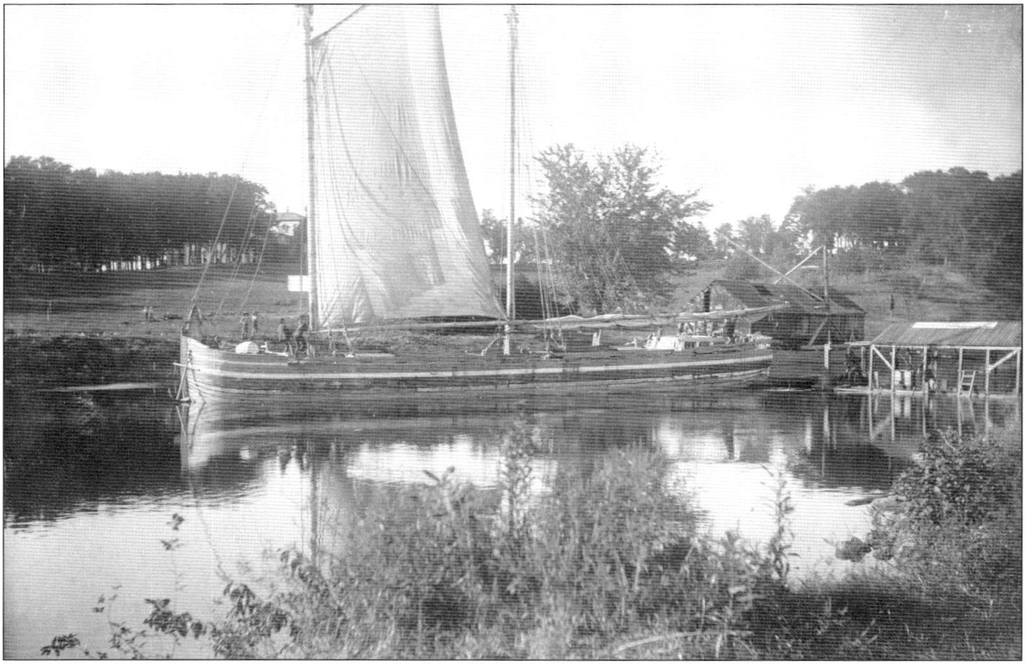

One of Lake Champlain's hardworking canal schooners is raising its foresail and leaving Vergennes, Vermont, on Otter Creek. These boats were designed to sail on Lake Champlain and then, at Whitehall, New York, take down the sailing rig and transit through the Champlain Canal towed by horses or mules. (UVM.)

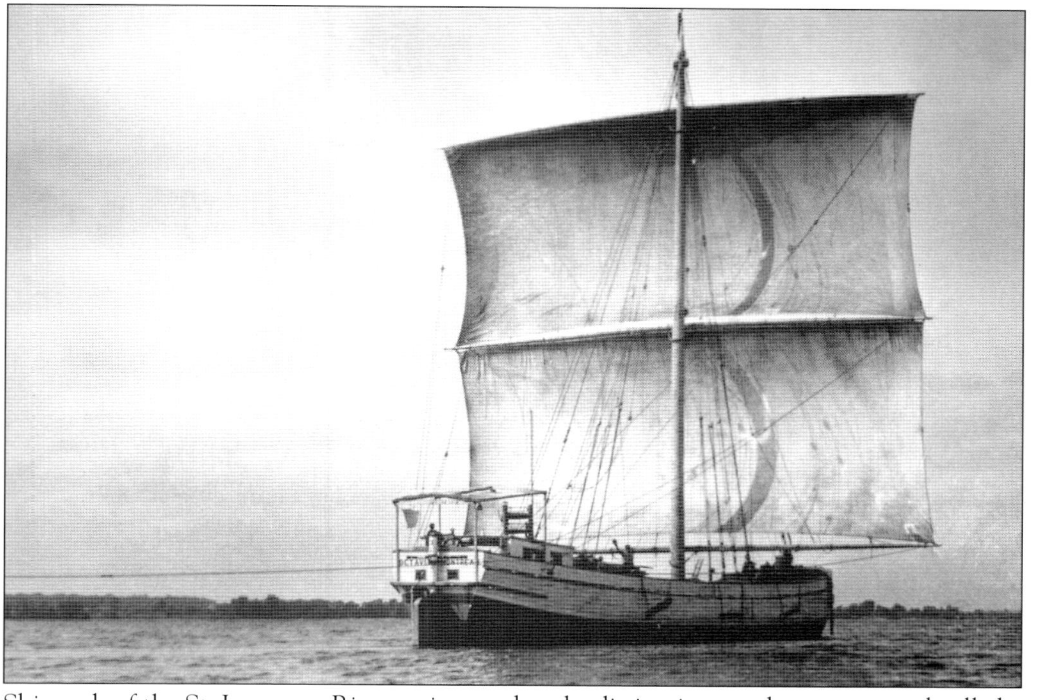

Shipyards of the St. Lawrence River region produced a distinctive wooden cargo vessel called a "pin plat" that had a different shape than Lake Champlain canal boats: a single mast with two square sails. They typically carried Canadian lumber to Burlington, Vermont, for processing. The *Burlington Free Press and Times* on July 7, 1871, noted, "The pin plat is a native of Canada and looks like an old fashioned country woodbox magnified fifty times." (ILM.)

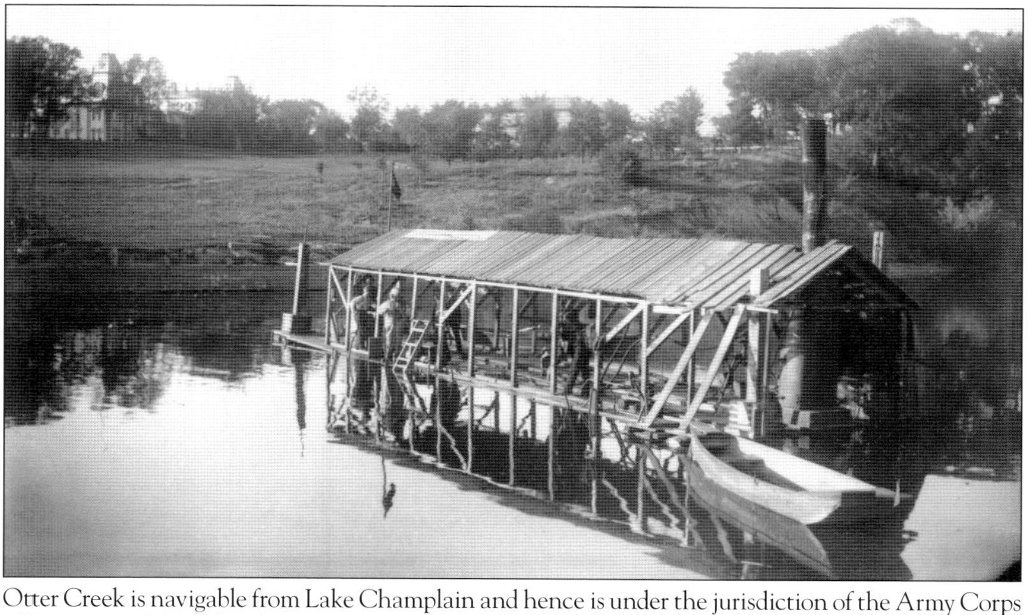

Otter Creek is navigable from Lake Champlain and hence is under the jurisdiction of the Army Corps of Engineers. A hard-hat diver can be seen at the left end of a work platform fitted with a steam engine. He may be setting underwater charges to remove an obstruction to navigation. (UVM.)

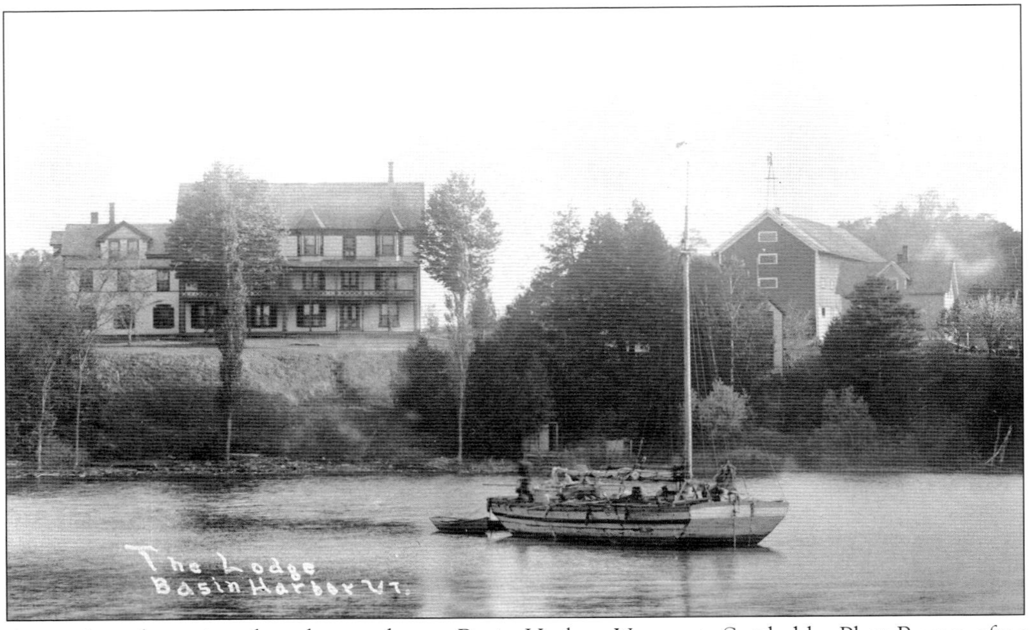

A wooden, sloop-rigged work scow leaves Basin Harbor, Vermont. Settled by Platt Rogers after the Revolutionary War, Basin Harbor was part of an early and well-traveled route across Lake Champlain. The ferry landing boasted a two-horse-powered boat in 1832. The Lodge was established in 1887; today, the fifth generation of the Beach family still welcomes visitors. (UVM.)

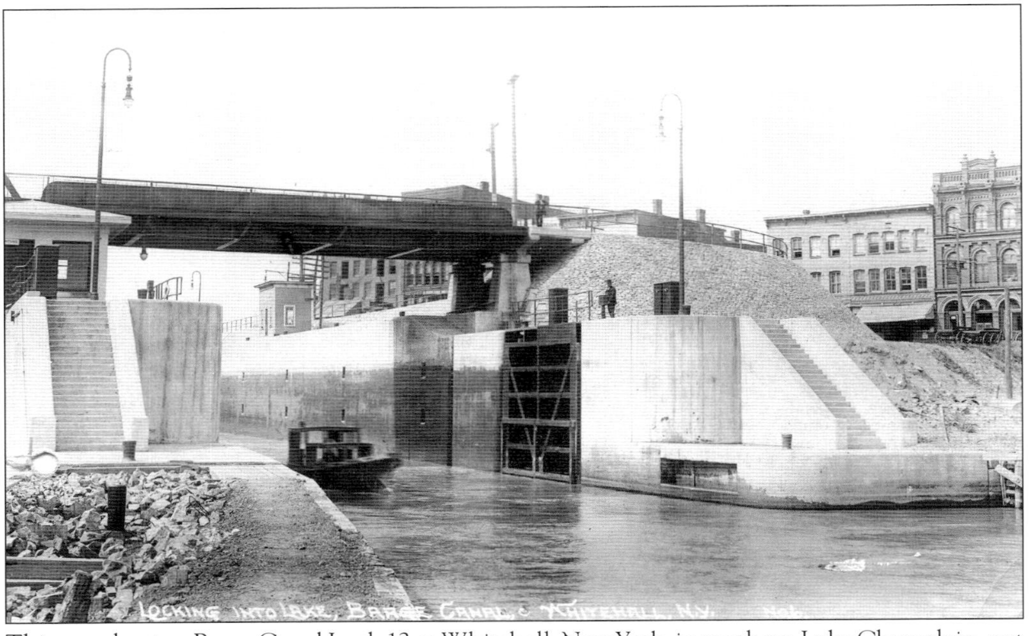

This vessel enters Barge Canal Lock 12 at Whitehall, New York, in southern Lake Champlain, not long after its 1918 opening. This enlarged version of the Champlain Canal allowed significantly larger vessels to transport more cargo to ports such as Buffalo, Albany, and New York City. A century later, the Barge Canal is still open today and is popular with recreational boaters. (UVM.)

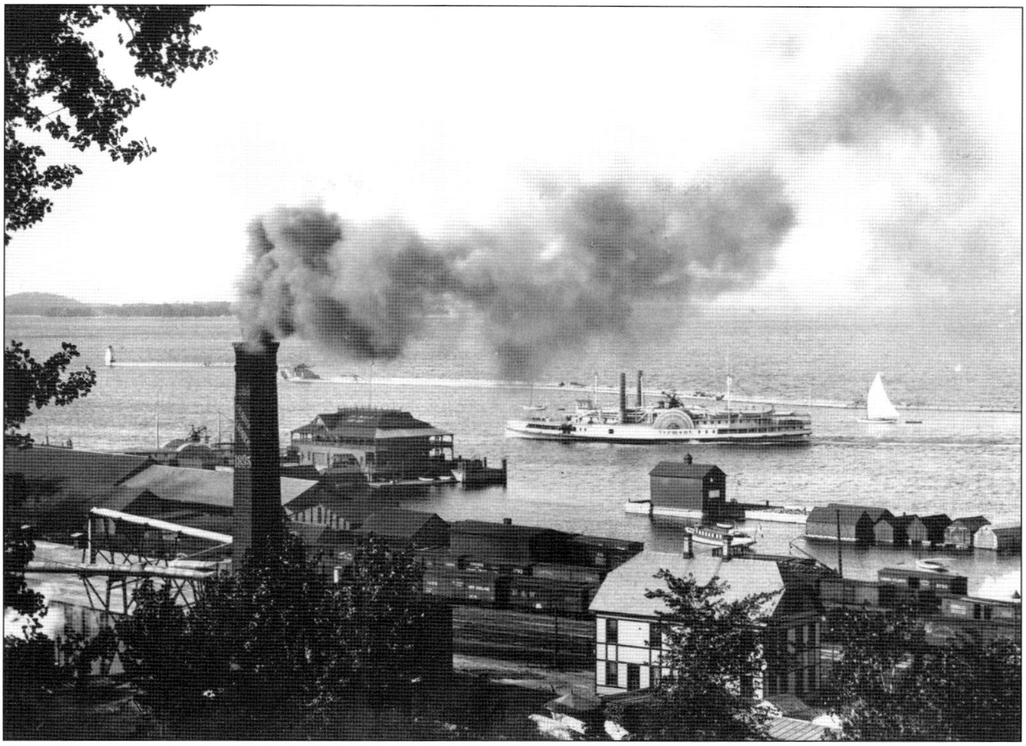

Above, the steamboat *Vermont II* (1871) passes the original Lake Champlain Yacht Club (1887) from the north end of Burlington Harbor, Vermont. The Burlington breakwater, seen beyond the steamboat, helped transform the exposed harbor into a safe haven for boats and commerce. Burlington's many lumber-processing companies imported and milled Canadian lumber and sent it out to market by rail and boat. The breakwater, begun in 1836 and regularly expanded through the end of the 19th century, is seen below under construction. (Both, UVM.)

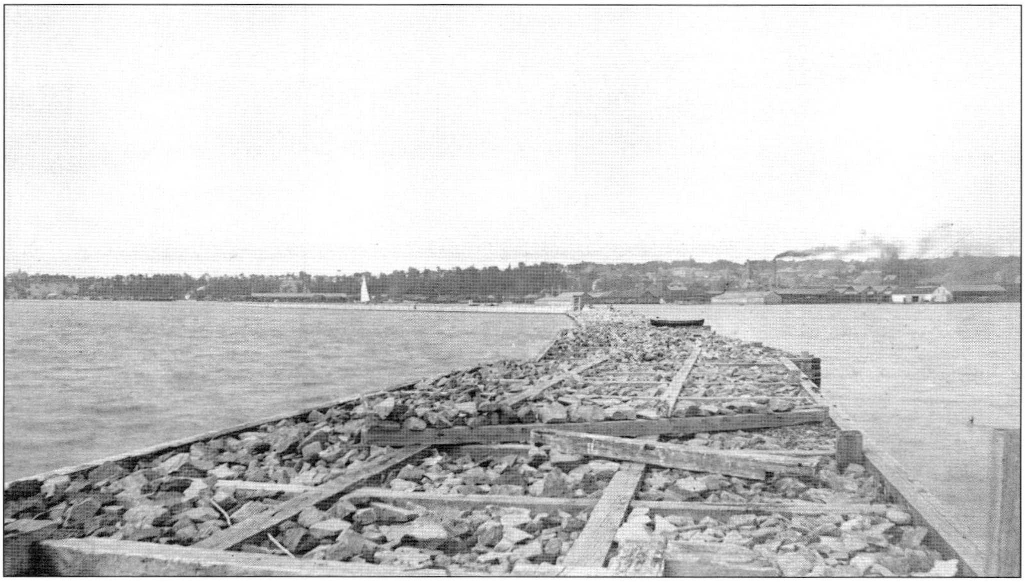

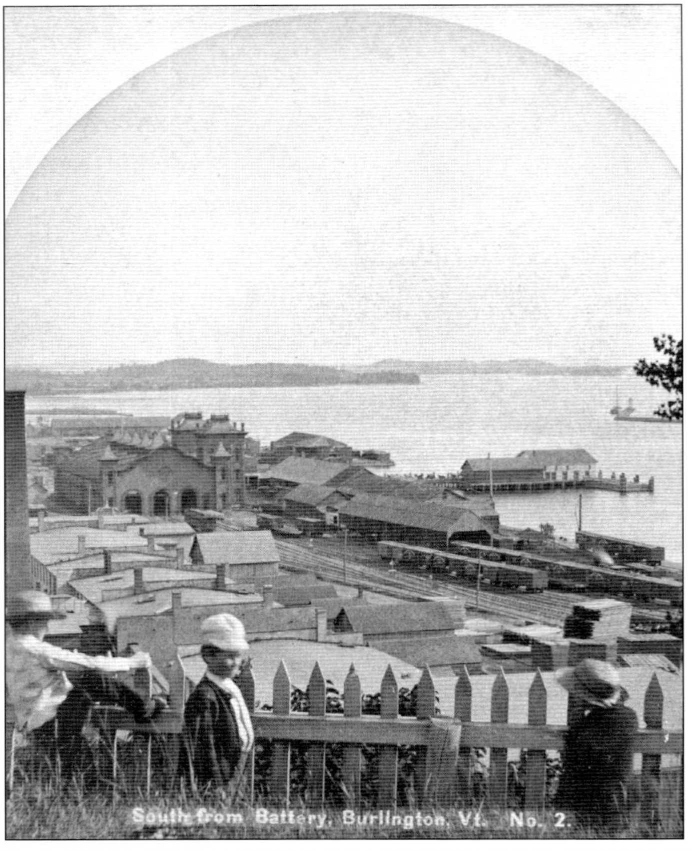

The early view of the Burlington, Vermont, waterfront at left, taken from the Battery, predates any of the boathouses, placing it prior to 1887. At this time, Burlington, the "Queen City," was the third-largest lumber port in the United States, a bustling economic hub connected to other markets by water and rail. The shoreline was repeatedly expanded with fill from the hillside, railway construction, and other locations. Below, a Civil War–era view of Rouses Point, New York, captures the 1847 steamboat *United States*, built in Shelburne, Vermont, docked alongside the 1848 schooner *American*, built in Willsboro, New York, and the canal schooner *S.H. Witherbee*, built in Essex, New York. (Left, UVM; below, LCMM.)

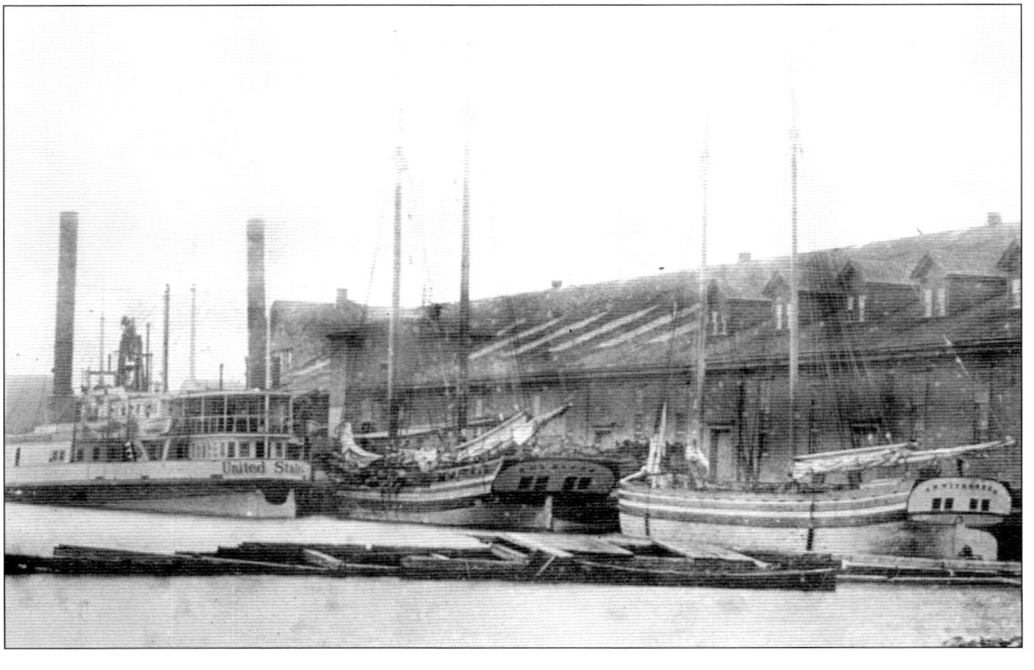

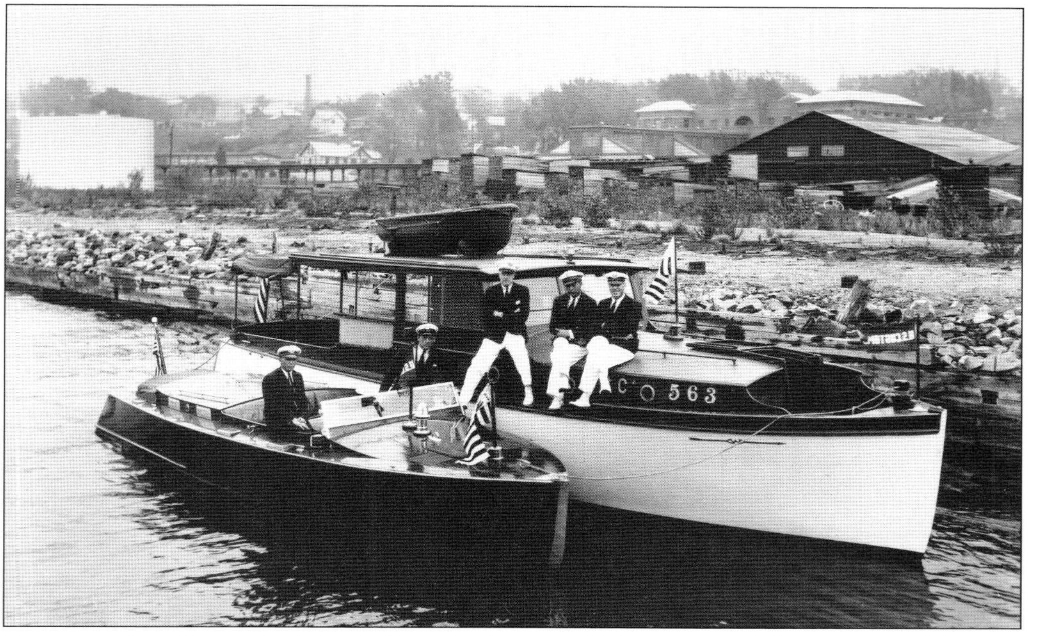

Commercial traffic on the lake declined in the early 20th century, while recreational boating expanded. The Burlington Harbor Coast Guard station was established in 1948 to maintain the lake's lighthouses, buoys, and other aids to navigation. (LCMM.)

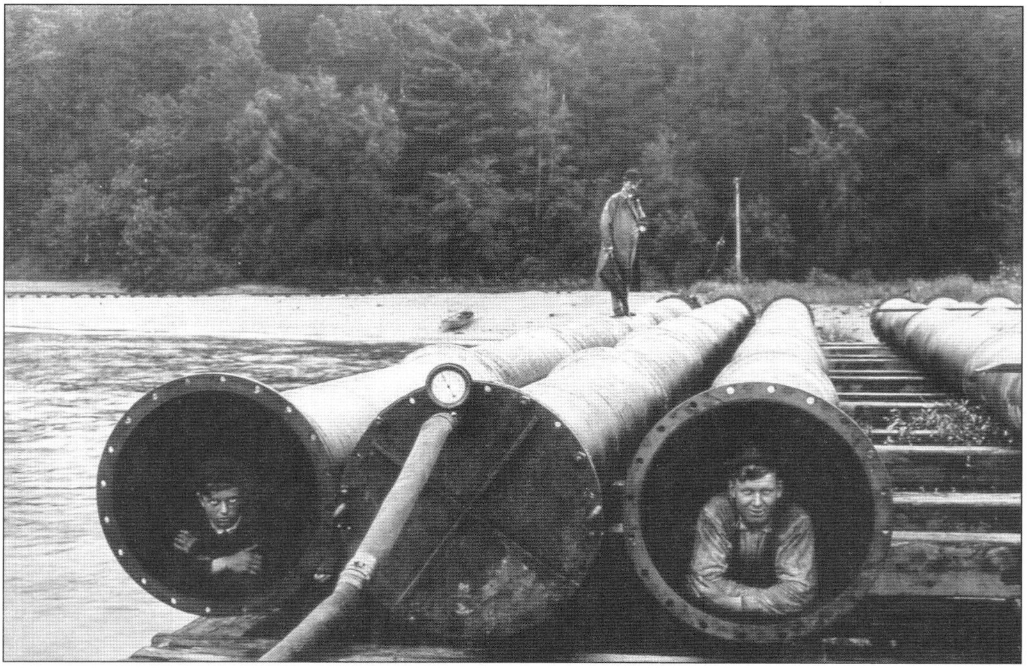

By the end of the 19th century, communities were becoming more aware of the importance of separating their sewer discharge from the point where water was taken for public use. This 1894 photograph captures some lighthearted workmen posing in the water pipes that were being readied for installation in Burlington Harbor. (VHS.)

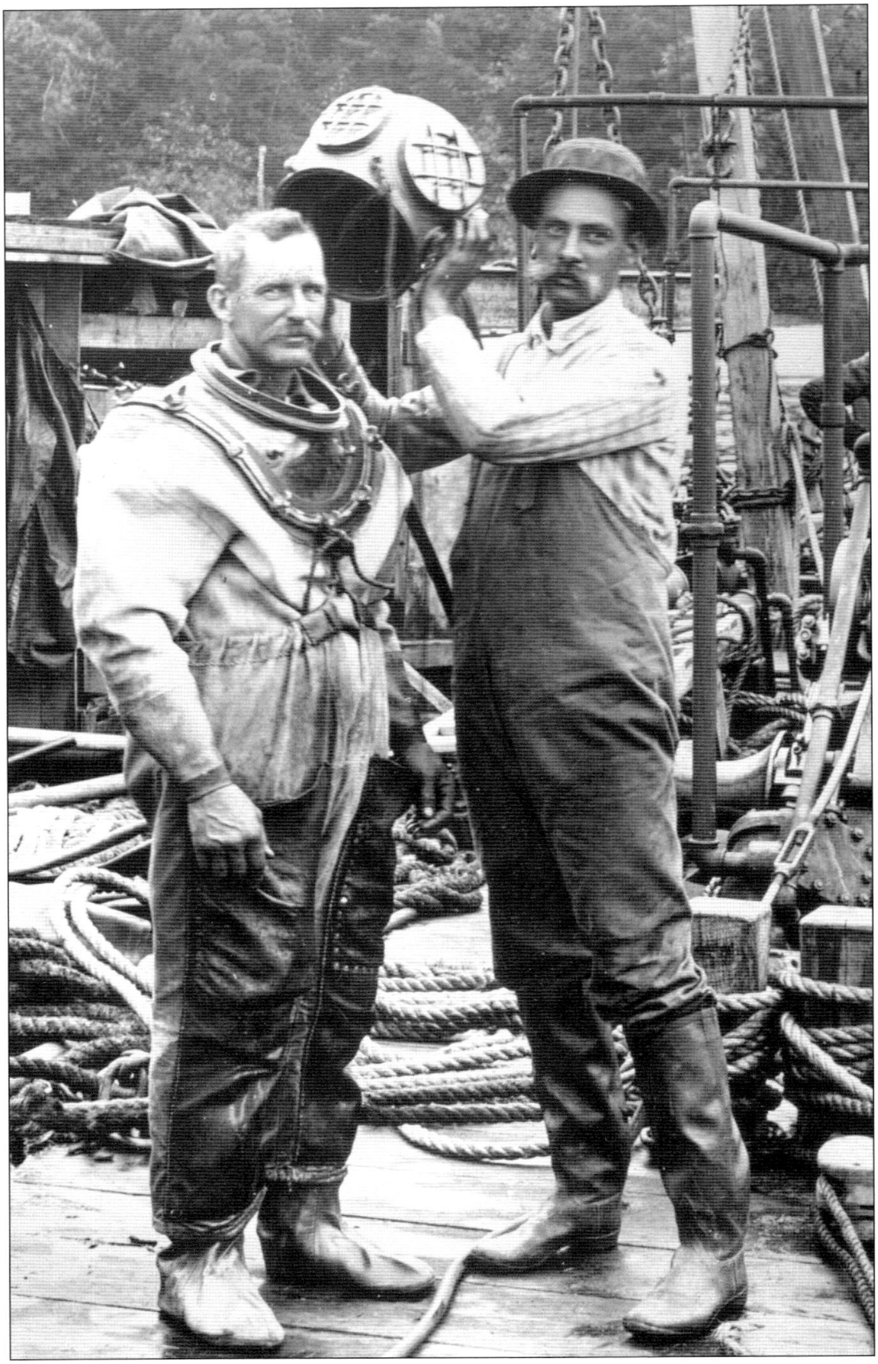

These men were likely working on the water intake project in Burlington, Vermont, shown on the previous page. This dangerous work entailed the diver donning a suit that could weigh 180 pounds before being lowered into the water to walk on the bottom of the lake. The diver then relied entirely on the surface to supply his air; early hand pumps were later replaced with steam compressors. (VHS.)

Three

Crossing Lake Champlain

Soon after the Revolutionary War, enterprising settlers began providing ferry service across the lake, as well as room and board for weary travelers. The earliest ferries were probably rowboats and canoes that carried passengers for a fee or barter. Later ferries were powered by sail, cable systems, horse tread-wheels, steam, and, ultimately, the diesel engines still used today.

Ferries were located at convenient points along the lake a few miles apart. The States of New York and Vermont licensed petitioners to operate a ferry at a particular location for a certain period of years. In the winter, markers on the ice guided travel. Communities that faced each other across the lake often shared churches and social events.

By the mid-19th century, trains needed to cross the lake. Trestles linked Swanton and Alburgh, Vermont, and Alburgh with Rouses Point, New York. Another trestle crossed the lake between Larrabee's Point, Vermont, and Ticonderoga, New York. A section of each trestle was engineered to permit lake vessels to pass.

Automobiles, introduced as the 20th century began, eventually replaced horse-drawn vehicles. Ferries were adapted, and roads began to dominate the transportation system. The Lake Champlain Bridge, the first permanent highway bridge to span the lake, was constructed in 1929, linking Crown Point, New York, and Chimney Point, Vermont. The second highway to cross the lake, between Rouses Point, New York, and Swanton, Vermont, was completed in 1938. This causeway required the construction of the Rouses Point Bridge and the Missisquoi Bay Bridge. By 1945, bridges connected almost all of the Champlain Islands, and the roads around Lake Champlain had been vastly improved. Even tourists abandoned the lake's excursion vessels and embraced the automobile.

Today, ferries cross Lake Champlain at four points. Three are operated by the Lake Champlain Transportation Company: Grand Isle, Vermont, to Cumberland Head, New York; Burlington to Port Kent, New York; and Charlotte, Vermont, to Essex, New York. A private cable ferry operates seasonally between Shoreham, Vermont, and Ticonderoga, New York.

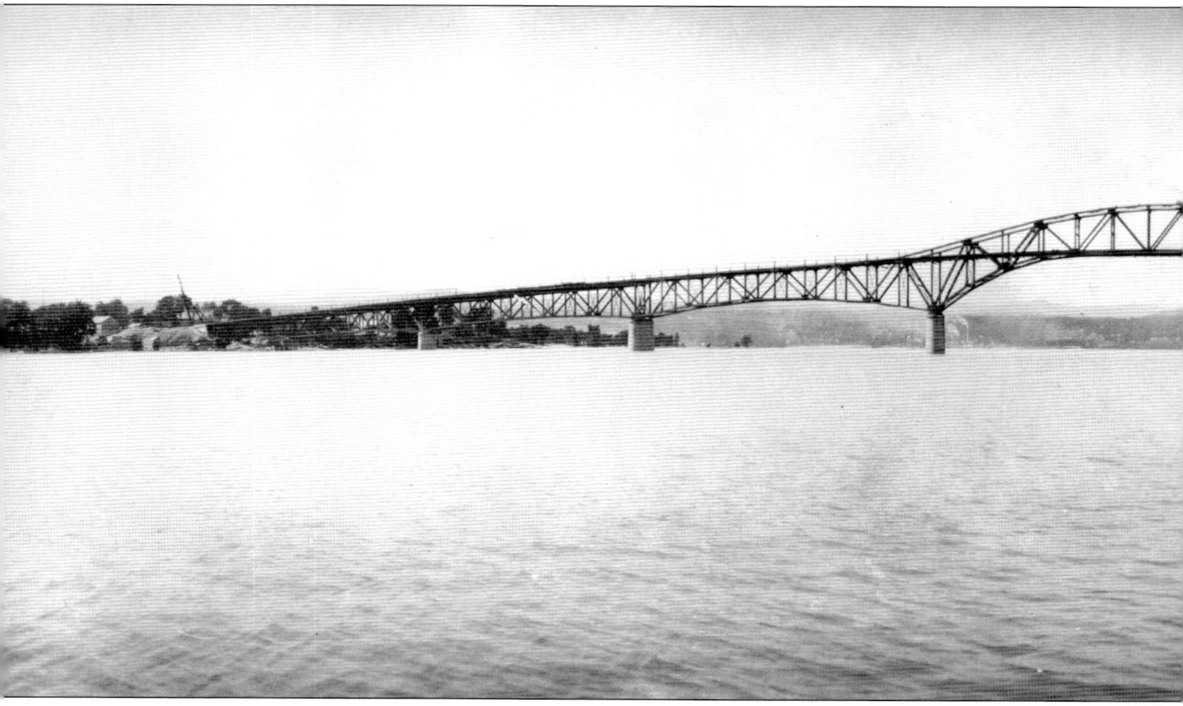

The Lake Champlain Bridge opened in August 1929, connecting Crown Point, New York, to Chimney Point, Vermont. This beloved local landmark was declared structurally unsound in

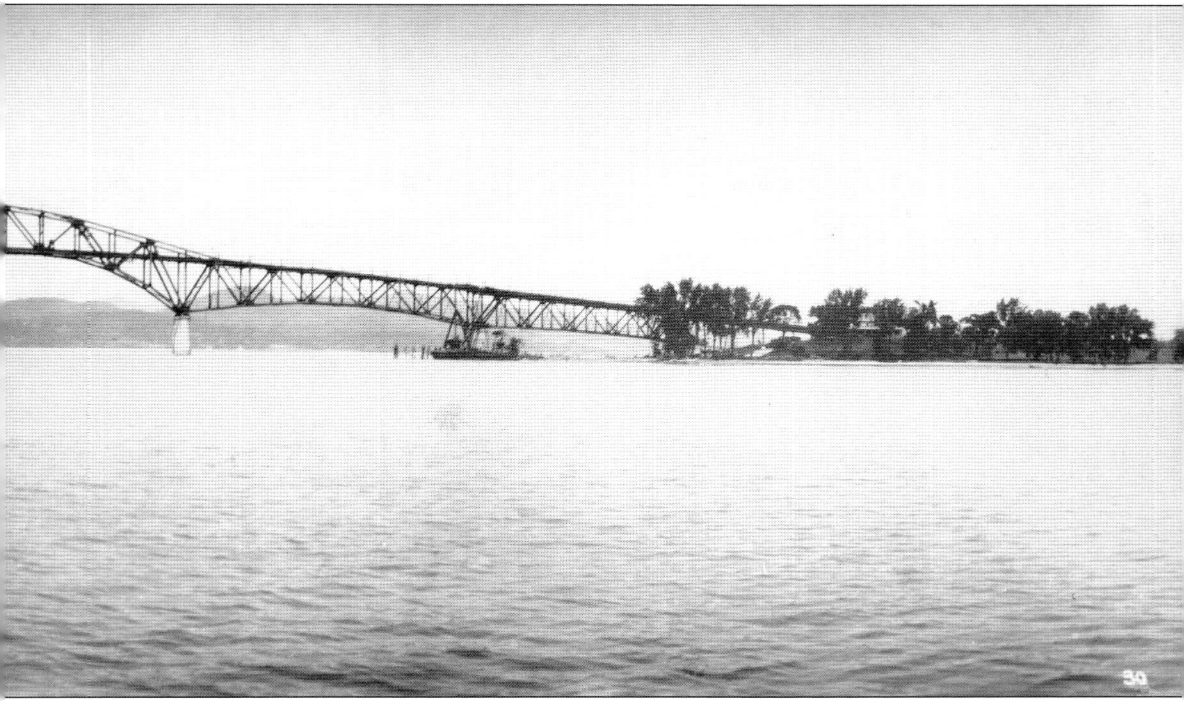

2009, and the final design selected for its replacement echoes the distinctive silhouette of the original. (LCMM.)

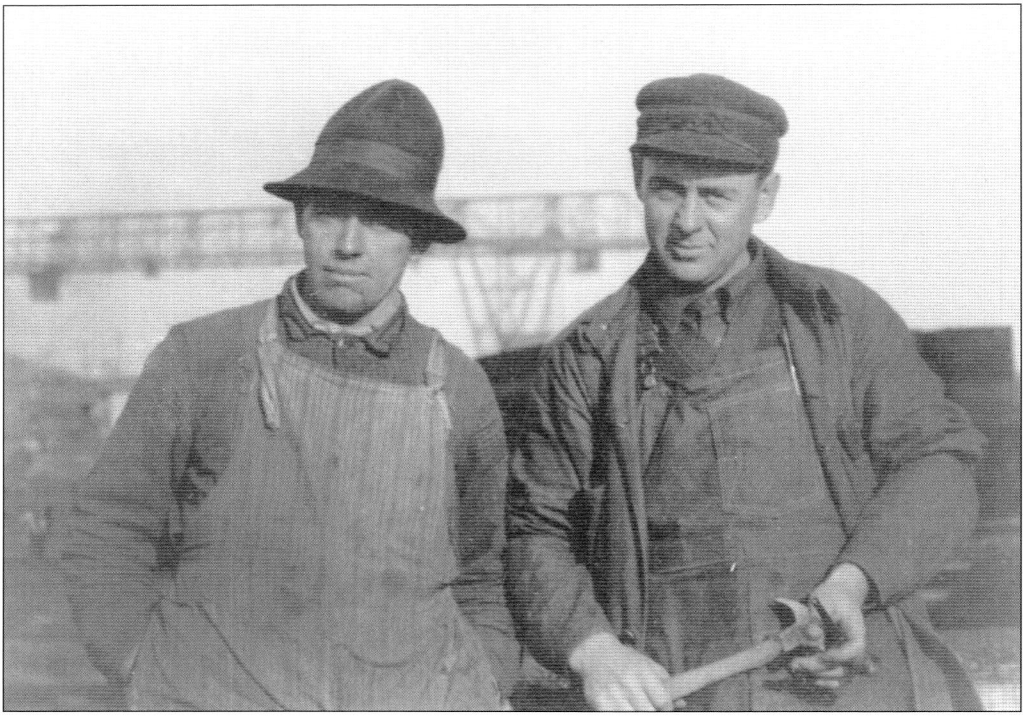

The community watched the construction of the Lake Champlain Bridge with fascination and great anticipation of the convenience it would bring. Above, bridge workers pause to record their participation in this momentous project. Below, photographer Louis L. McAllister captured the steamboat *Vermont III* passing beneath the bridge. The channel clearance of 90 feet was designed to accommodate this vessel's smokestack. (Above, BF; below, UVM.)

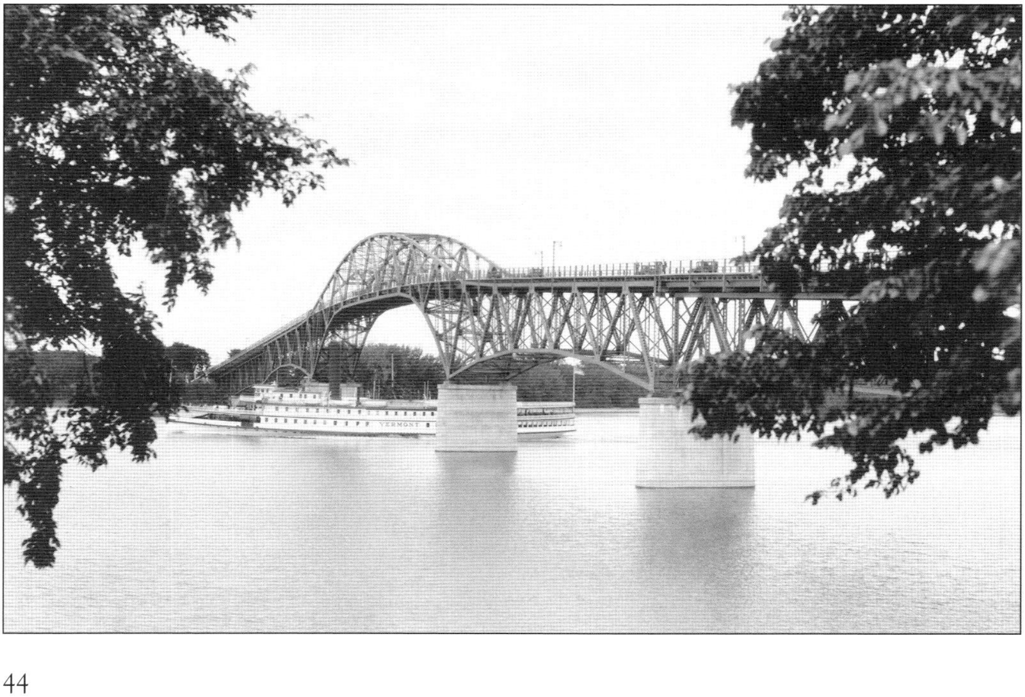

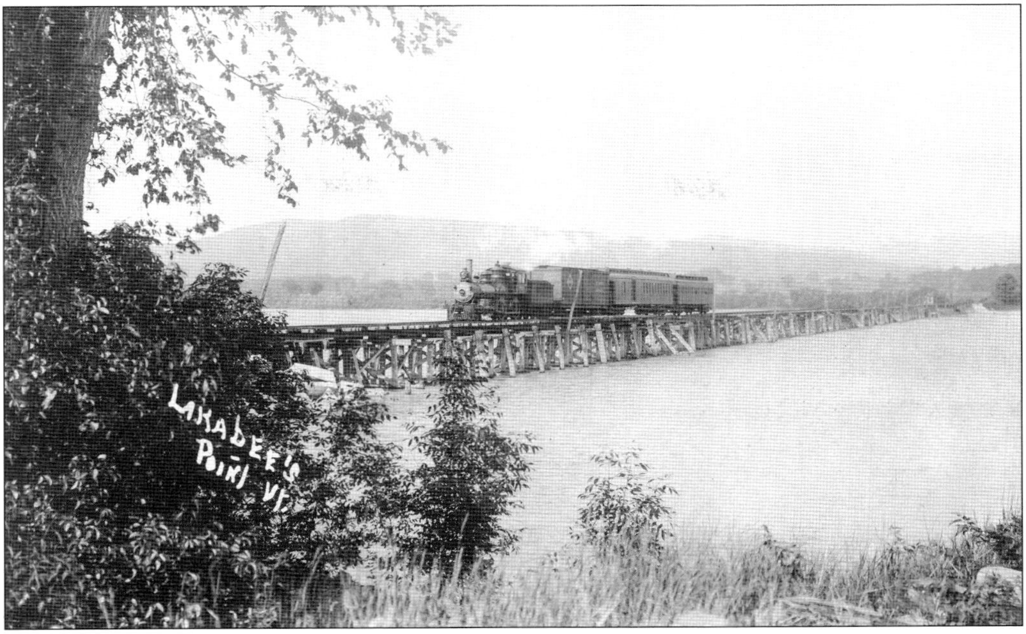

An Addison Railroad Company train crosses the trestle between Larrabee's Point, Vermont, and Ticonderoga, New York. A section of the track was supported by a floating draw-boat that was moved out of the way for marine traffic and filled the gap when the train was scheduled. This section can be seen by carefully looking at the right side of the photograph. The bridge was abandoned in 1923 due to competition from trucking. (UVM.)

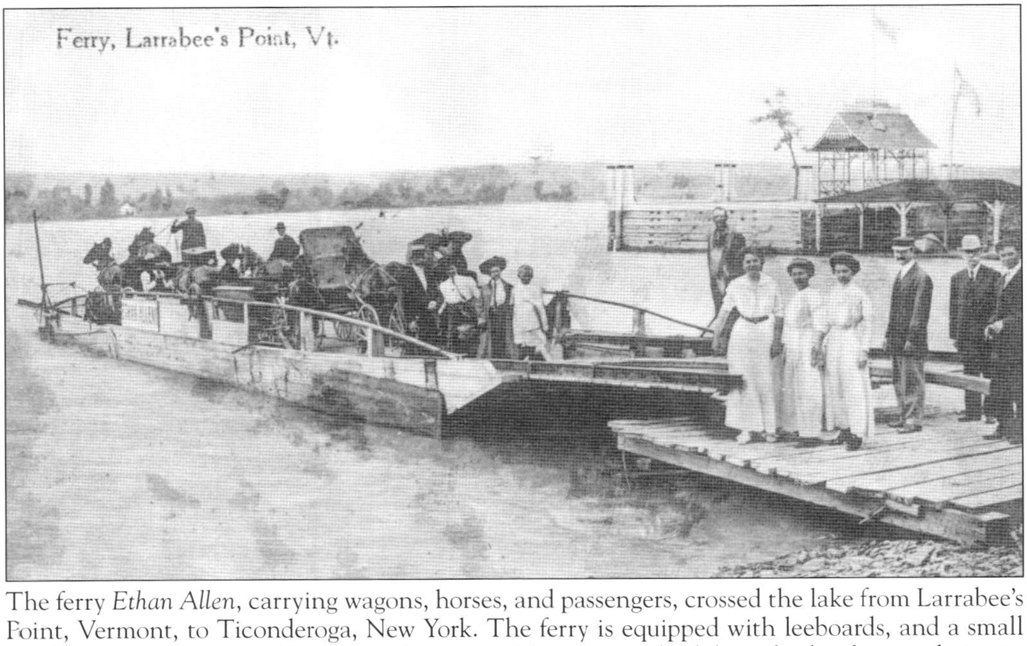

The ferry *Ethan Allen*, carrying wagons, horses, and passengers, crossed the lake from Larrabee's Point, Vermont, to Ticonderoga, New York. The ferry is equipped with leeboards, and a small auxiliary vessel (not visible) probably powered her across the lake. The landing and pier in the background are still in use, and a steel barge ferry operates by cable on the route of *Ethan Allen*. (UVM.)

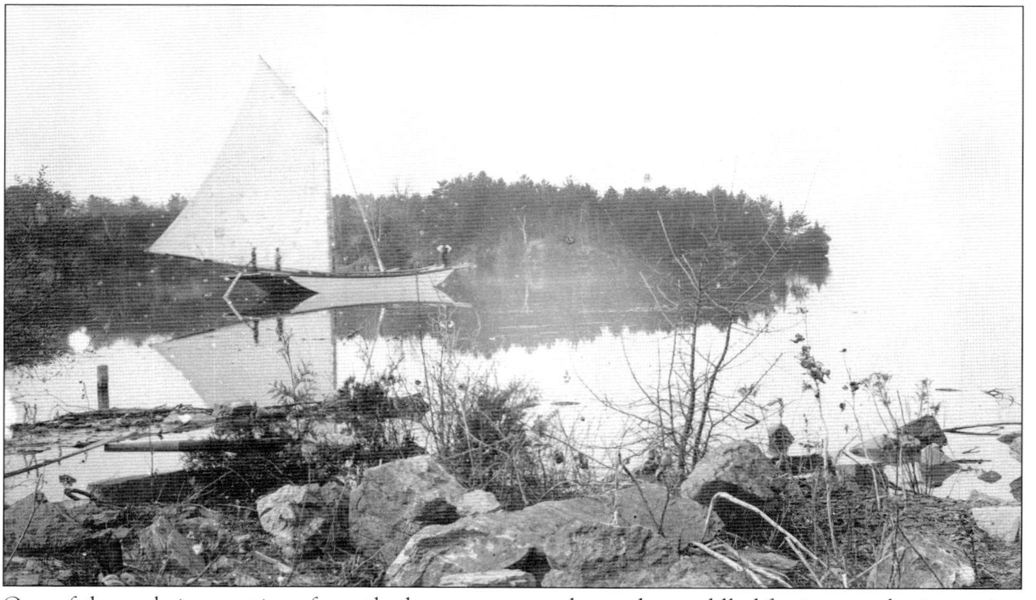

One of the early innovations from the human-powered rowed or paddled ferries was the invention of the Lake Champlain sail ferry, like this one at Arnold's Bay. This wooden, barge-like hull supported a single mast and sail, with an offset mast to keep the center free for loading cattle or horse-drawn wagons. The sail ferry was steered with a long sweep from the stern. (BMFL.)

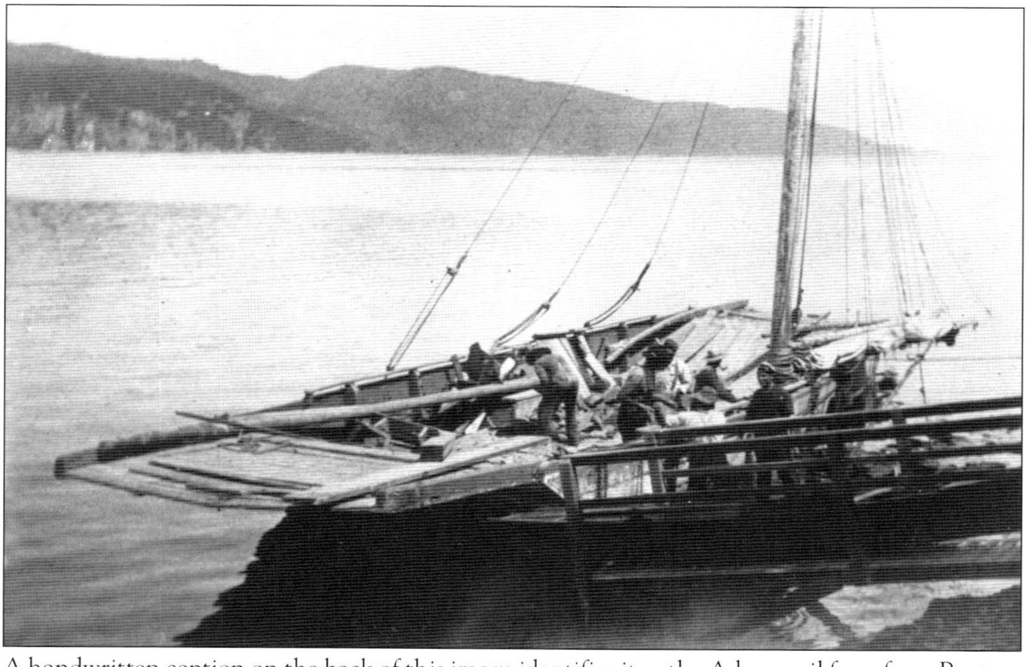

A handwritten caption on the back of this image identifies it as the Adams sail ferry from Panton, Vermont, to Westport, New York, around 1905. Operations at the site began in 1799, ceasing in 1929 with the opening of the Lake Champlain Bridge. (LCMM.)

The wooden scow ferry *Champlain* was built in 1922 to serve the expanding motor vehicle traffic at the Larrabee's Point–Ticonderoga crossing. Powered by an auxiliary vessel secured to its side, many of these cross-lake ferries were double-ended and designed to drop a ramp on shore for vehicle boarding. A modern-day steel barge and auxiliary vessel on a cable still operates at this crossing today. (LCMM.)

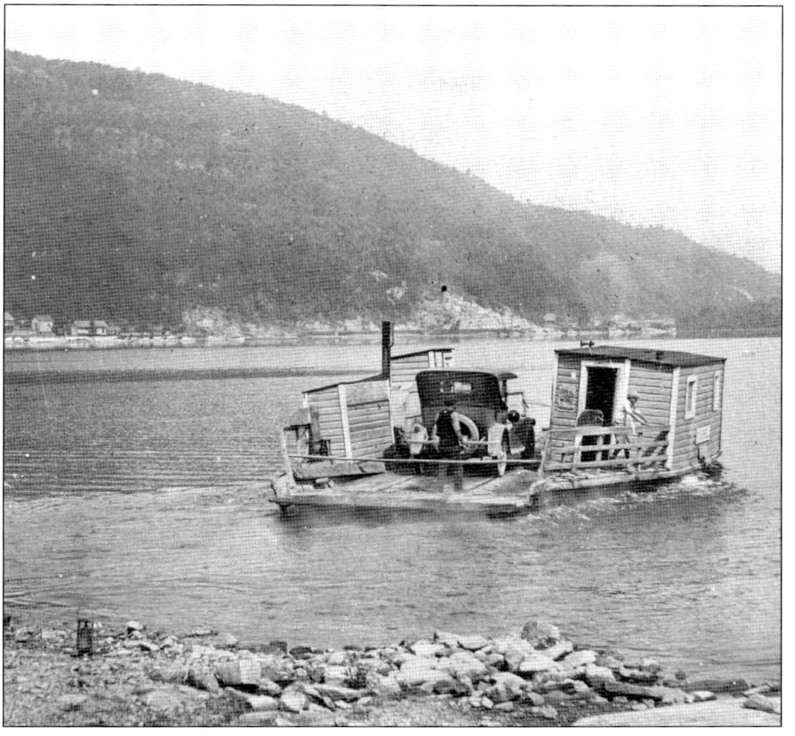

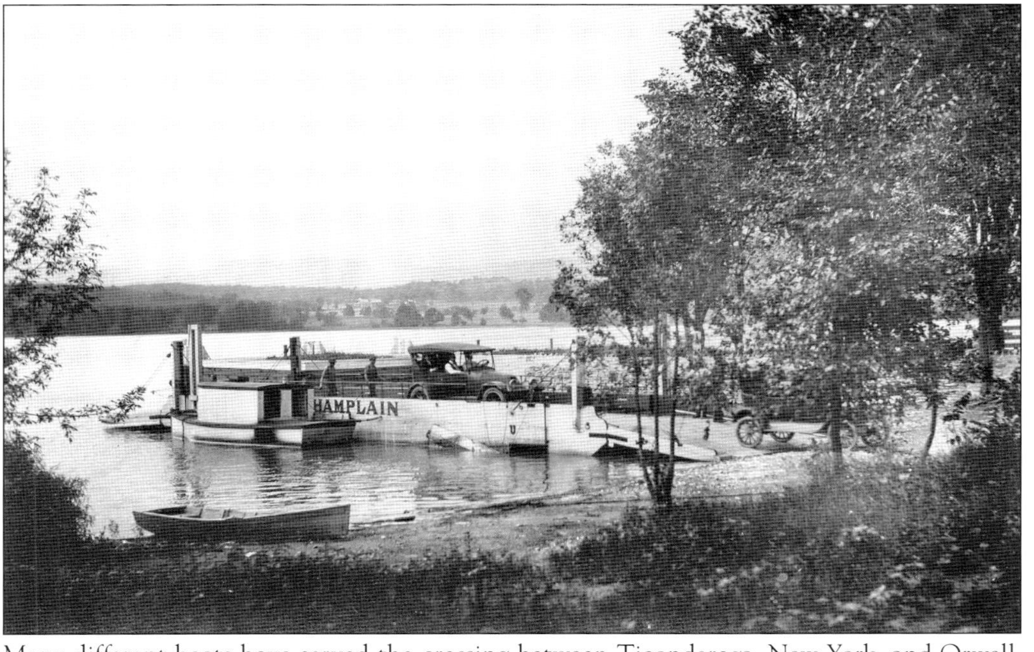

Many different boats have served the crossing between Ticonderoga, New York, and Orwell, Vermont, including a barge with auxiliary power. The rustic cabins and rail fencing give this ferry a domestic look. (LCMM.)

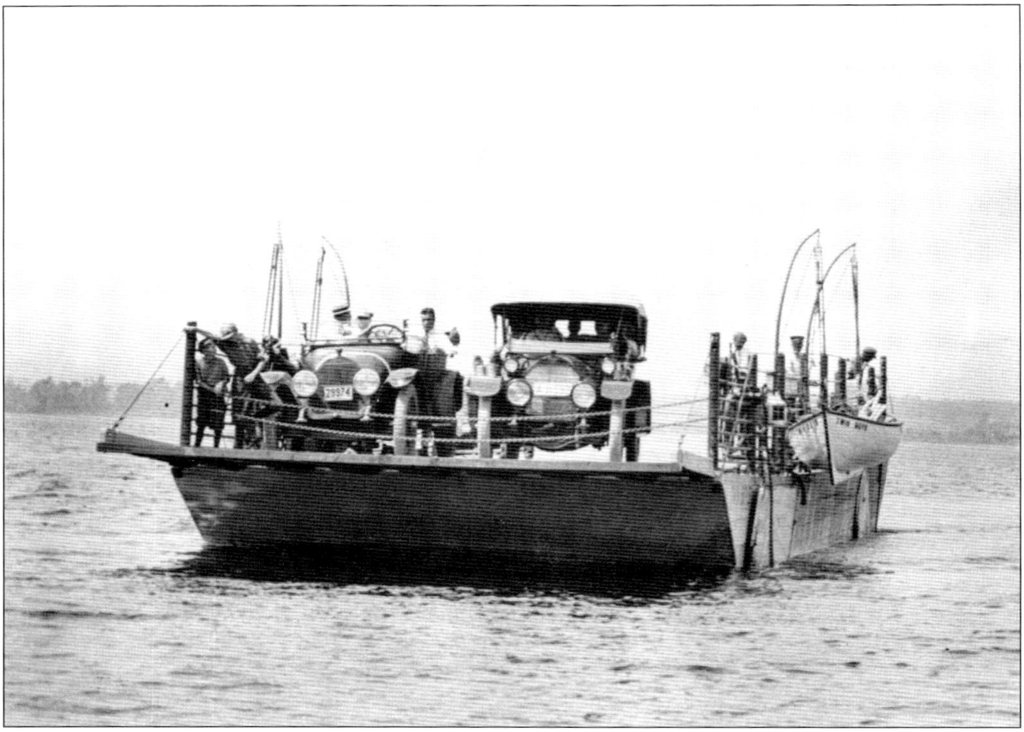

The gasoline-powered, propeller-driven ferry above was built in 1916 at Champlain, New York, with a lifeboat named *Twin Boys*. Below, the ferry *The Twins* was operated by William Sweet from Chazy, New York, to Isle La Motte, Vermont, and the boats were named for his twin sons Gerald and Clinton. Thomas Edison, Harvey Firestone, and Henry Ford used this ferry to cross Lake Champlain on their camping trips. (Both, UVM.)

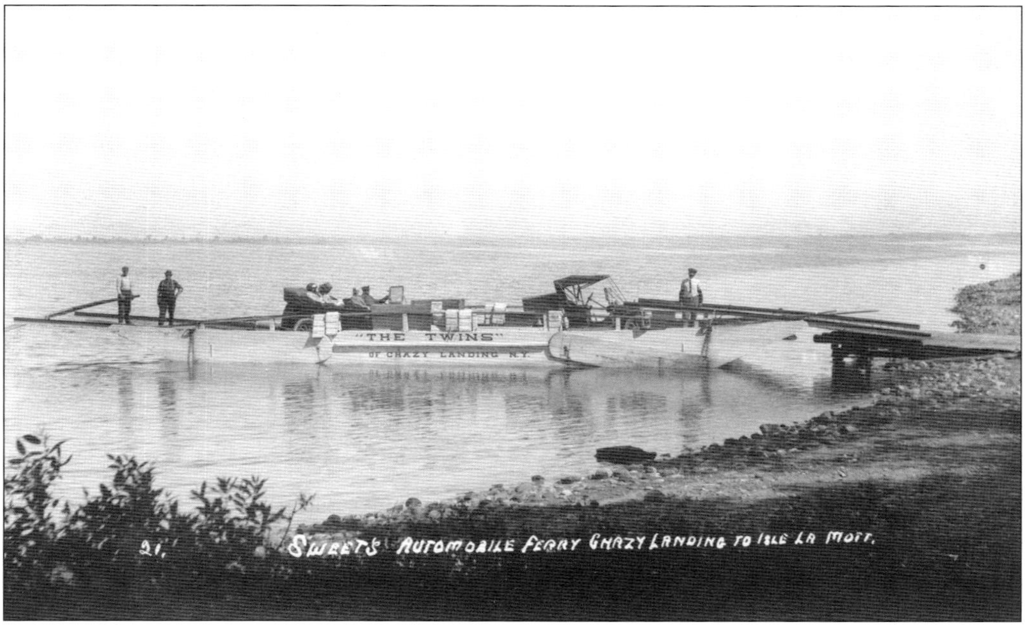

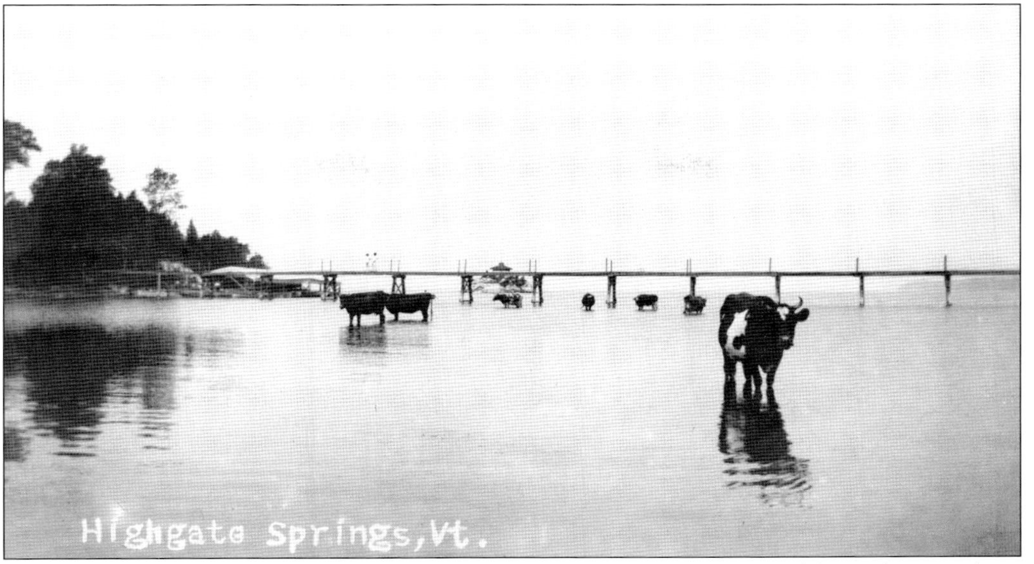

Vermont's Franklin County, where Highgate Springs is located, was renowned for its dairy products in the 19th century. Mineral springs in Highgate and Sheldon attracted tourists. Railroad service was essential for getting dairy products to the marketplace. (UVM.)

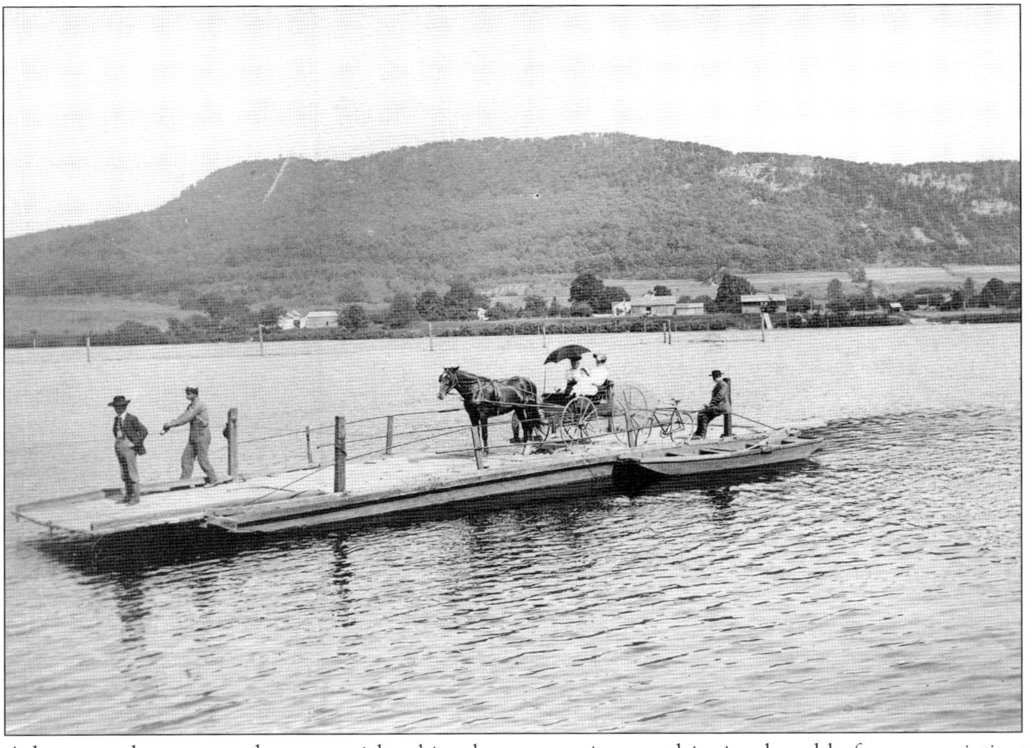

A horse and wagon and a man with a bicycle are crossing on this simple cable ferry, consisting of a small scow barge with ends that facilitate landing on the shoreline. This ferry was probably used in Addison County, Vermont. The small rowing boat tied to its side would have been used if there were any problems during the passage. (UVM.)

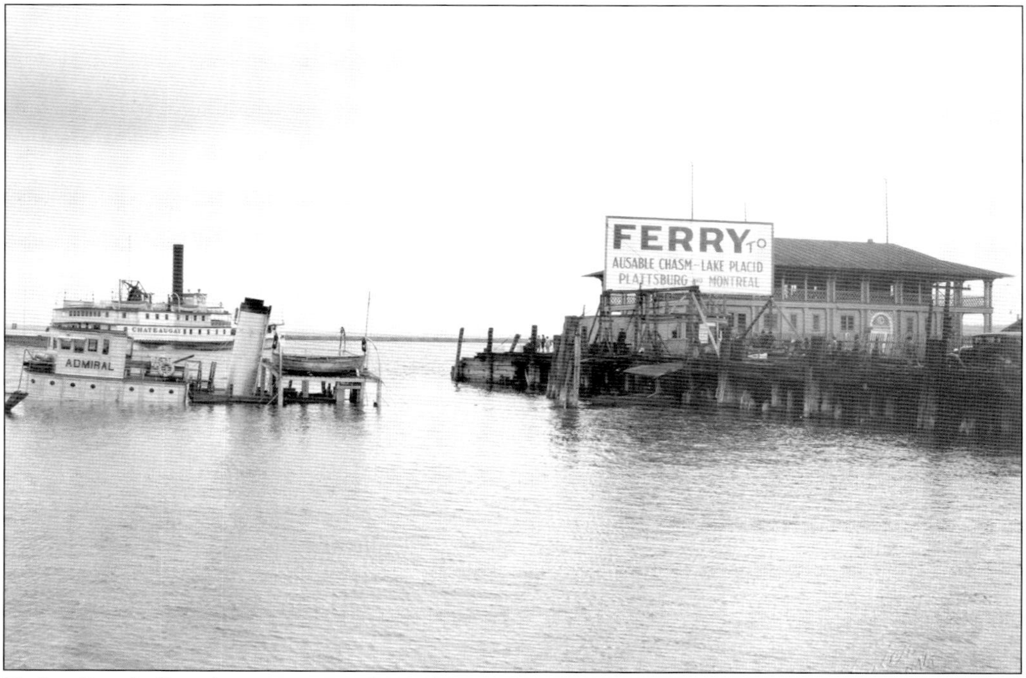

Elisha Goodsell, a ferry operator from the northern Champlain Islands, purchased several old steam yachts and adapted them to carry cars, with mixed success. When the crew arrived to find their boat *Admiral* (above) resting on the lake bottom, Goodsell directed them to pump her out, get her floating, and resume service. As competition from railroads increased and automobiles appeared on the scene, the Champlain Transportation Company adapted, offering ferry service, excursions, and freight delivery. (Above, UVM; below, LCMM.)

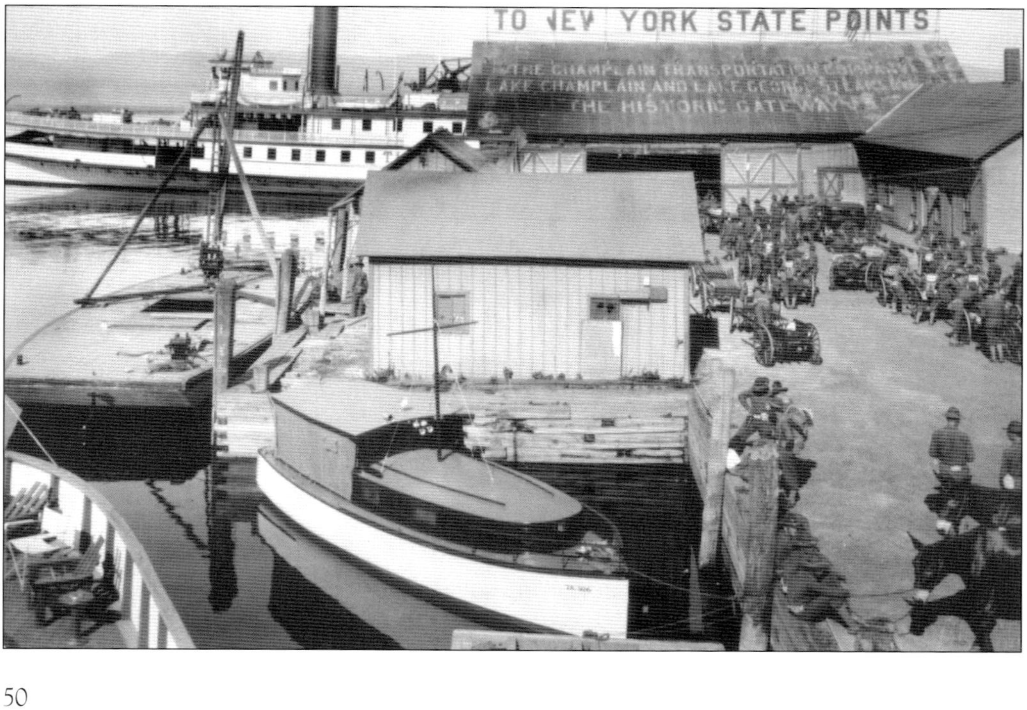

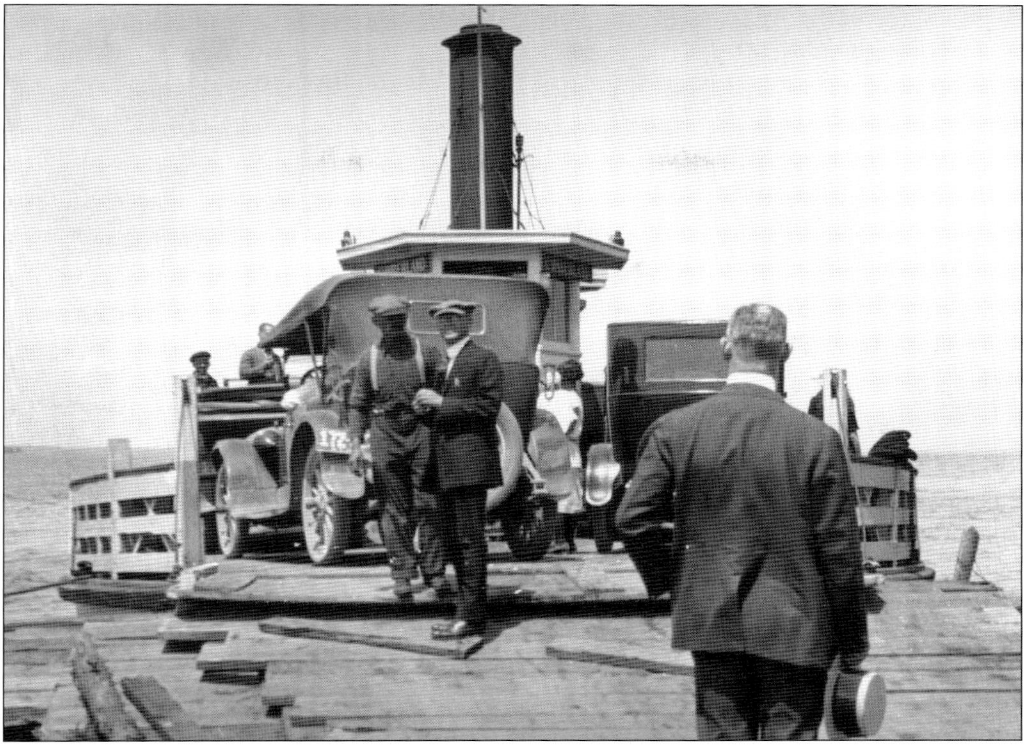

As steam engines became easier to manufacture and more cost-effective, they began to be used in ferry boats serving some of the longer cross-lake locations. This photograph captures the changing landscape, which included more and more automobiles wanting to cross Lake Champlain. The *Cumberland* ferry was specifically designed to load and carry automobiles across the lake. (VHS.)

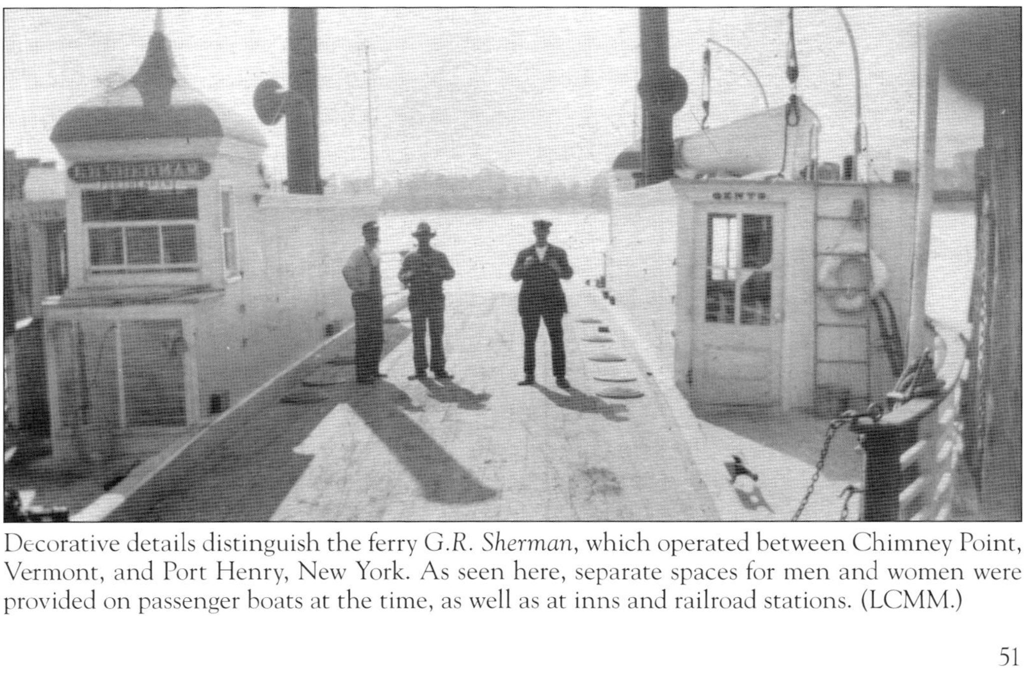

Decorative details distinguish the ferry G.*R. Sherman*, which operated between Chimney Point, Vermont, and Port Henry, New York. As seen here, separate spaces for men and women were provided on passenger boats at the time, as well as at inns and railroad stations. (LCMM.)

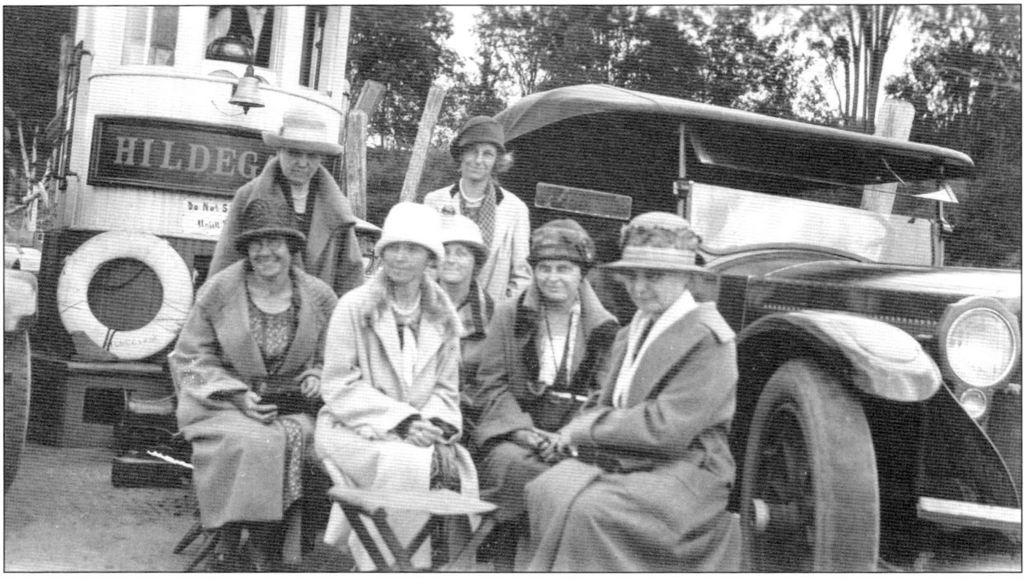

Hildegarde was built in Islip, New York, in 1876 as the yacht *Niantic*. She was brought to Lake Champlain about 1915 by Clarence Morgan of New York City. Converted into a steam-screw ferry, *Hildegarde* served the crossing from Chimney Point, Vermont, to Port Henry, New York. She was then converted to a working boat and, in her new life in the 1930s, served as a tugboat for a stone barge from Fiske's Landing in Isle La Motte to Burlington Harbor. (BHC.)

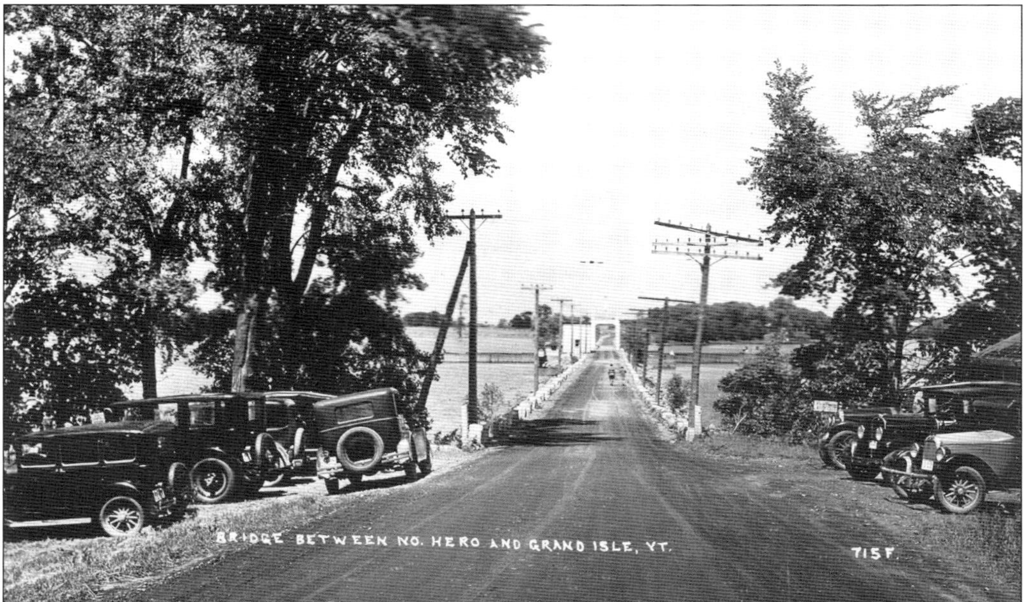

As the automobile continued to expand its presence in and around Lake Champlain, bridges replaced some of the shorter ferry crossings. This causeway and bridge connects North Hero, Vermont, and Grand Isle, Vermont. Short crossing bridges were often fitted with a lift section or a swivel arrangement that would permit vessels to continue to pass. (UVM.)

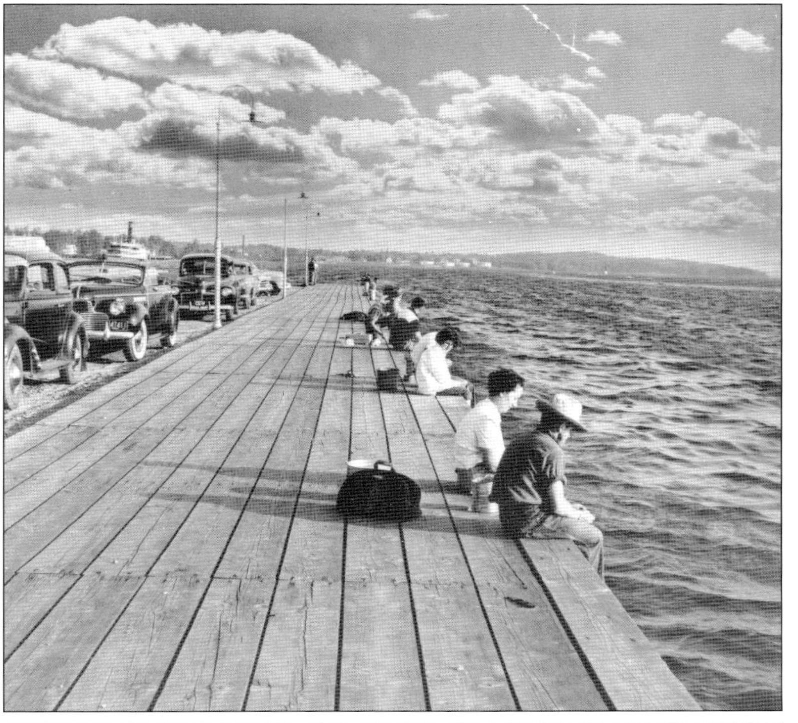

This photograph looks south at Burlington Harbor, Vermont, from the present-day Coast Guard area. People are fishing and picnicking, with the steamboat *Ticonderoga* (1906) in the background. At the end of its career, *Ticonderoga* operated excursions out of this location until she was finally acquired by the Shelburne Museum. (UVM.)

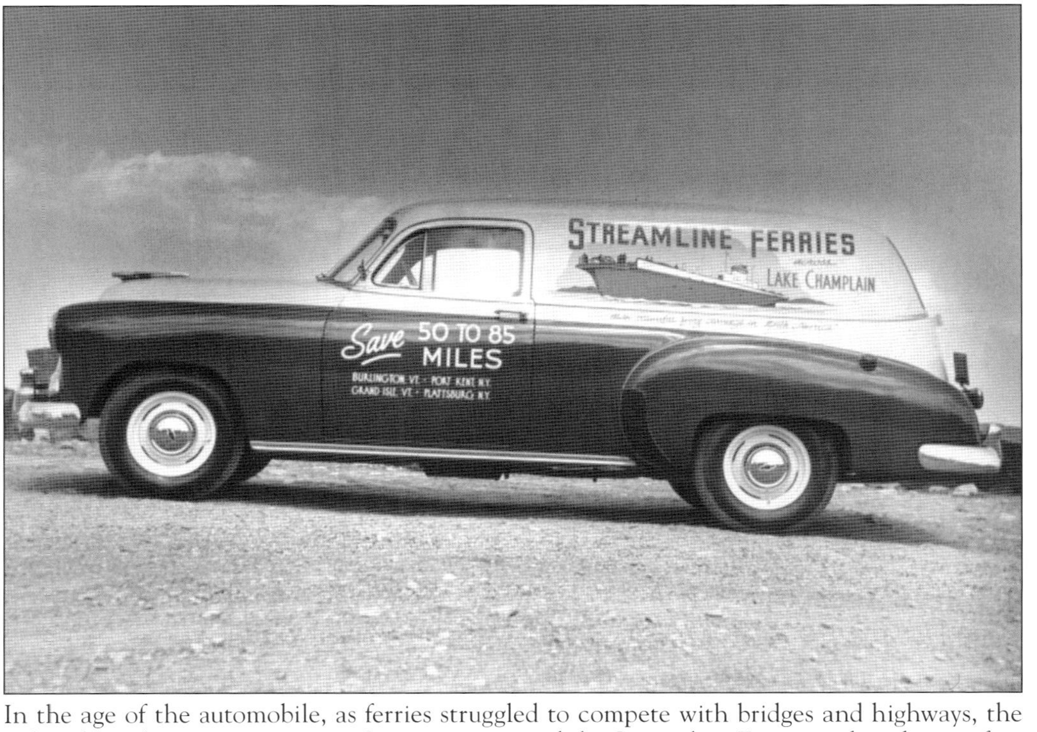

In the age of the automobile, as ferries struggled to compete with bridges and highways, the Lake Champlain Transportation Company operated the Streamline Ferries and made use of an automobile to attract customers. (LCMM.)

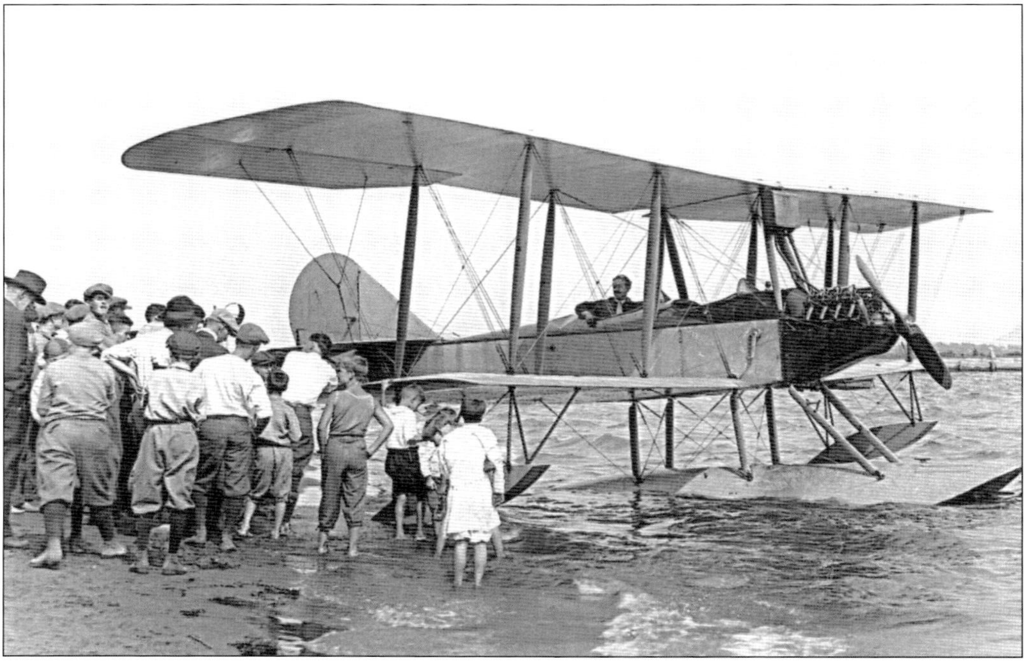

In the early decades of the 20th century, as air travel began to emerge, amphibious planes began to appear on Lake Champlain. They drew admiring and curious crowds, as seen above in Essex, New York. Below, the Basin Harbor Club is visited by the biplane that flew under the Champlain Bridge the day it opened. The pilot, a Mr. Velez, was training with Charles Lindbergh. (Both, BHC.)

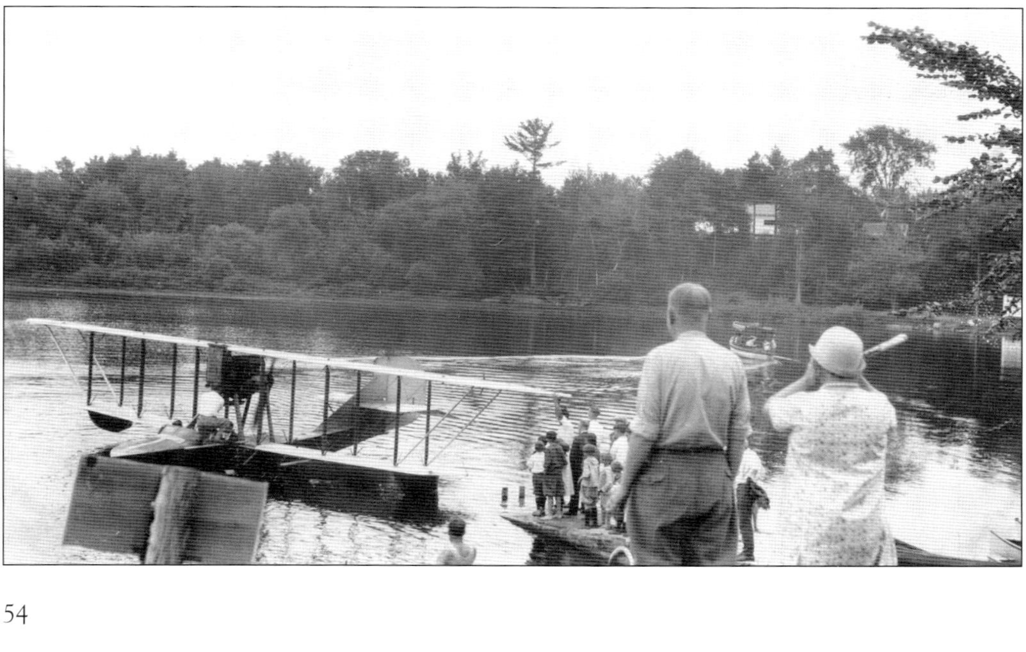

Four

Age of Steam

Since ancient times, the unpredictability of wind-powered vessels limited their effectiveness, and alternatives were sought. By the 18th century, many inventors were to trying to harness steam to propel watercraft. In 1807, Robert Fulton, working on the Hudson River, successfully launched and operated the *Clermont*, ushering in a revolution. The very next year, the world's second successful steamboat was laid down on Lake Champlain "under an old oak tree" at Burlington Harbor.

Vermont I was built by brothers James and John Winans, who came to Lake Champlain from the Hudson River. Although primitive by later standards and subject to frequent breakdowns, *Vermont I* began service in 1809, ushering in a century of steam boating on Lake Champlain. With each new launching, the steamboats on the lake increased in size, power, and finish. Steamboats soon became the primary mode of transportation for travelers on Lake Champlain, the Hudson River, and the St. Lawrence River. Railroads reached Lake Champlain about 40 years later, and they were so successful that they soon bought the controlling interest in both the Lake Champlain and Lake George Steamboat Companies.

While grand steamboats traveled the long north-south axis of the lake, smaller steamboats navigated waterways like Otter Creek at Vergennes, Vermont, and provided a link to the big lake steamers. They also towed canal boats to and from canals at each end of Lake Champlain and offered excursions to beautiful and historical sites. But when automobiles, trucks, and buses powered by internal combustion engines came on the scene, steam engines became obsolete and disappeared from the lake. *Chateaugay* (1888) was cut into 20 sections and sent to Lake Winnipesaukee, where she still operates as *Mount Washington II*. *Vermont III* (1903) was modified and served as a coastwise freighter until she was sold for scrap. *Ticonderoga* (1906), the last of the Lake Champlain fleet, survived on the water until the mid-1950s, when she was moved overland to the Shelburne Museum. The venerable *Ticonderoga* has been restored and is annually opened to the public to transport them back to the days when steam power ruled the world.

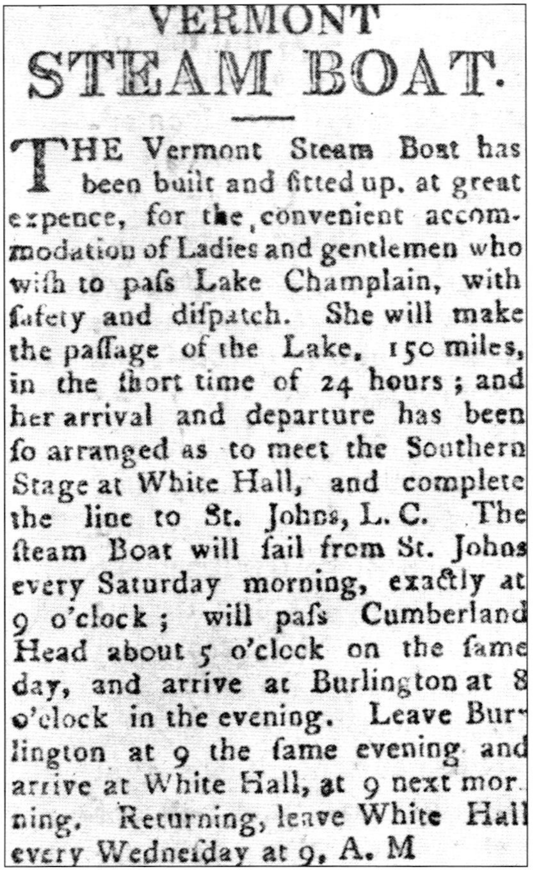

VERMONT

STEAM BOAT.

THE Vermont Steam Boat has been built and fitted up, at great expence, for the convenient accommodation of Ladies and gentlemen who wiſh to paſs Lake Champlain, with ſafety and diſpatch. She will make the paſſage of the Lake, 150 miles, in the ſhort time of 24 hours; and her arrival and departure has been ſo arranged as to meet the Southern Stage at White Hall, and complete the line to St. Johns, L. C. The ſteam Boat will ſail from St. Johns every Saturday morning, exactly at 9 o'clock; will paſs Cumberland Head about 5 o'clock on the ſame day, and arrive at Burlington at 8 o'clock in the evening. Leave Burlington at 9 the ſame evening and arrive at White Hall, at 9 next morning. Returning, leave White Hall every Wedneſday at 9, A. M

This advertisement appeared in the *Vermont Centinel* on June 30, 1809, announcing the first ever through-lake steamboat service aboard *Vermont I*. During the War of 1812, she was said to travel with a barrel of gunpowder so she could be blown up rather than captured. She suffered frequent machinery breakdowns, the final of which sank her on the Richelieu River. The hull was recovered in 1953 by salvage expert Col. Lorenzo Hagglund. (Courtesy of *The Steamboats of Lake Champlain, 1809–1930* by Ogden Ross.)

This commemorative postcard falsely identifies the vessel shown as *Vermont I*. It is in fact another early steamboat, *General Greene*. (LCMM.)

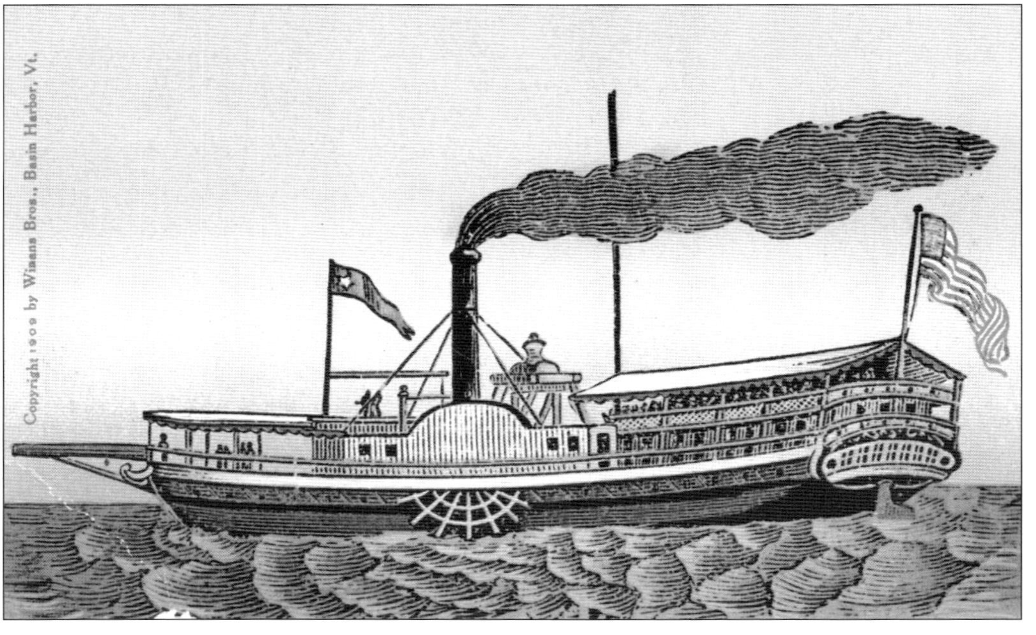

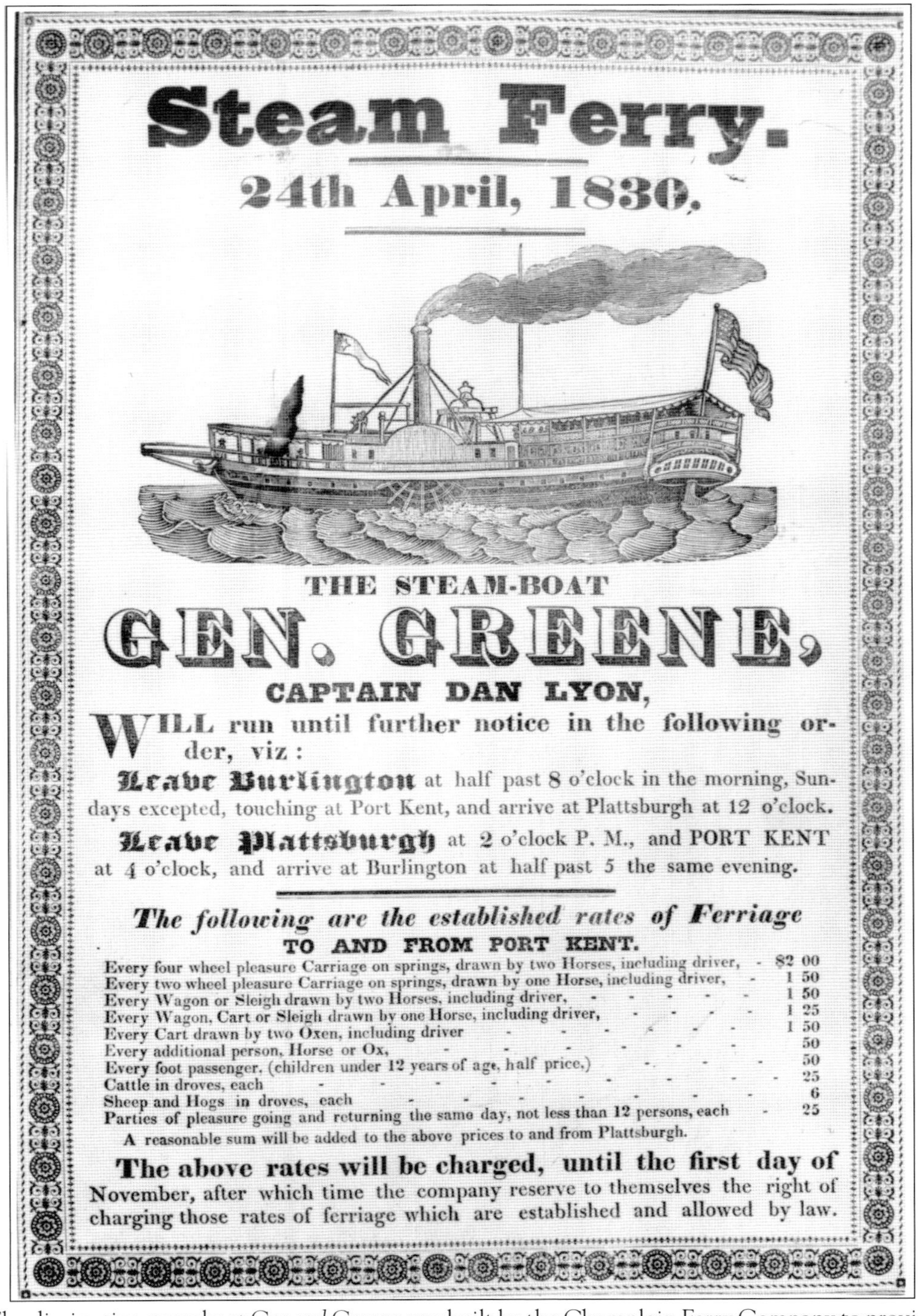

Steam Ferry.

24th April, 1830.

THE STEAM-BOAT

GEN. GREENE,

CAPTAIN DAN LYON,

WILL run until further notice in the following order, viz :

Leave Burlington at half past 8 o'clock in the morning, Sundays excepted, touching at Port Kent, and arrive at Plattsburgh at 12 o'clock.

Leave Plattsburgh at 2 o'clock P. M., and PORT KENT at 4 o'clock, and arrive at Burlington at half past 5 the same evening.

The following are the established rates of Ferriage
TO AND FROM PORT KENT.

Every four wheel pleasure Carriage on springs, drawn by two Horses, including driver,	$2 00
Every two wheel pleasure Carriage on springs, drawn by one Horse, including driver,	1 50
Every Wagon or Sleigh drawn by two Horses, including driver,	1 50
Every Wagon, Cart or Sleigh drawn by one Horse, including driver,	1 25
Every Cart drawn by two Oxen, including driver	1 50
Every additional person, Horse or Ox,	50
Every foot passenger, (children under 12 years of age, half price,)	50
Cattle in droves, each	25
Sheep and Hogs in droves, each	6
Parties of pleasure going and returning the same day, not less than 12 persons, each	25

A reasonable sum will be added to the above prices to and from Plattsburgh.

The above rates will be charged, until the first day of November, after which time the company reserve to themselves the right of charging those rates of ferriage which are established and allowed by law.

The diminutive steamboat *General Greene* was built by the Champlain Ferry Company to provide daily service from Burlington, Vermont, to Port Kent, New York, and Plattsburgh, New York. She operated until 1833, when her engine and boilers were removed and she was converted into a sloop. The ferry service was then undertaken by the larger steam ferry *Winooski*. (UVM.)

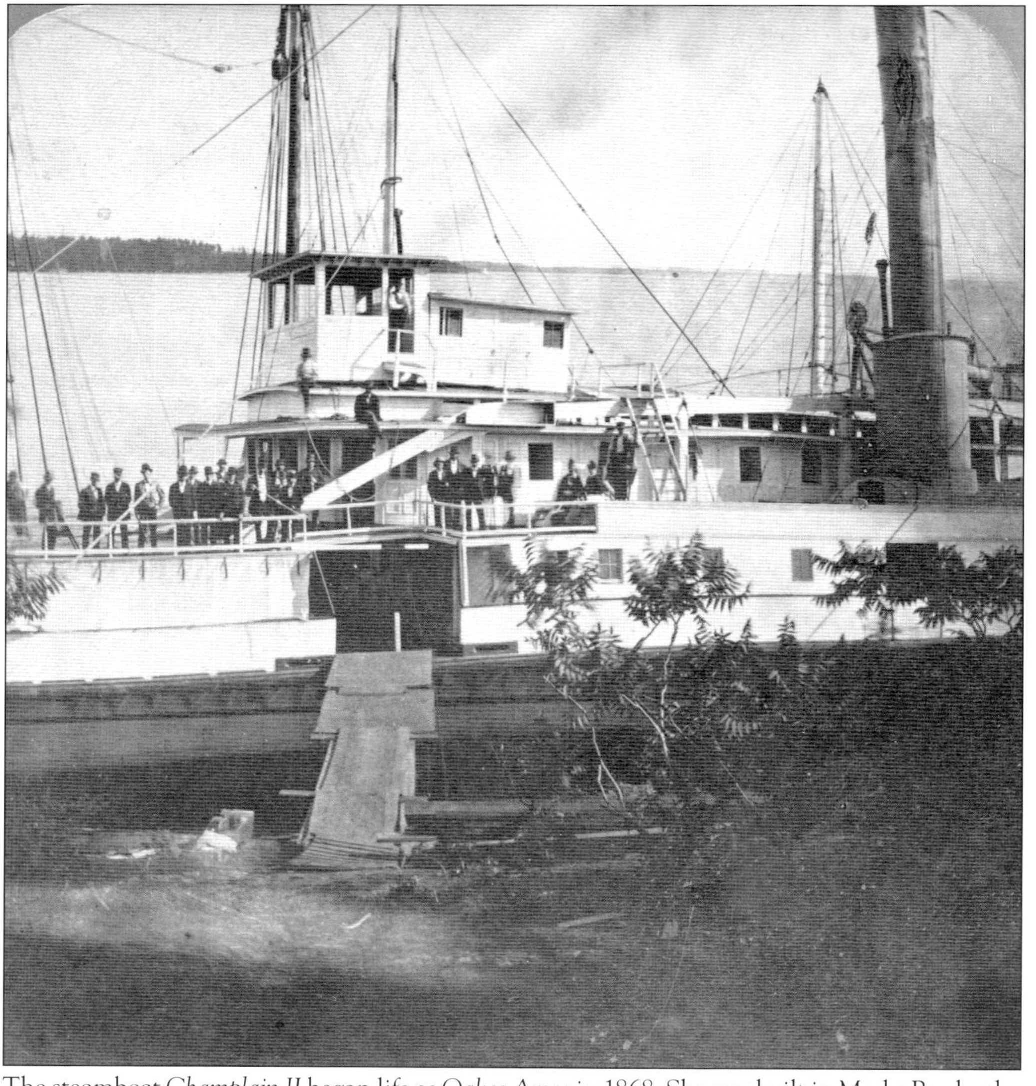

The steamboat *Champlain II* began life as *Oakes Ames* in 1868. She was built in Marks Bay by the Rutland Railroad Company to ferry railroad cars between Burlington, Vermont, and Plattsburgh, New York. Converted into a passenger steamer and renamed *Champlain II*, her new career came to an abrupt end on July 16, 1875, when, leaving Westport, New York, she struck Split Rock Mountain. Note the improvised ramp to shore seen here. (UVM.)

The pilot of *Champlain II*, John Eldredge, was addicted to morphine and had fallen asleep at the wheel while under way at dusk in July 1875 along the New York shoreline. No lives were lost, but *Champlain II* was deemed a total loss. The backbone of the steamboat was broken, so all useful material was salvaged and the hull was abandoned. The pilothouse became part of a summer camp in Vermont, and the stairway went into a church in Essex, New York. The wreckage of *Champlain II* is now part of the Lake Champlain Underwater Historic Preserve system of shipwrecks designated for public access. (Both, UVM.)

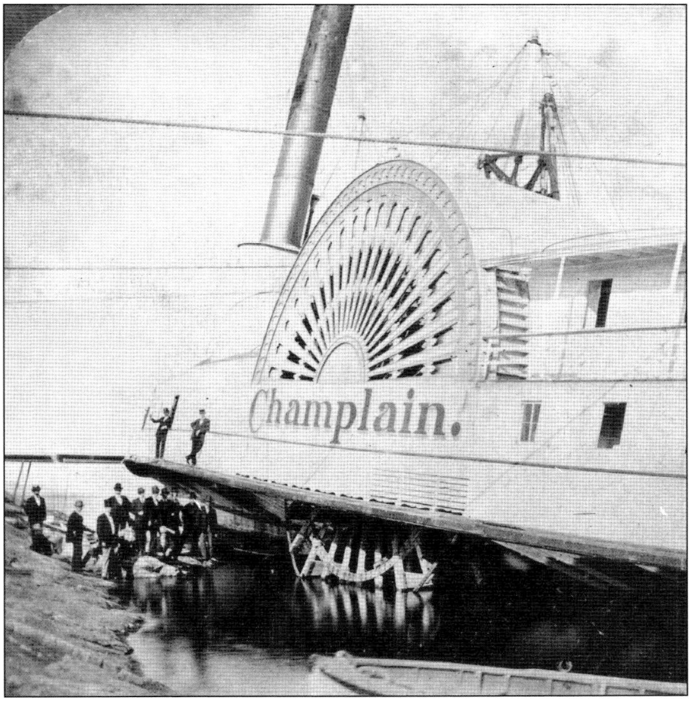

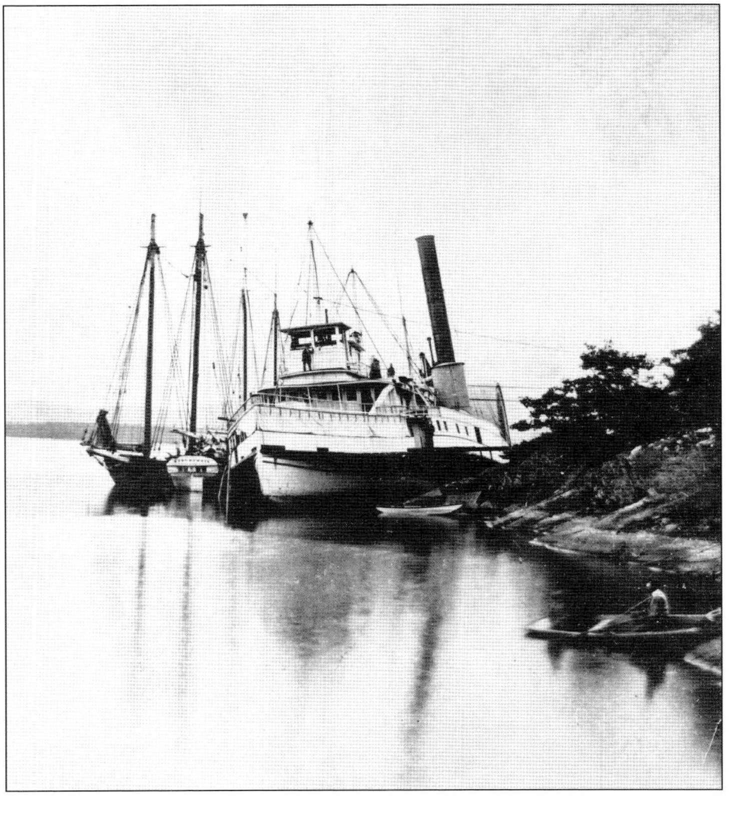

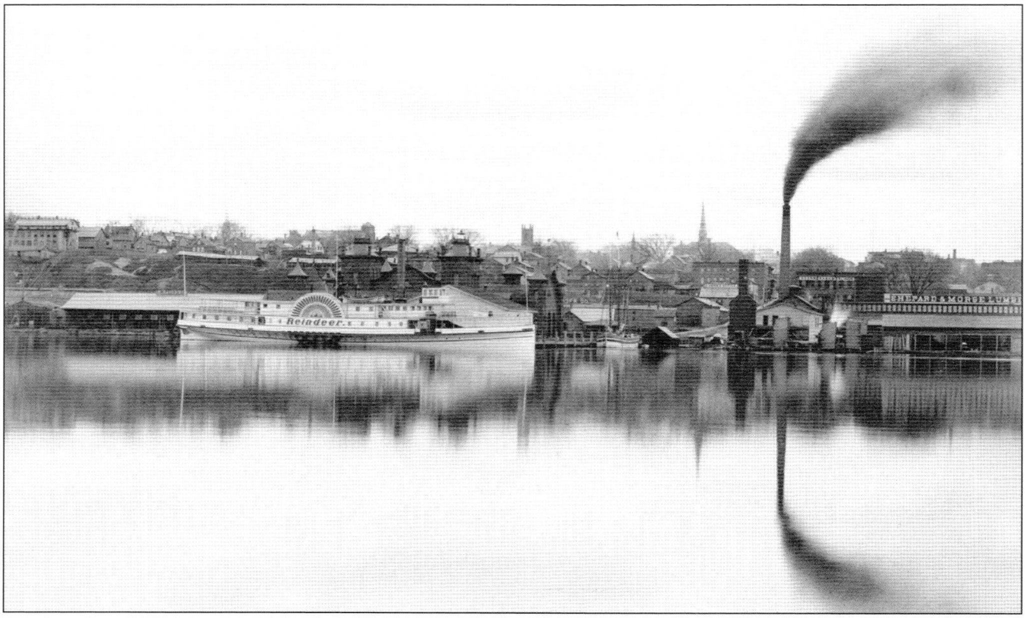

In this lovely photograph, the steamboat *Reindeer* (1882) is lying at the King Street dock in Burlington. To the right of the *Reindeer*'s bow, a Lake Champlain canal schooner sits facing bow out. The calm water provides the perfect reflection of the Shepard & Morse Lumber Company on the right. The photographer presumably took this long-exposure photograph from the stability of Burlington breakwater. (UVM.)

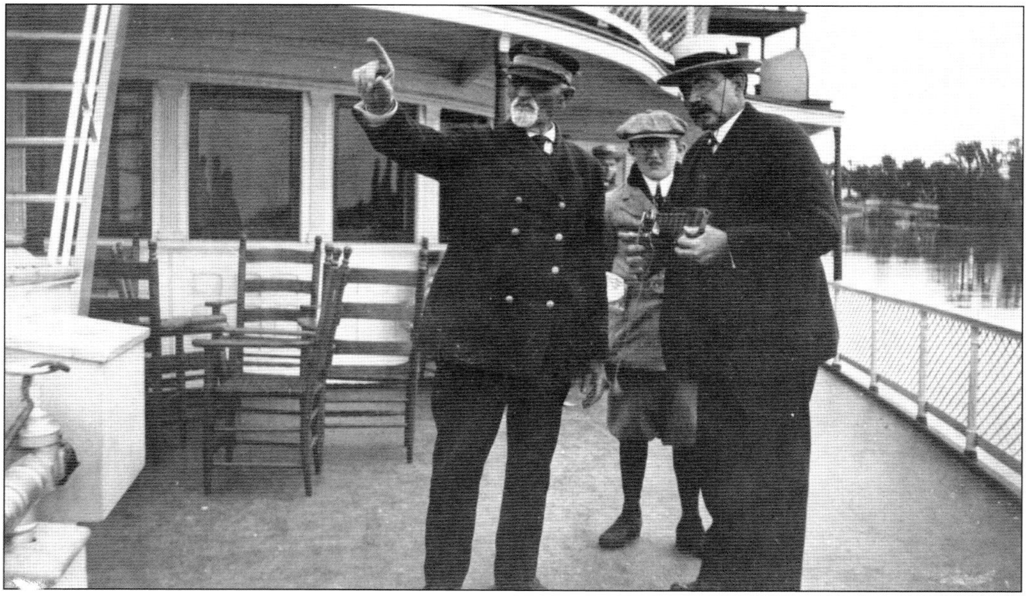

Mariners on the inland seas often came from communities and families that bordered the lake. Perhaps no family better exemplifies the multigenerational calling than the Rockwell family of the Champlain Islands. Ell Rockwell began his career as a cabin boy aboard his father's schooner and made the transition to the expanding steamboat operations. Captain Rockwell became the lake's most celebrated mariner, captaining steamboats until his passing in 1928 at age 98. (UVM.)

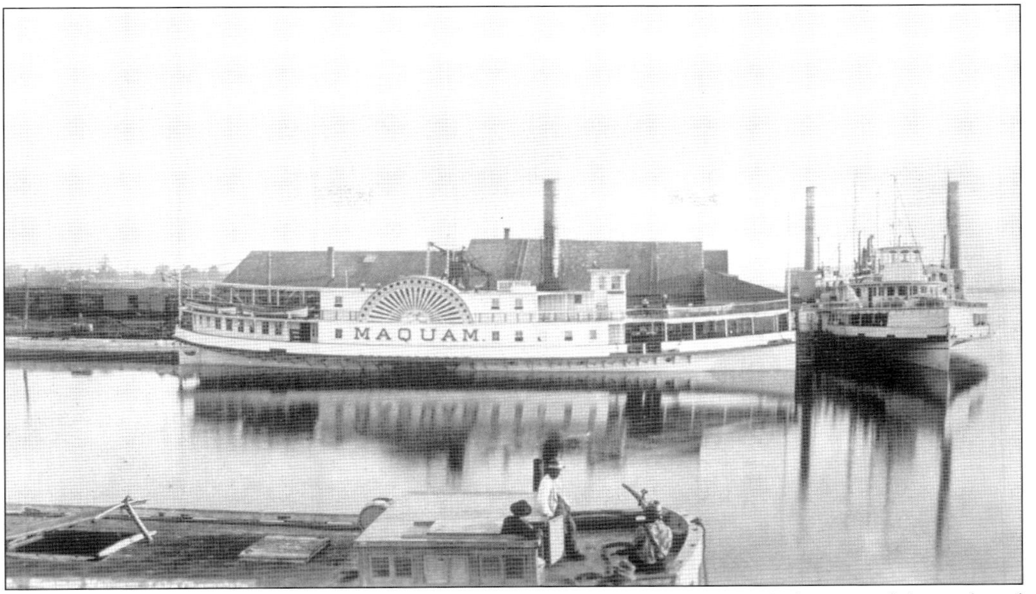

Maquam was built on the Maquam shore near Swanton, Vermont, in 1881 by one of the railroad companies and was later purchased by the Champlain Transportation Company. *Maquam* had a tendency to roll, and, on occasion, some excursion-passenger "merrymakers" would run from side to side to get her rolling. Note the steamboat *Vermont II* on the outer berth, and, in the foreground, a canal boat and her crew. (UVM.)

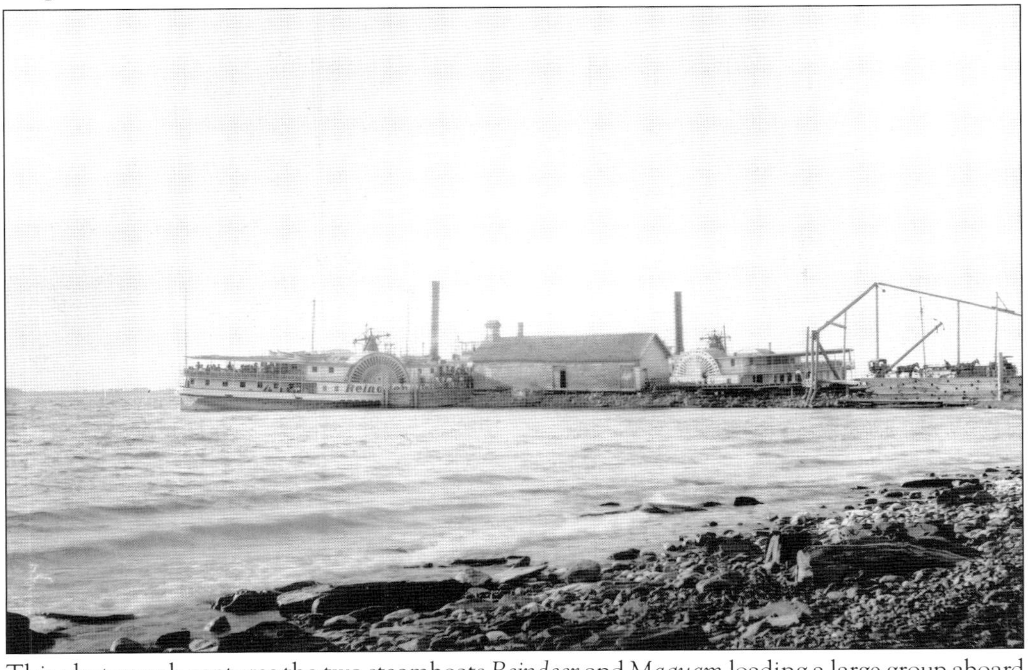

This photograph captures the two steamboats *Reindeer* and *Maquam* loading a large group aboard for an excursion in St. Albans Bay, Vermont, in 1899. In competition with railroads for ridership, steamboats were an attractive opportunity to get out on the lake with a large social, church, civic, or school group. A band would often accompany the revelers. (UVM.)

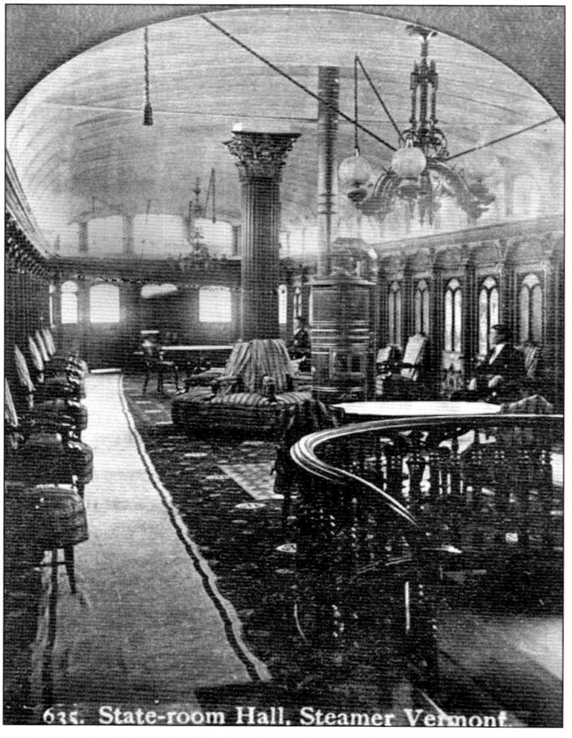

As the steamboat era advanced, steamboats became more dependable, larger, and more elegant. This opulence was captured by Charles Dickens in 1842, who wrote, "The *Burlington* is a perfectly exquisite achievement of neatness, elegance and order. The decks are drawingrooms; the cabins are boudoirs, choicely furnished and adorned with prints, pictures, and musical instruments; every nook and corner of the vessel is a perfect curiosity of graceful comfort and beautiful contrivance." (UVM.)

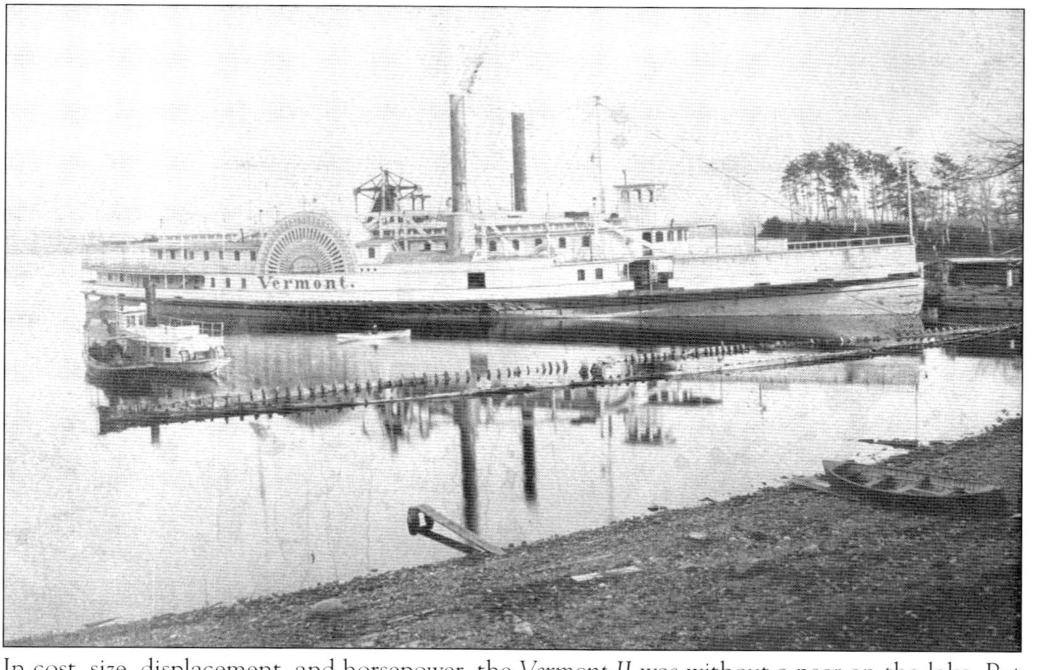

In cost, size, displacement, and horsepower, the *Vermont II* was without a peer on the lake. Put into service in 1871, she is seen here at Shelburne Shipyard. After the Civil War, she carried a distinguished party of Union generals, including Generals Grant, Sheridan, and Porter. After 30 years of service, she was replaced by the *Vermont III* in 1903. (UVM.)

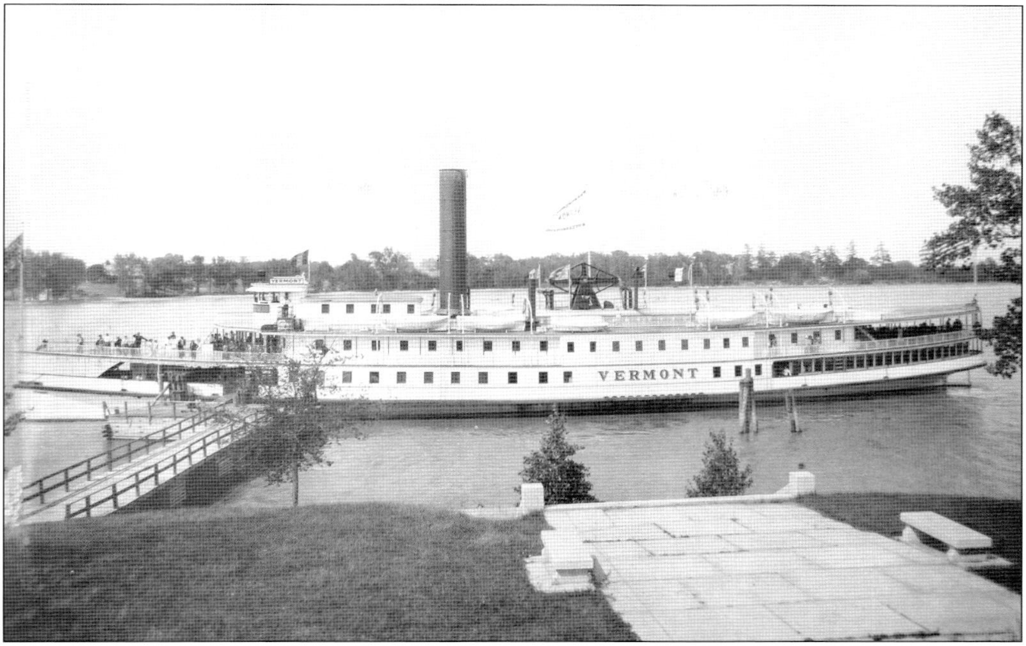

Vermont III, finished in the fine tradition of the expanded steamboats, is seen here in 1920 at Crown Point, New York. The 262-foot *Vermont III* was the second Champlain Transportation Company steamboat with an iron hull, transporting 900 passengers in luxury at up to 23 miles per hour. Each of its 50 staterooms was equipped with running water. (UVM.)

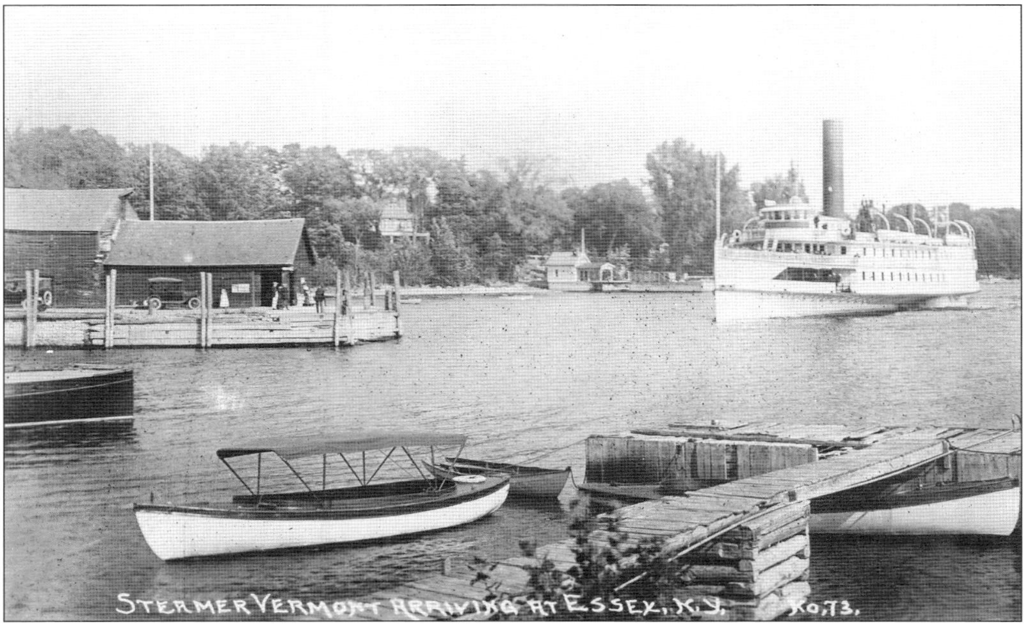

The steamer *Vermont III* transported passengers to ports across Lake Champlain, including here in Essex, New York. Historically, many canal schooners were constructed in Essex, and this active waterfront still hosts an active ferry landing today, connecting Essex to Charlotte, Vermont. (UVM.)

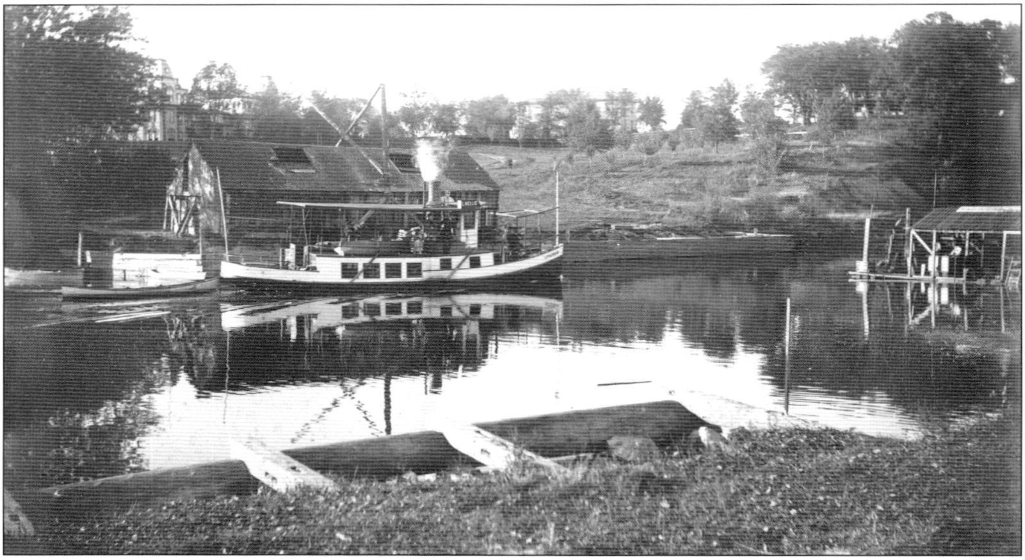

Multiple industries harnessed the power of the falls in Vergennes, Vermont, ideally located on Otter Creek with access to Lake Champlain. Products and personnel could get to market on boats such as the Daniels Line of steamboats, including the 45-foot-long *Little Nellie*, shown here, which was bought and repaired by the Daniels family after she had sunk in an 1890 storm. (UVM.)

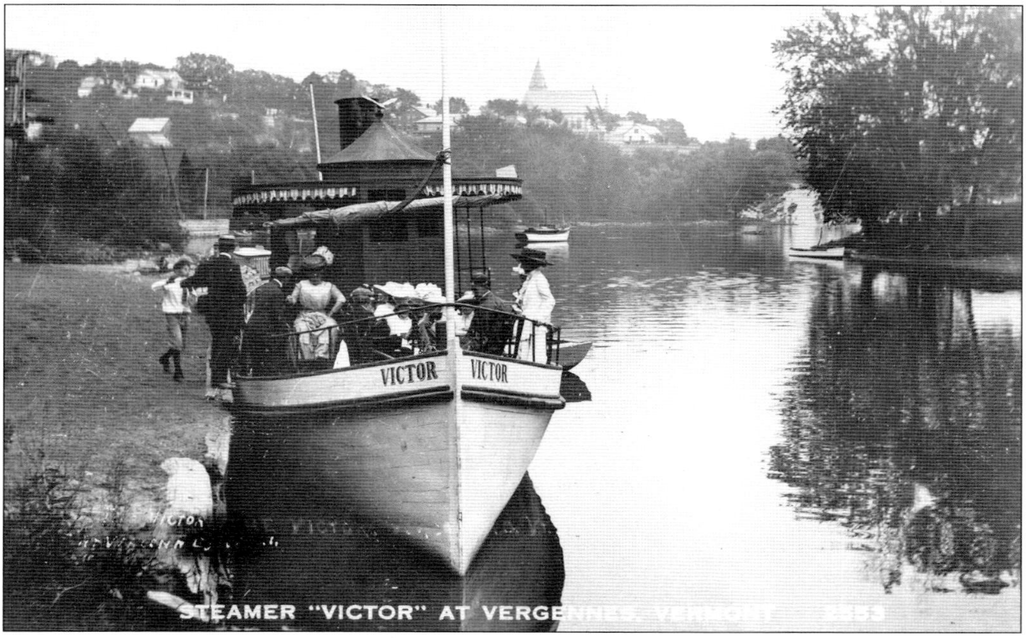

The steamboat *Victor* was "handsome and seaworthy" and could accommodate 275 passengers in service to nearby communities such as Westport and Port Henry, New York. She was one of the vessels in the family-owned Daniels Line, operated by members of the Daniels family, including Capt. Louis Daniels and his wife, Philomena. She is reported to be the first woman in the world to earn her master's license for captaining boats. (BMFL.)

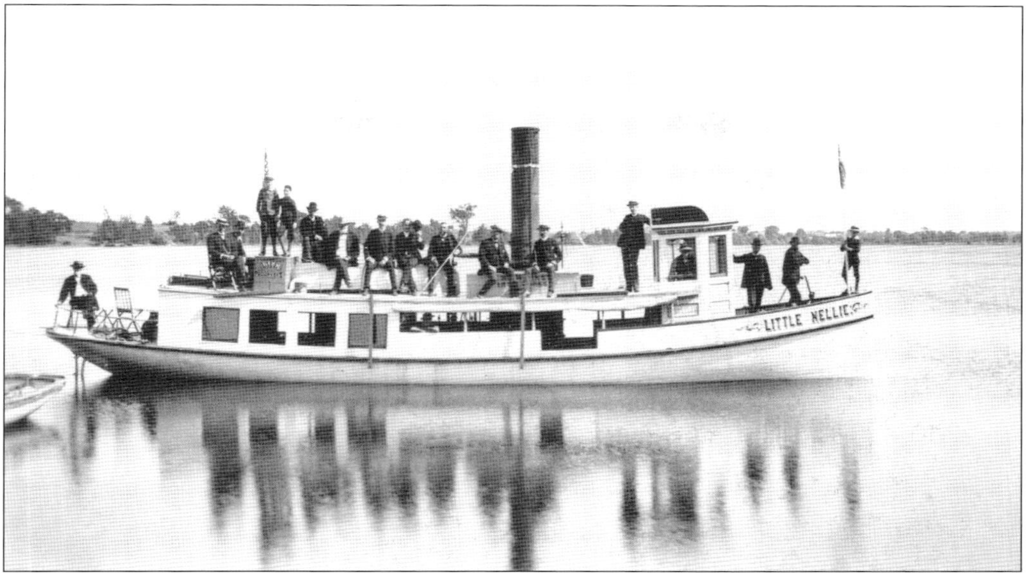

The steamer *Little Nellie*, seen above in St. Albans Bay, Vermont, took passengers all around Lake Champlain. Note the box of life preservers on the rear of the cabin roof. In the scene below, with the falls of Vergennes, Vermont, in the background, a group of men, women, and children get ready to enjoy a pleasure cruise on Otter Creek. The Daniels Line was a family affair led by Captains Louis and Philomena Daniels and their sons Mitchell and Frederick Daniels, a captain and an engineer, respectively. After Louis died in 1897, Mitchell's wife, Helen, the mother of eight children at home, carried on the family tradition by becoming a licensed pilot. (Above, UVM; below, BMFL.)

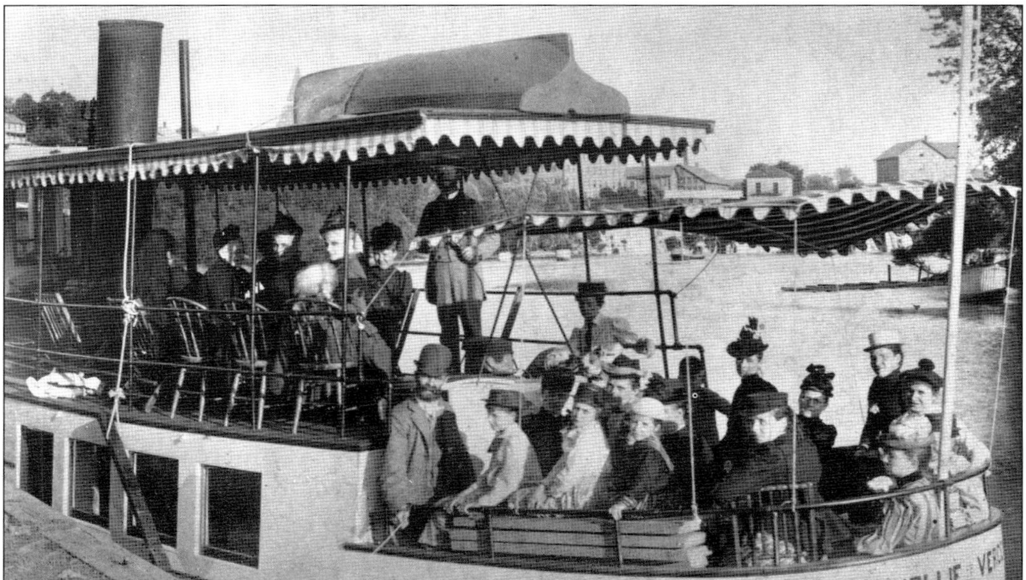

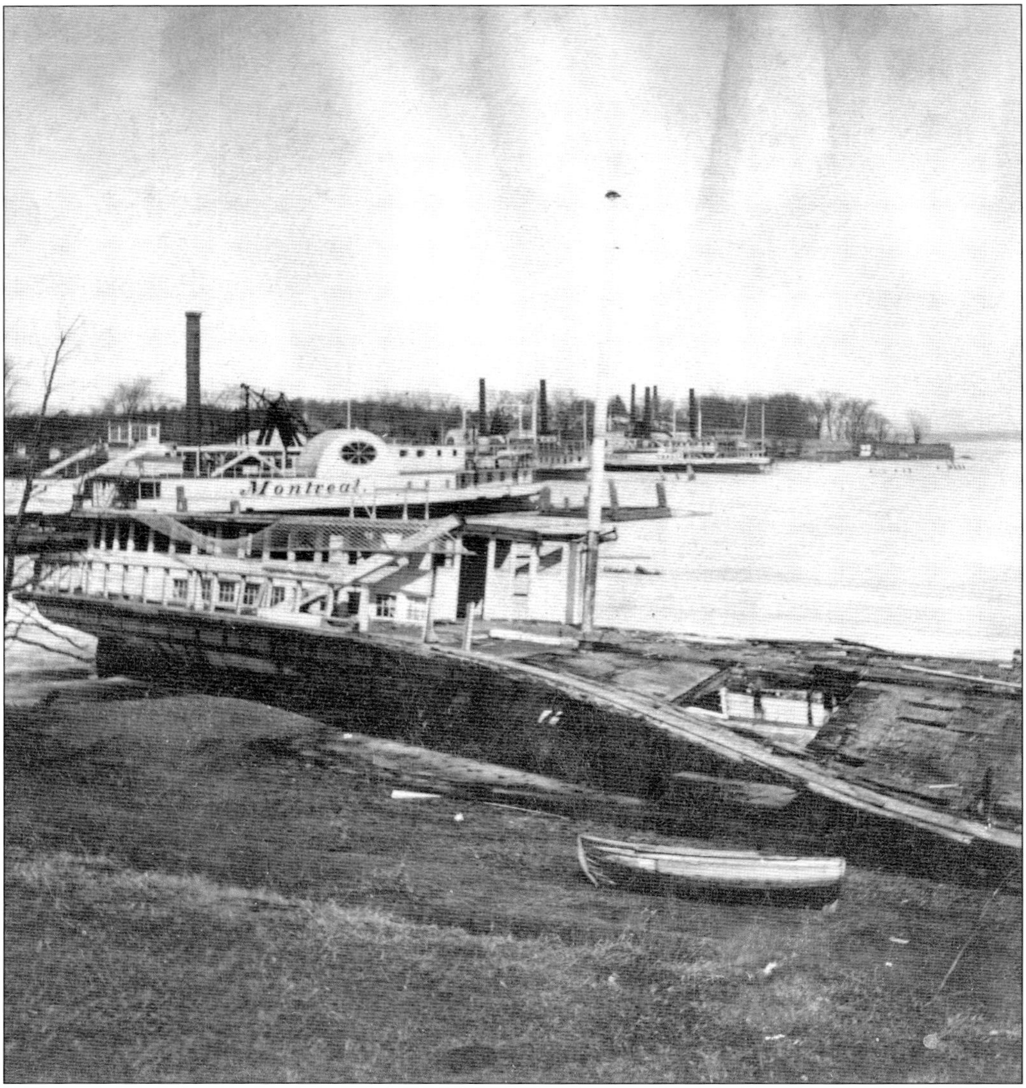

Originally based on Otter Creek, the Lake Champlain Steamboat Company searched for new headquarters that would be less vulnerable to early and late ice than the creek. The protected tip of the east side of Shelburne Bay was deemed the perfect choice, and, from 1825 on, the Shelburne Shipyard was the construction site of almost all of the lake steamers. This construction, repair, and maintenance facility supported a large year-round population of skilled maritime workers. It was also the place where retiring vessels were brought to be dismantled and recycled. Fortuitously, many of the steamboat hulls were stripped and allowed to sink around the harbor, as seen here with the active steamboat *Montreal* in the background. Today, Shelburne Shipyard contains a legacy of more than a dozen shipwrecks that are in active study by the Lake Champlain Maritime Museum. (UVM.)

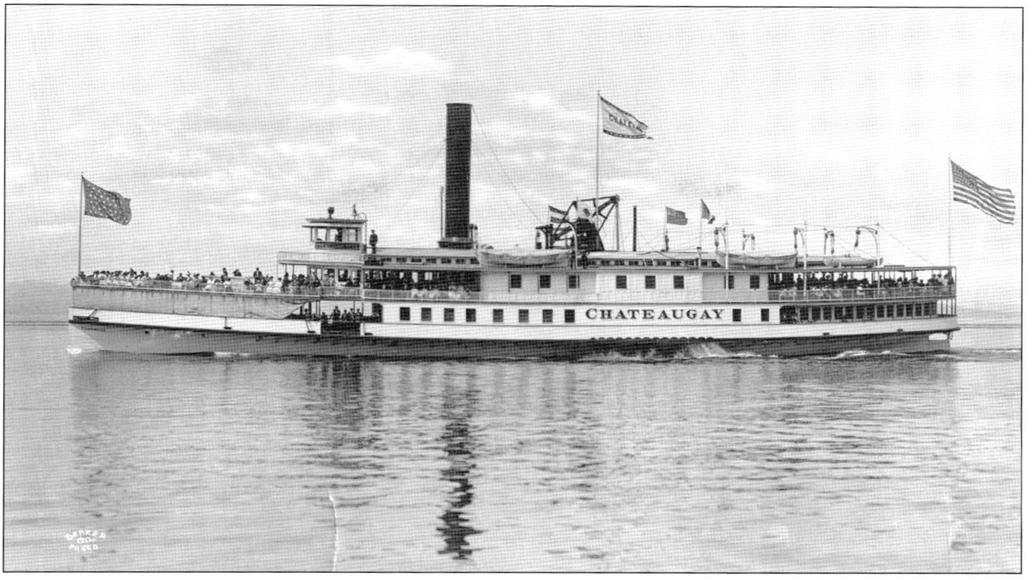

In 1888, the steamboat *Chateaugay* was the first Lake Champlain steamboat built with an iron hull, a major departure from previous wooden-hulled steamboats. She operated excursions and a shortened north-south run from Port Henry to Rouses Point, New York, until the outbreak of World War I, when declining lake travel resulted in her being laid up at the dock. In an effort to adapt to the ever more dominant automobile, she was converted into an automobile ferry for cross-lake service. With the onset of the Depression, however, she was retired to Shelburne Harbor in 1933 with an uncertain future. But that was not the end. *Chateaugay* was hauled out, cut into 20 sections, and transported to New Hampshire for reassembly and a new life as the excursion vessel *Mount Washington II* on Lake Winnipesaukee, where she is still in operation today. (Both, UVM.)

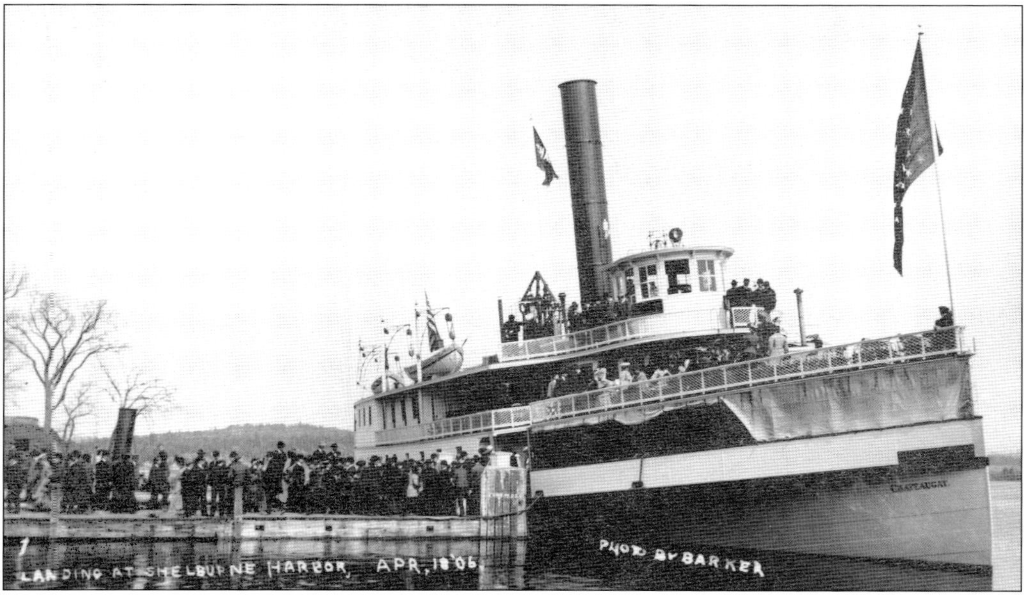

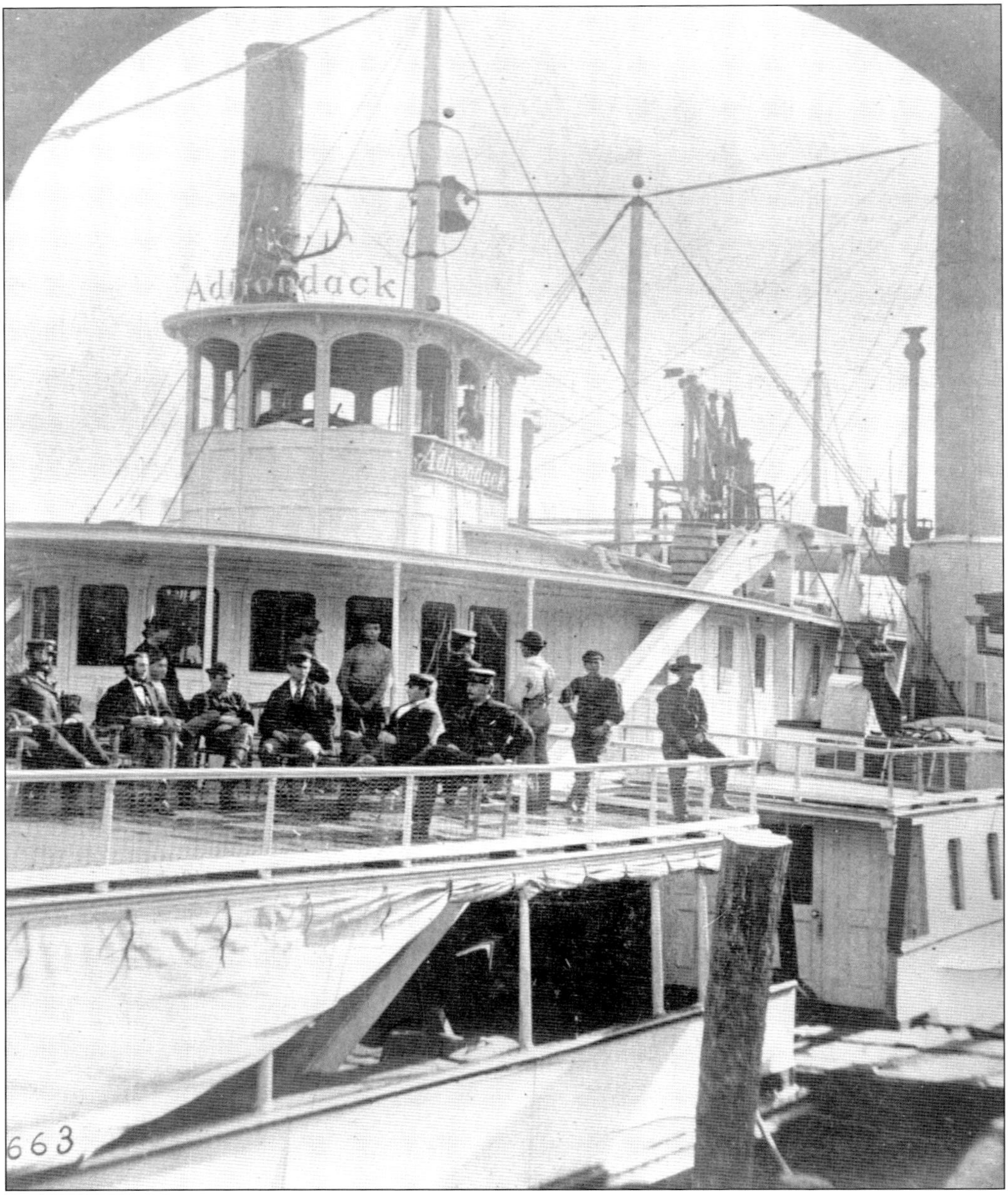

In this casual scene, some of the crew of the steamer *Adirondack* (constructed 1867) wait for the vessel's scheduled departure. Two officers are visible in the pilothouse, suggesting that they expect to be in motion soon. Note the *Adirondack*'s distinctive deer horns mounted on the pilothouse roof. (UVM.)

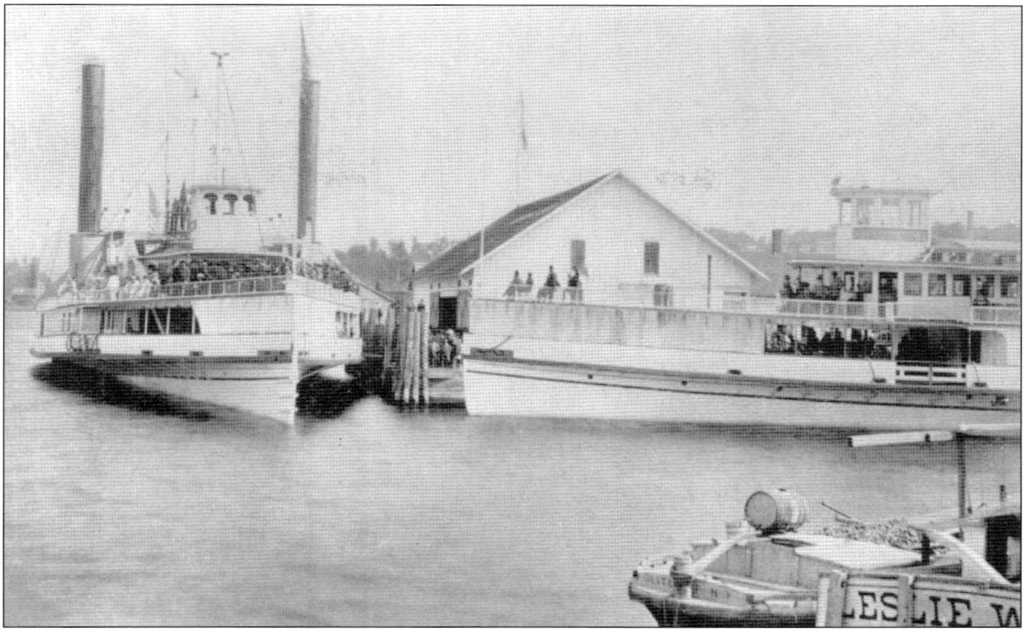

In this photograph taken from the Burlington, Vermont, Maple Street Pier (now Perkins Pier), the two distinctive stacks of *Vermont II* identify what many believed to be the most impressive steamboat of the line. Writes Ogden Ross in *Steamboats of Lake Champlain*, "Her size and speed, the dignity and richness of her fittings and equipment contributed greatly to her popularity." Also pictured are the steamboat *Chateaugay*, pointing west, and the sterns of two canal boats in the foreground. (UVM.)

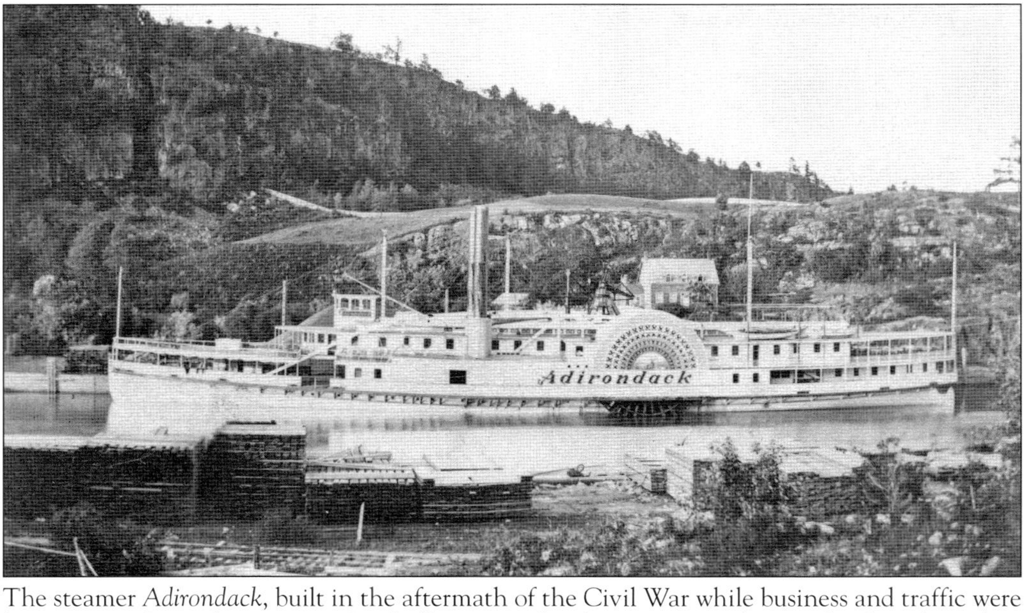

The steamer *Adirondack*, built in the aftermath of the Civil War while business and traffic were booming, is shown here near Whitehall, New York. These were good times for the Champlain Transportation Company, and steamboats were being built and retired with regularity. Today, the hull of the *Adirondack* lies in the shallow waters of Shelburne Bay. (UVM.)

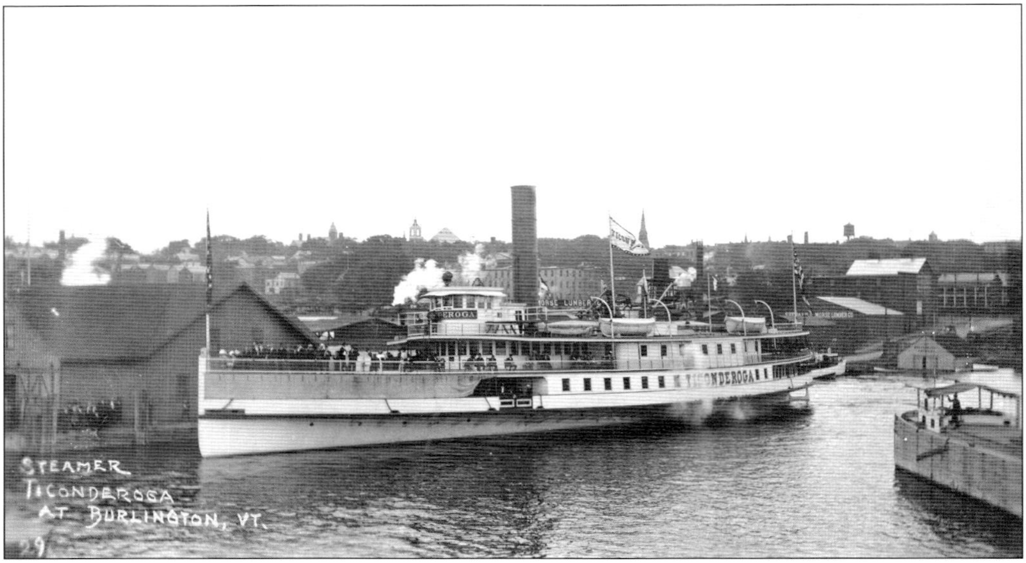

The steamboat *Ticonderoga* (1906) was the last of the large Lake Champlain steamboats. Constructed almost a century after Robert Fulton initiated the steamboat era with his successful *Clermont* run to Albany, *Ticonderoga* would become a bridge from the steam-powered boats of the past to the internal combustion engines of the future. *Ticonderoga* could not survive by the sentimental recollections of public excursions alone. The lack of business and the scarcity of licensed steam engineers required a more radical solution: preservation in a museum environment. In the mid-1950s, *Ticonderoga* was towed to the southern end of Shelburne Bay, where she was transferred to land and pulled on railroad tracks to her new home at the Shelburne Museum. Today, the venerable, restored *Ticonderoga* can be boarded on land, returning the visitor to the era of steam boating. (Both, LCMM.)

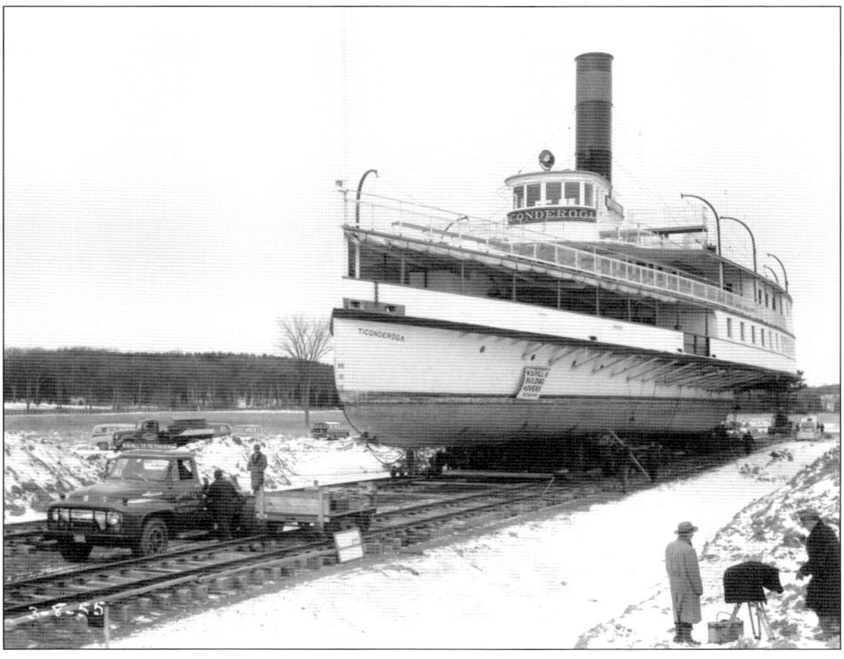

Five

Fishing and Hunting

Lake Champlain and the lands that surround it are more than just beautiful scenery. Together they form a complex, living ecosystem that encompasses plants and animals, including people. The open waters of the lake, the rivers and streams that flow into it, the wetlands along its shores, and the adjacent forests and agricultural lands seem timeless. But throughout history, human activity in the Champlain Valley has resulted in changes to the environment and wildlife of the area.

Lake Champlain's diverse geography—sandy shorelines at the mouths of rivers and streams, rocky places from steep cliffs to sloping ledges, islands large and small, and waters that range from shallow to cool and deep—provides habitat for more than 80 species of fish. For centuries, Abenaki villages, fishing camps, and hunting territories were located along rivers on the eastern side of the lake, and many Abenaki families maintain their connection to these locations.

Over the centuries, human occupation and activity changed the habitat, causing some species to diminish or even disappear. Cutting the original-growth forest to create farmland and damming streams for waterpower had the unintended consequence of eroding valuable topsoils and washing silt into rivers and the lake. Dams and mills blocked access to spawning grounds. The construction of canals, a tremendous economic benefit to the region, also opened pathways for invasive species of plants, shellfish, and fish. Each of these changes of habitat has altered the population of indigenous fish. Today, fisheries biologists are working to restore the populations of native fish species, including salmon and sturgeon.

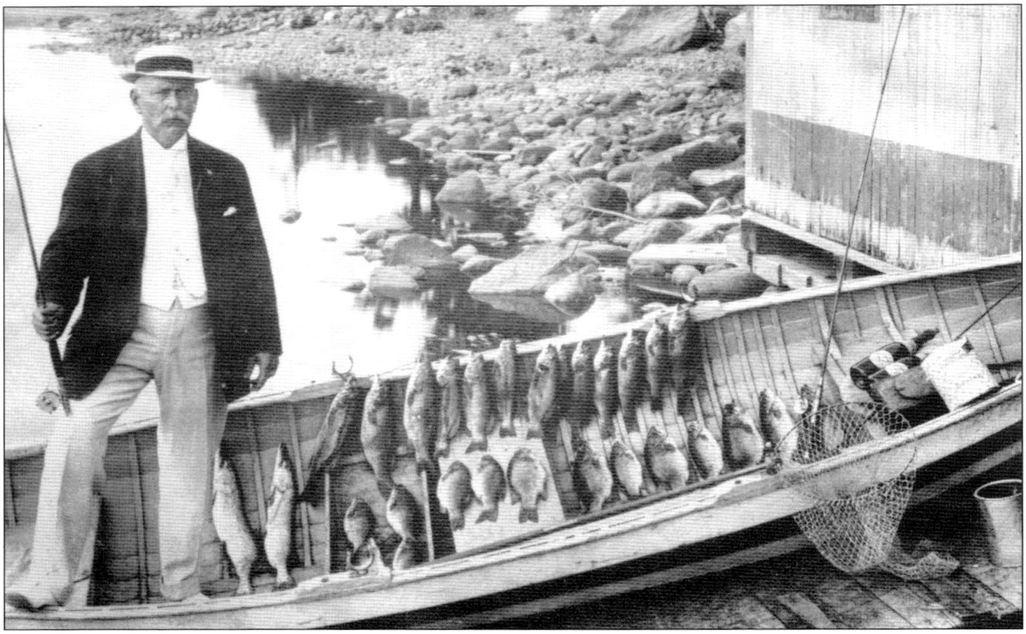

After a day's fishing, this unidentified man poses with his catch, a representative sampling of the lake's shallow-water fish. Smallmouth bass can be seen in the upper row, while the lower row includes the two lengthy pike, or pickerel, near the man's leg, and, to the right, pumpkinseed, bluegill, rock bass, and perch. Their neatly stowed equipment includes rods with reels, a net, a bait pail, and refreshments. (UVM.)

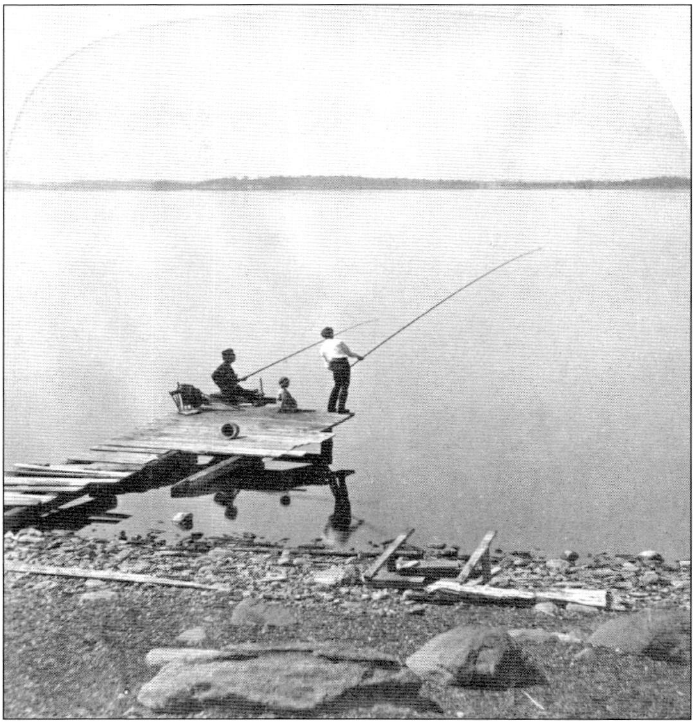

The landing at Lake View House, at St. Albans Point, Vermont, is the setting for this trio. Sturdy long poles, heavier than those used for fly-fishing, would extend the line out beyond the shadows cast by the fishermen, and a jigging motion would attract the fish. The cribbing of old piers and waterfront structures provides attractive habitat for many shallow-water fish. (UVM.)

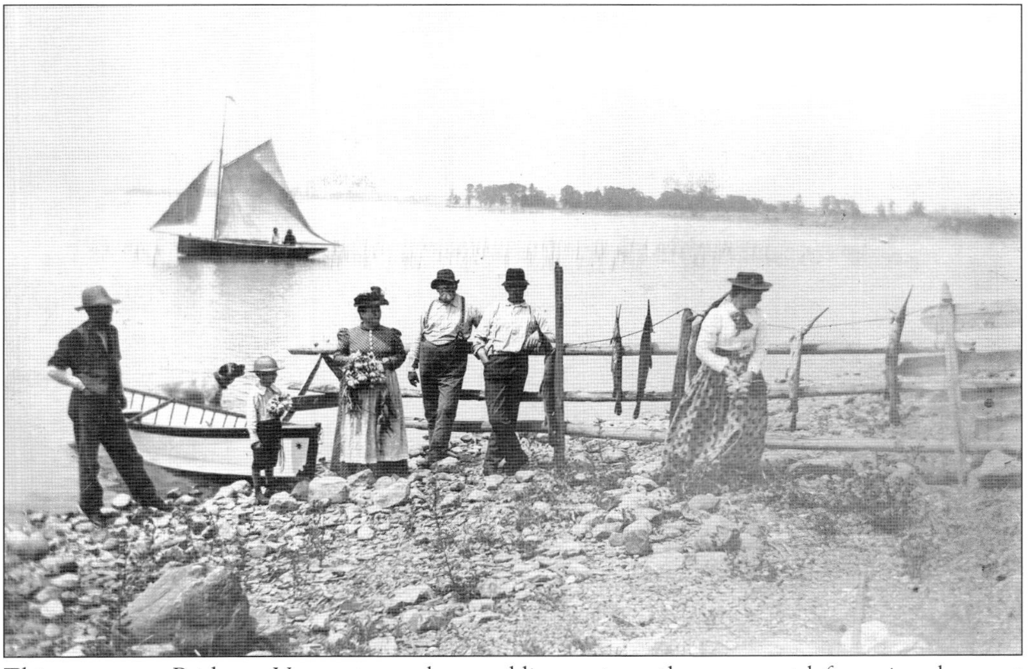

This scene near Bridport, Vermont, may be a wedding party, as the woman at left carries a bouquet and the boy beside her holds a nosegay. Several large garfish hanging from the fence raise the question of whether the men leaning against the fence are there for the wedding or the fishing. In the background, a gaff-rigged sloop is under way under a light breeze. (UVM.)

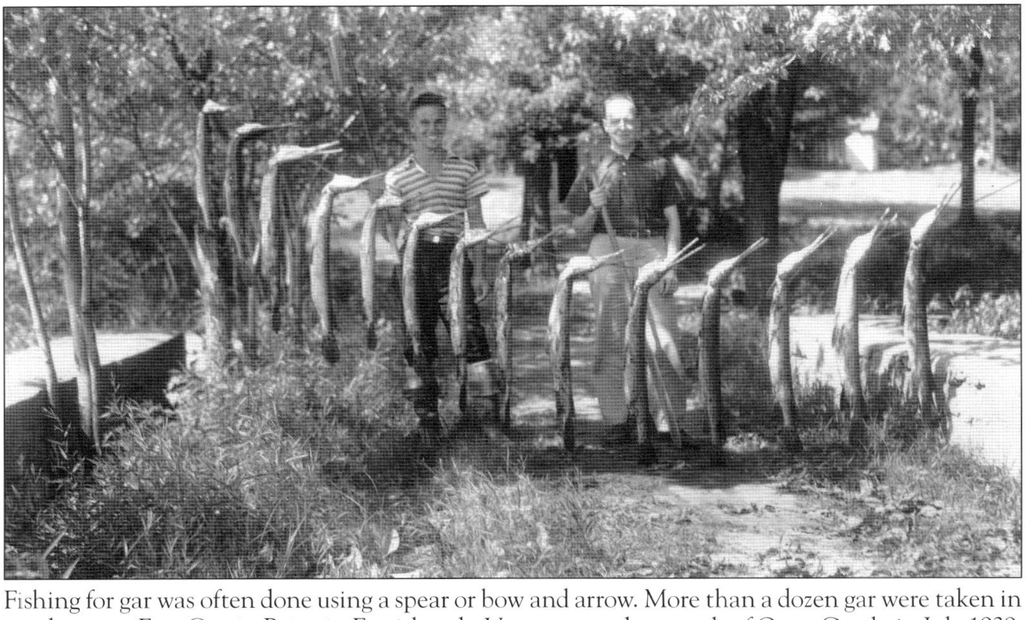

Fishing for gar was often done using a spear or bow and arrow. More than a dozen gar were taken in two hours at Fort Cassin Point in Ferrisburgh, Vermont, at the mouth of Otter Creek, in July 1939. Large gar are still found there, as well as in Otter Creek's warm tributary Dead Creek. (BHC.)

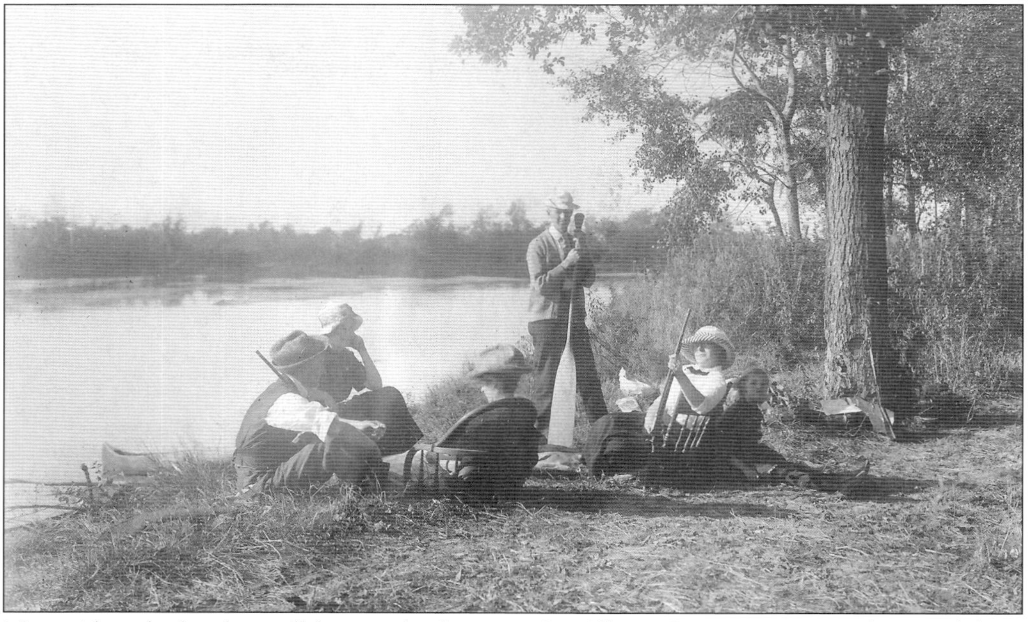

Many Abenaki families still live in the Swanton-St. Albans, Vermont, area and enjoy fishing and hunting along the waterways. In the 1910 photograph above, picnickers include Fred W. Wiseman (standing) and Josephine Wiseman (right), leaning against a young Dorothy Wiseman. Their canoe can be seen on the riverbank at left. The man fishing from his guide boat (below) is identified as "Chief of the Wabanacus, Highgate Springs." (Both, FMW.)

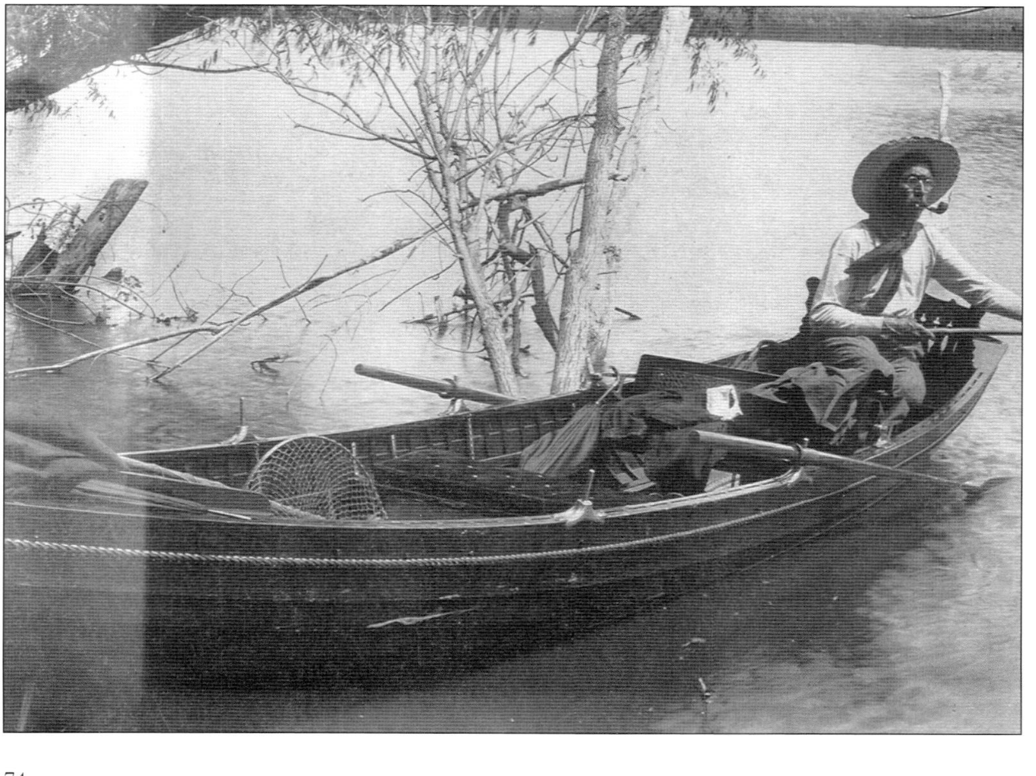

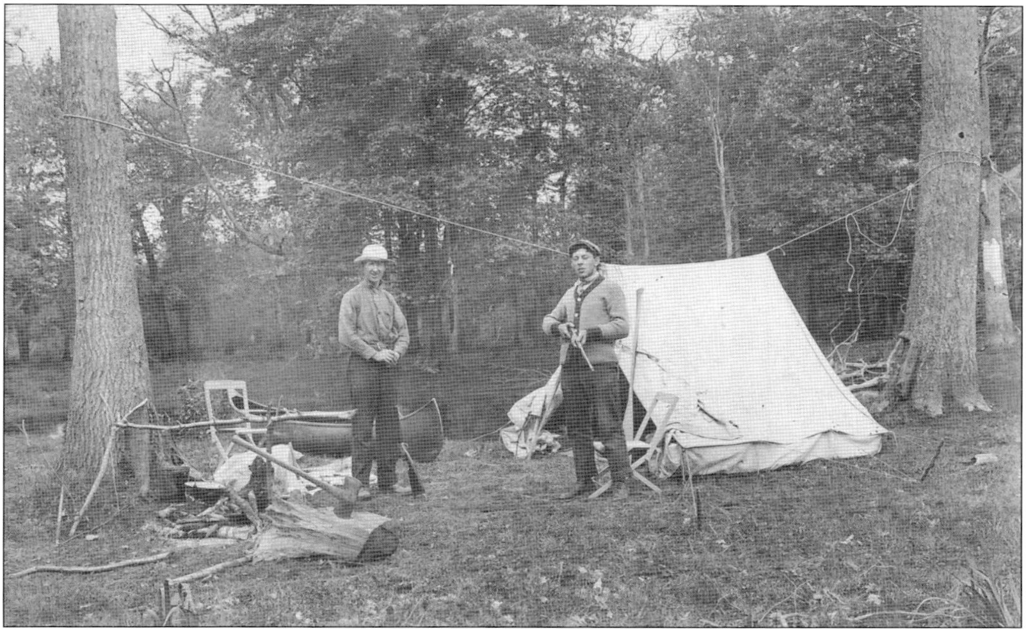

Above, Fred W. Wiseman (left) and an Abenaki guide evidently traveled by canoe to this hunting camp, packing their tent, folding chairs, and cook pot. The hunters in the photograph below are, from left to right, Judson Hilliker, Fred W. Wiseman, and Bill Borden. (Both, FMW.)

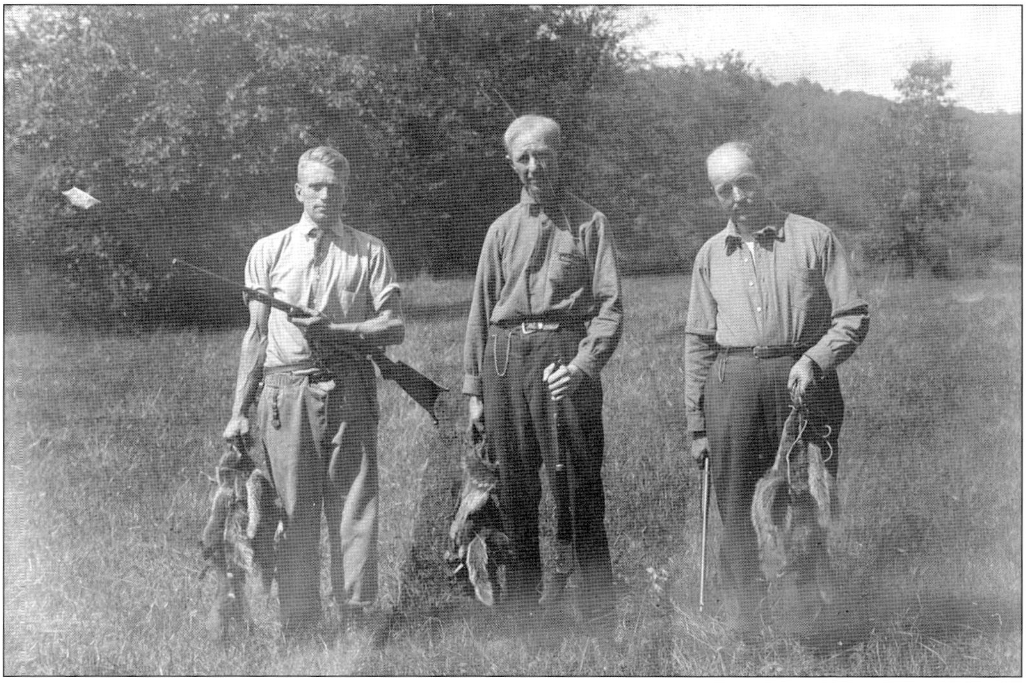

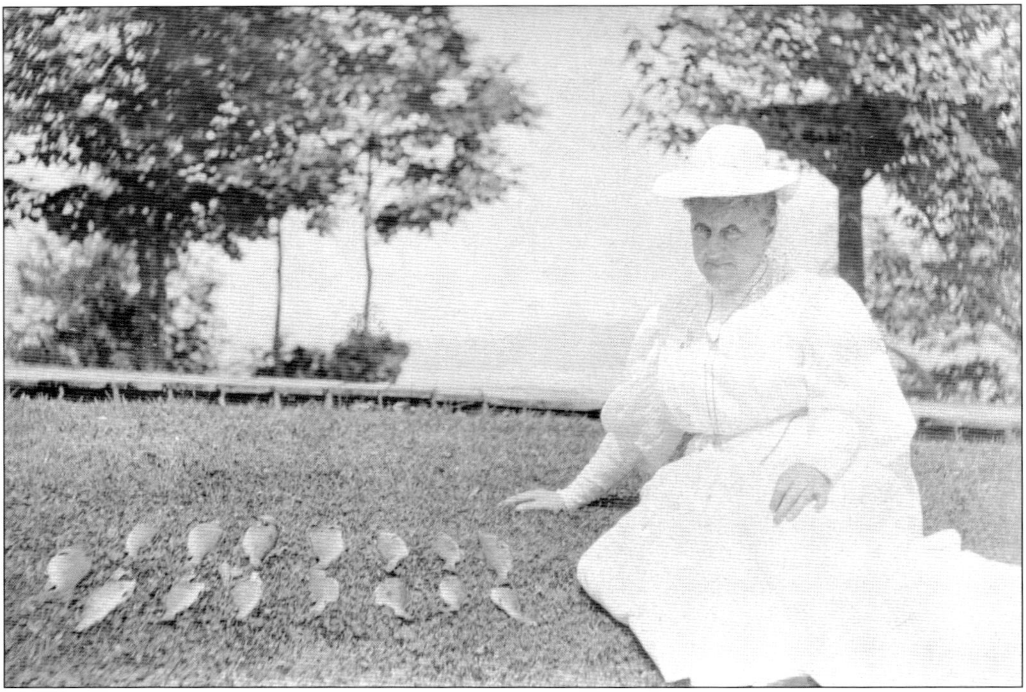

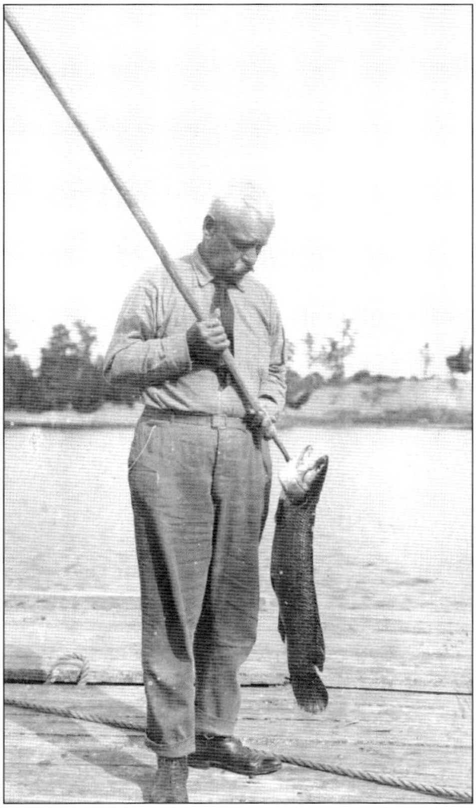

A woman elegantly attired in summer white displays her catch of bluegills on the lawn at Button Island, now part of Vermont's Button Bay State Park in Ferrisburgh. From the late 1800s through the 1970s, Button Island was the summer home of Samuel P. Avery and his descendants. (LCMM.)

The bowfin is one of the most unusual and ancient fish in Lake Champlain, with a single dorsal fin along its body. It is no surprise that this man looks warily at his catch and keeps his hands clear—the bowfin most likely fought against his hook, and its jaws are armed with pointed teeth that eagerly snap at nearly anything that moves. Bowfin can survive long periods of breathing air. (BHC.)

Standing on the rocky ledge at the shore of Button Island in Ferrisburgh, Vermont, this woman has caught a yellow perch using a fairly heavy bamboo rod. Amy Welcher inherited Button Island from her uncle Samuel P. Avery in 1904 and continued to summer on the island with friends and family members for many years. (LCMM.)

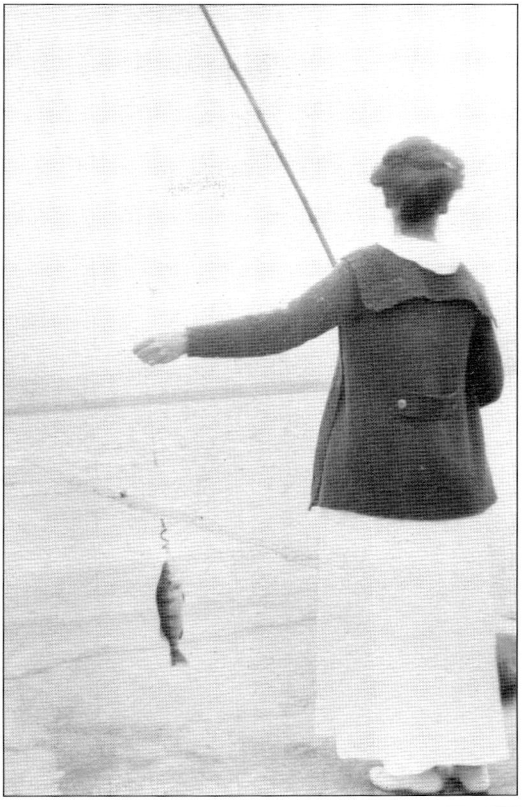

Yellow perch are abundant in Lake Champlain and are in season all year. Any size and any number can be taken. This image from the Basin Harbor Club album shows two fishermen delighted with their success, perhaps after visiting nearby Button Bay. (BHC.)

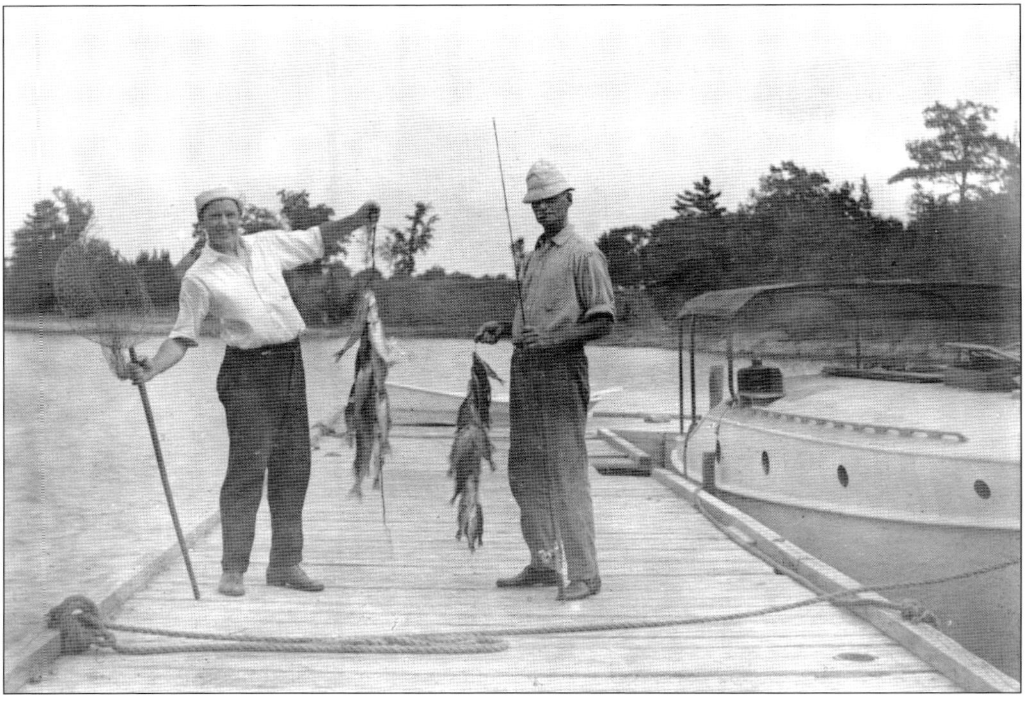

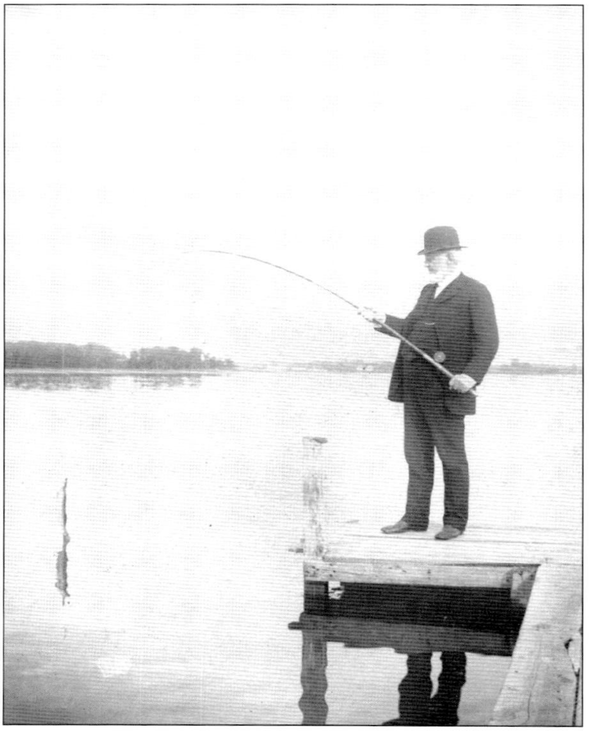

This image of a man in business attire fishing at the dock was found among the papers of Charles Edmund Parker (1839–1923). A prominent businessman and Civil War veteran from Vergennes, Vermont, Parker's collection of photographs suggest that he enjoyed recreation on the lake and Otter Creek. The photograph may be an example of fishing humor, as a small fish can be seen in the water trailing from his line. (UVM.)

Flat-bottomed skiffs made a stable platform for fishing and were easily pulled up on rocky ledges or wooden docks around the shoreline. Here, a long fishing pole can be seen in the stern of the boat as the fisherman lifts his oar. (LCMM.)

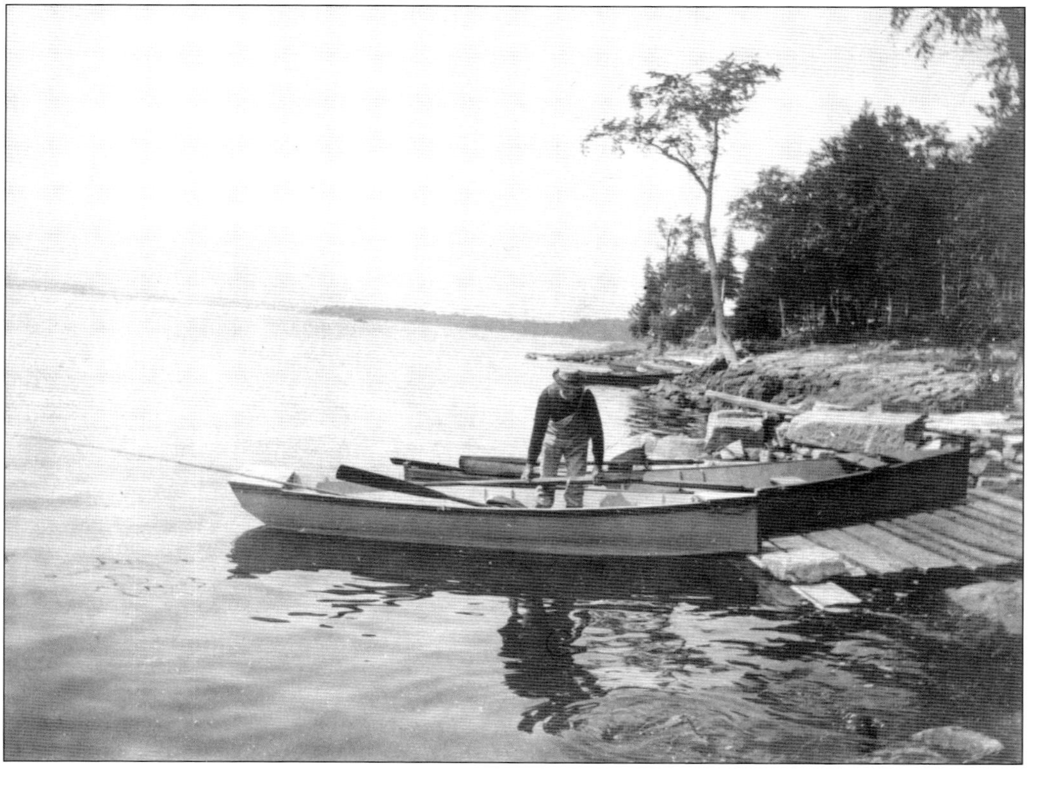

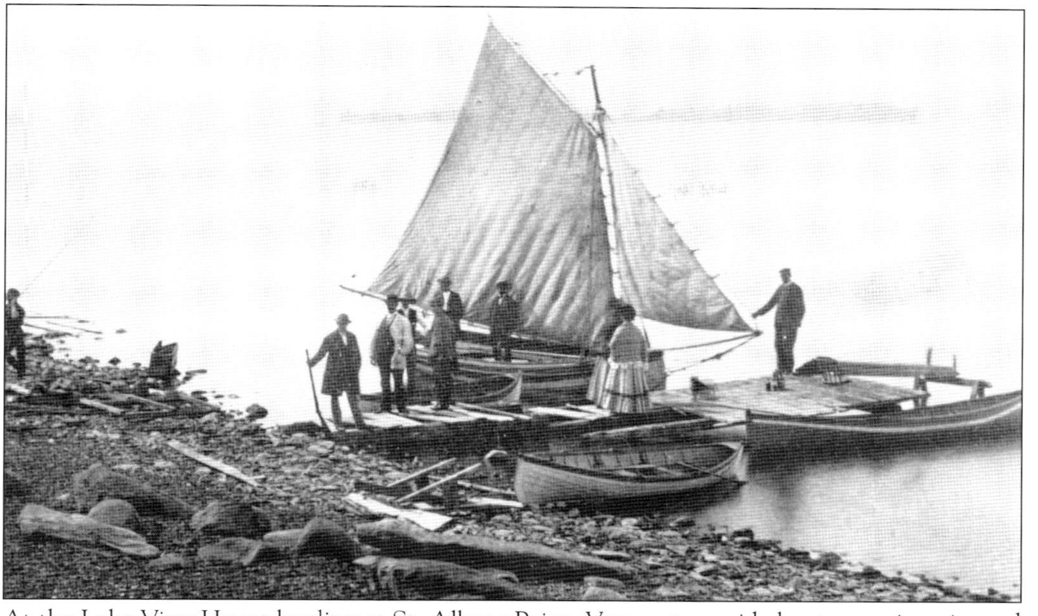

At the Lake View House landing at St. Albans Point, Vermont, a guide boat, a rowing gig, and the yacht *Sea Bird* await passengers. The Back Bay fishing grounds may be the destination of these hotel guests, as the man at the far left has a fishing pole. However, the cold-weather clothing and the long gun held by the man second from left may indicate fall duck hunting or spring pickerel shooting. The photograph was taken by T.G. Richardson. (LCMM.)

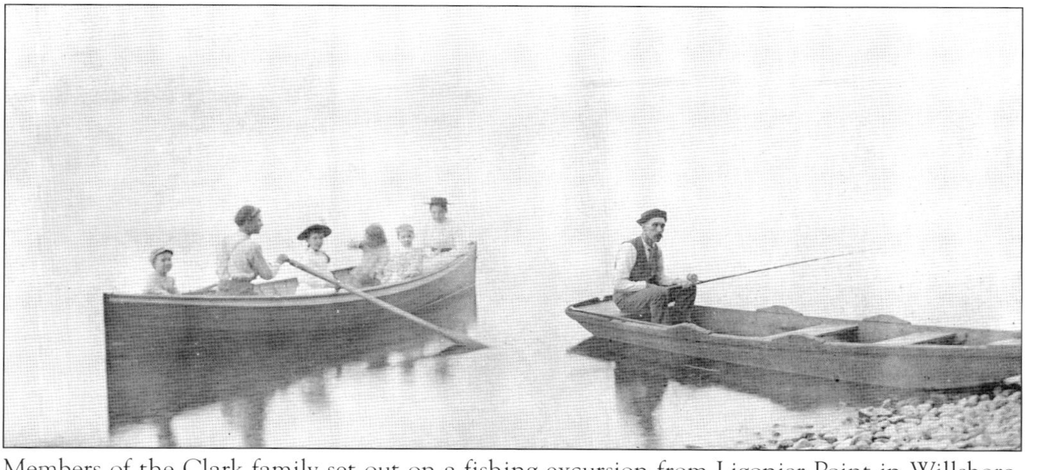

Members of the Clark family set out on a fishing excursion from Ligonier Point in Willsboro, New York. The Four Brothers Islands can be seen in the background. The Clarks operated a blue limestone quarry, shipyard, and dairy farm in the 19th century, and they took to the lake for recreation at every opportunity. The boat on the left was one of a number collectively referred to by the family as the "*Comet* boats." (HHRF.)

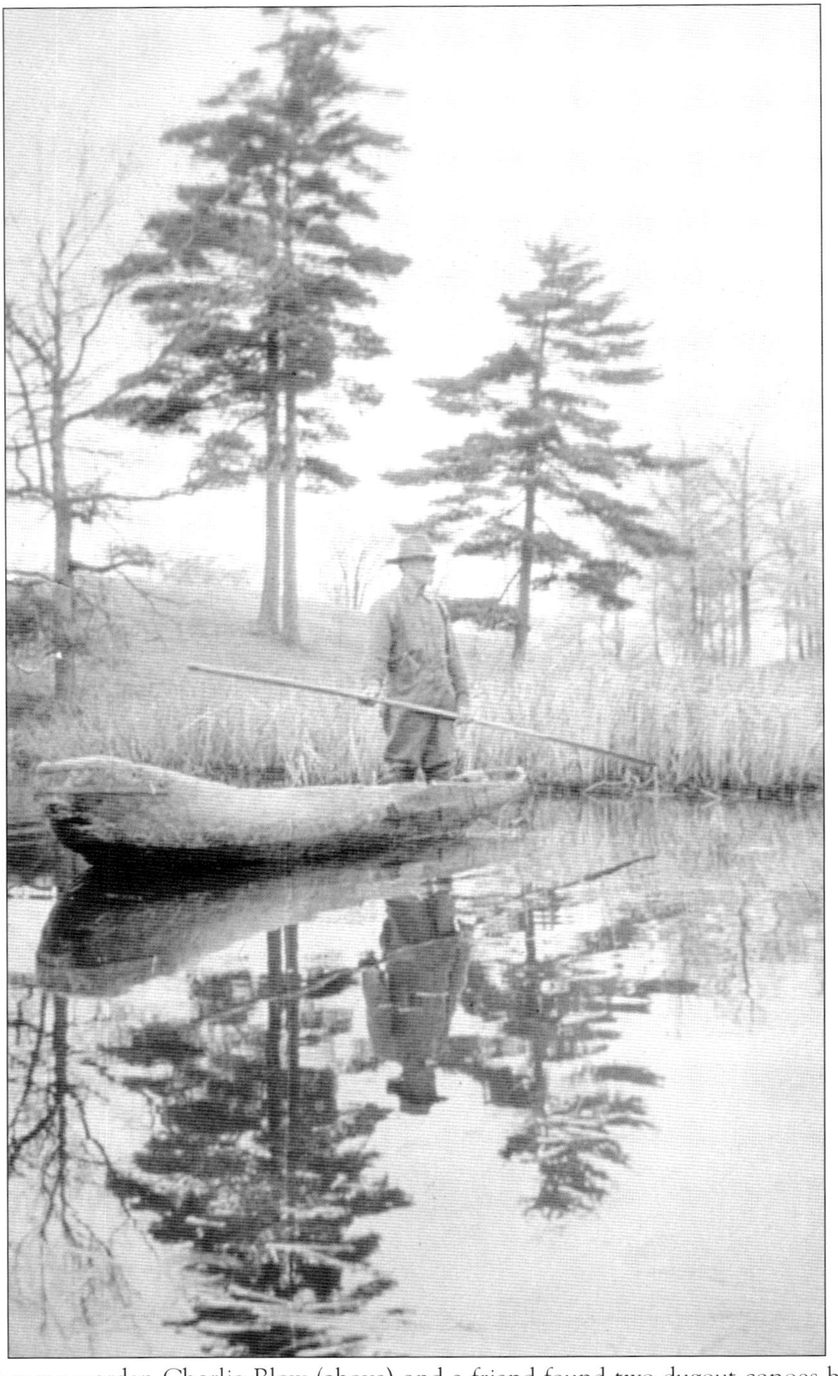

Vermont game warden Charlie Blow (above) and a friend found two dugout canoes buried in mud in a marsh, a traditional North Country method of preserving wooden boats. Blow, seen here with one of the canoes, used them in the 1920s and 1930s. The photographer, Rollin Tilley, later told this story to his son Russell. The marshy borders of Lake Champlain were popular for duck hunting, fishing, and trapping. (LCMM.)

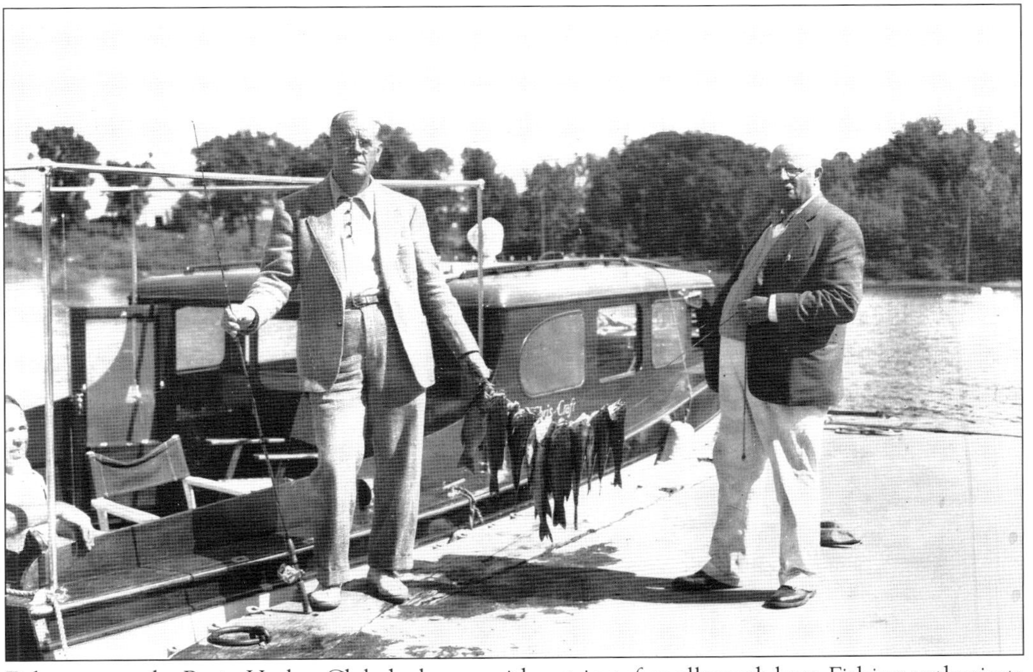

Fishermen at the Basin Harbor Club dock pose with a string of smallmouth bass. Fishing enthusiasts find lots of opportunities to follow their passion in the waters of this century-old resort. (BHC.)

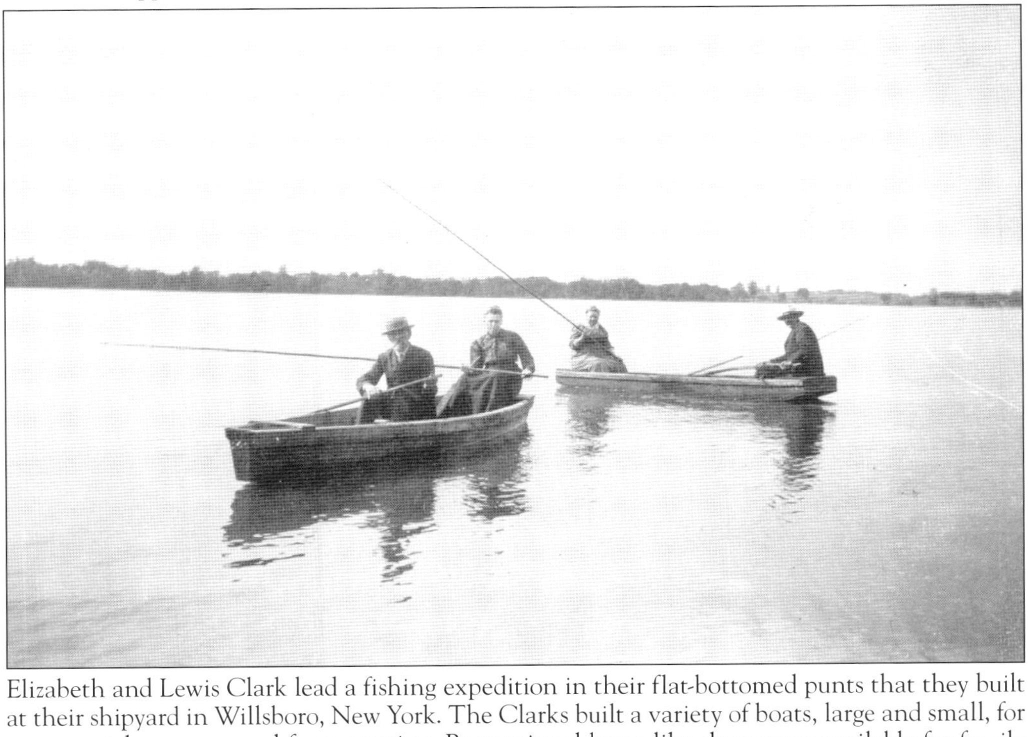

Elizabeth and Lewis Clark lead a fishing expedition in their flat-bottomed punts that they built at their shipyard in Willsboro, New York. The Clarks built a variety of boats, large and small, for commercial purposes and for recreation. Recreational boats like these were available for family and friends for outings on the lake. (HHRC.)

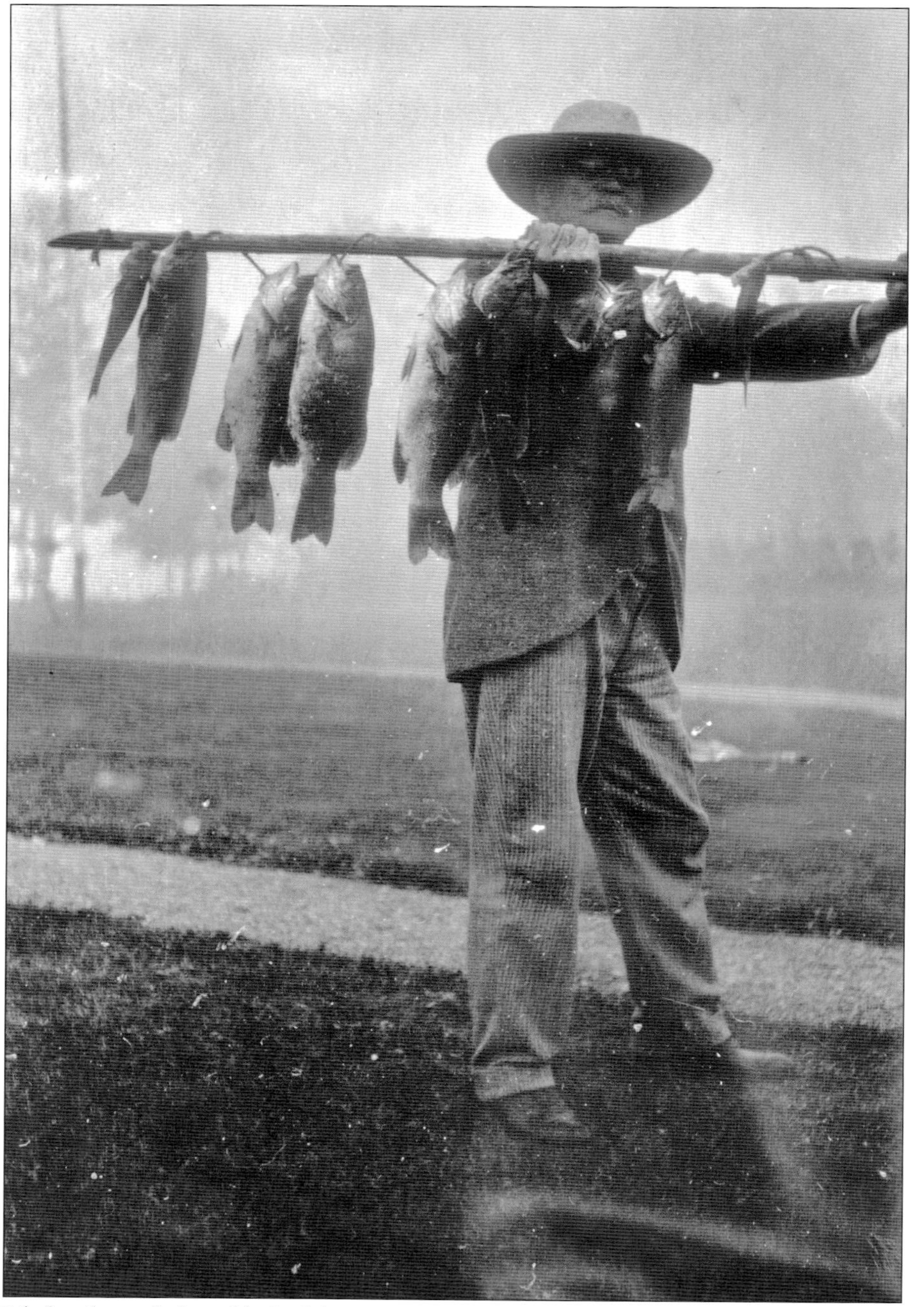

The Fisk family settled on Isle La Motte in 1788, near a quarry used by the French in 1666. The family operated the quarry and farmed for three generations. On September 6, 1901, Vice Pres. Theodore Roosevelt was at the Fisk Farm for a meeting of the Vermont Fish and Game League when he received word that Pres. William McKinley had been shot. Just eight days later, Roosevelt became the 26th president. This photograph of an unidentified man with a string of fish probably dates from that same era. The Isle La Motte Preservation Trust now administers the Fisk Quarry, and Fisk Farm hosts music and arts programming. (ILM.)

Six

Summer and Summer Folk

As the use of the north-south waterway as a commercial conduit was coming to an end, people increasingly came to regard the lake and its surrounding mountains as a haven for fishing, hunting, and boating. Local families migrated to the lake to escape the heat of the summer and began to dream about owning a piece of the shoreline. City dwellers from distant urban areas were attracted by inns and resorts that advertised the rejuvenating powers of a stay on Lake Champlain.

A few enterprising lakeside residents began converting their property to accommodate the growing population that had free time and the means to travel. They came to the lake by rail and automobile to spend vacation time basking in Lake Champlain's healthy and aesthetic environment. Special summer camps catered to children, particularly ones from urban areas, and provided them with opportunities to learn about nature. At a summer camp, young people could develop traditional skills in swimming, hiking, boating, and woodcraft in an atmosphere of fellowship. Summer camps on Lake Champlain remain popular today.

Some summer enclaves were seasonal communities under canvas tents. Others were multistoried resorts with porches facing the lake, docks, and boathouses. Champlain Valley families planned to spend time each summer at a "camp" on the lake, either owning or renting. Families that returned to summer on Lake Champlain year after year often established a more permanent family camp. At Long Point, Cedar Beach, and Thompson's Point, families gradually converted summer camps of canvas tents into more permanent, although still seasonal, rustic wooden structures. Over the years, many of these camps have been further adapted into year-round dwellings that permit the Lake Champlain enthusiast to remain beside the lake throughout its four seasons. Today, public recognition of the many ways that Lake Champlain enriches lives has inspired widespread efforts to preserve and protect the natural and cultural legacy of the lake.

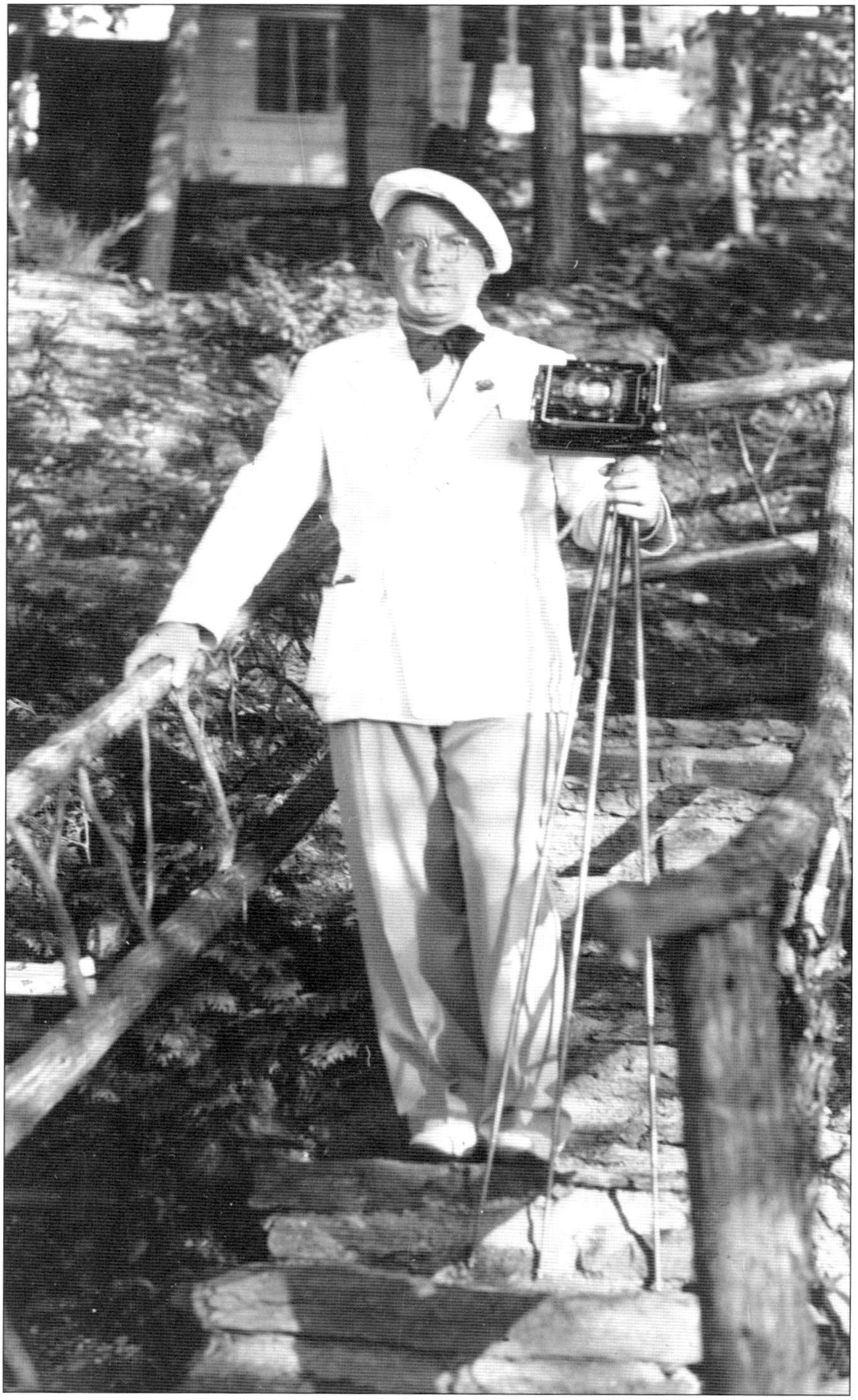

Allen Penfield Beach nurtured the fledgling Basin Harbor Club into the modern age. Seen here with his Graflex camera in hand at a Melius picnic below Greystone Cottage in Vermont, Beach was always ready to capture an engaging moment in the life of the resort. (BHC.)

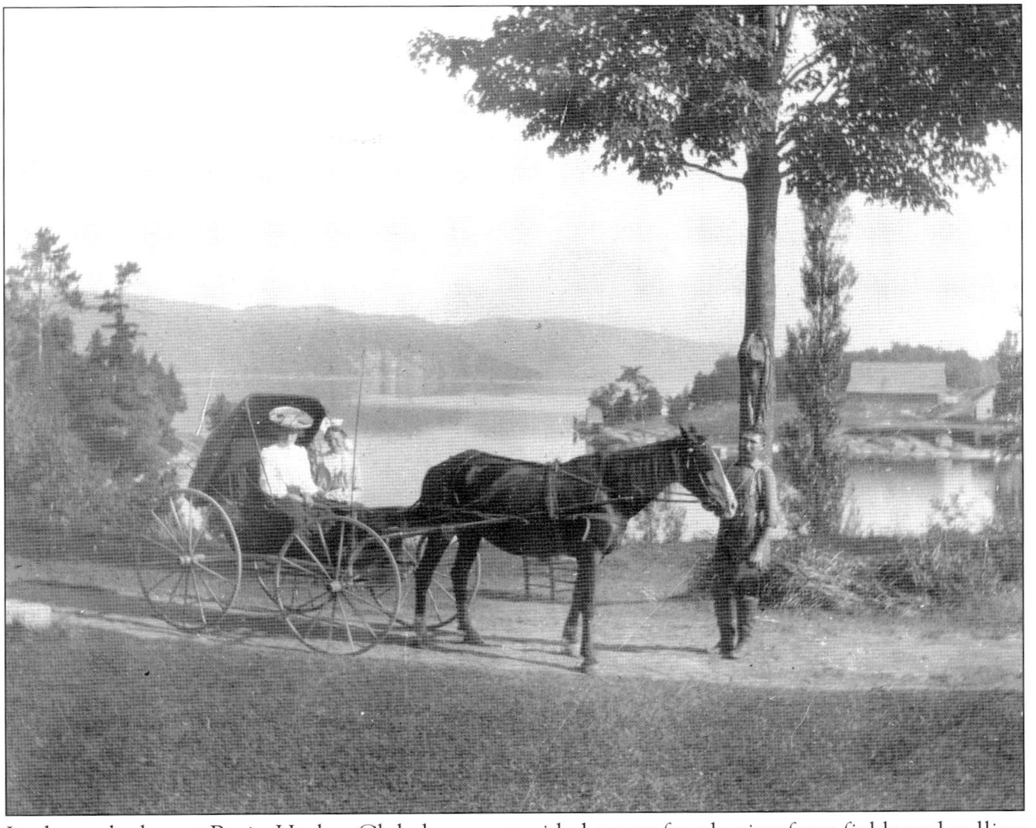

In the early days at Basin Harbor Club, horses provided power for plowing farm fields and pulling carriages (above), while steamboats made deliveries and naphtha launches carried guests on excursions (below). (Both, BHC.)

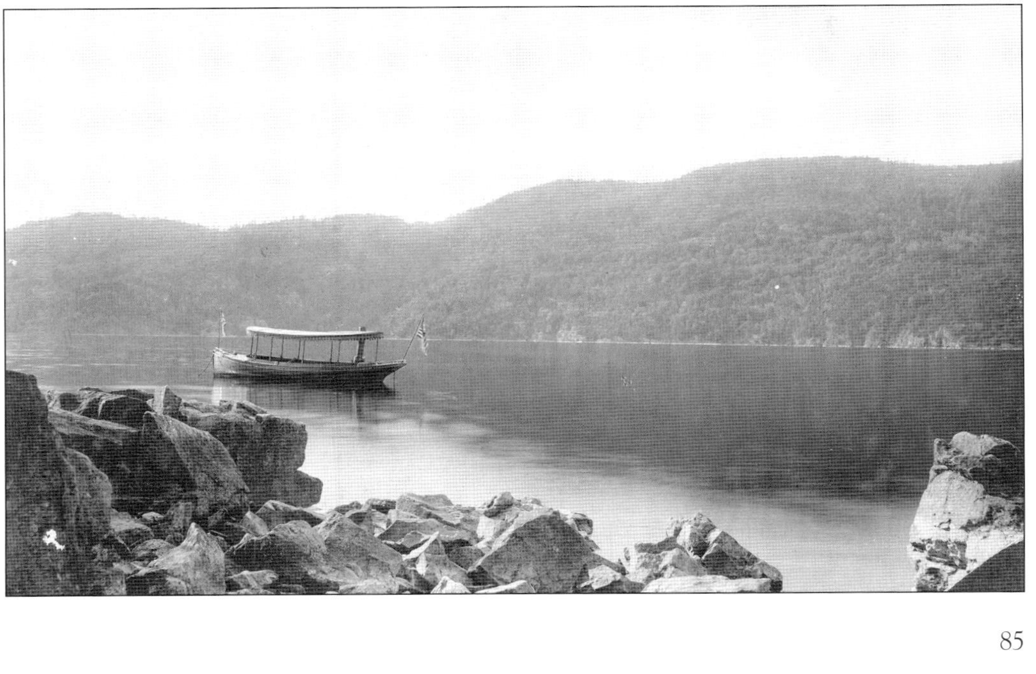

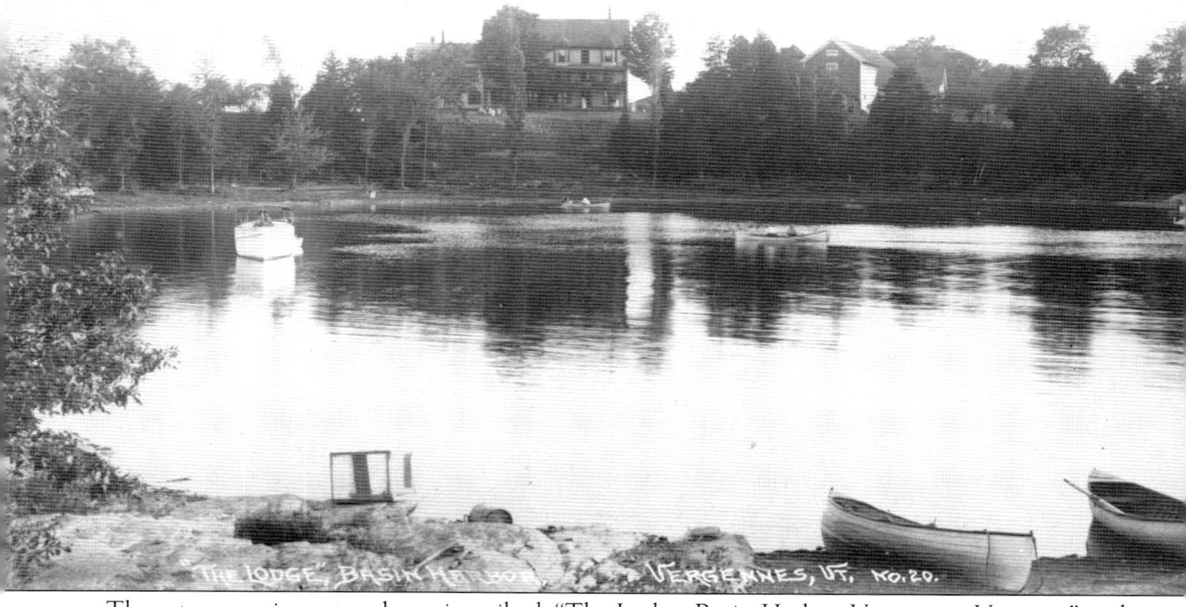

These two scenic postcards are inscribed, "The Lodge, Basin Harbor, Vergennes, Vermont" and "Basin Harbor Entrance, Westport, New York, in distance." The paired captions emphasize the connection with the neighboring community of Westport, directly west across the lake. An array

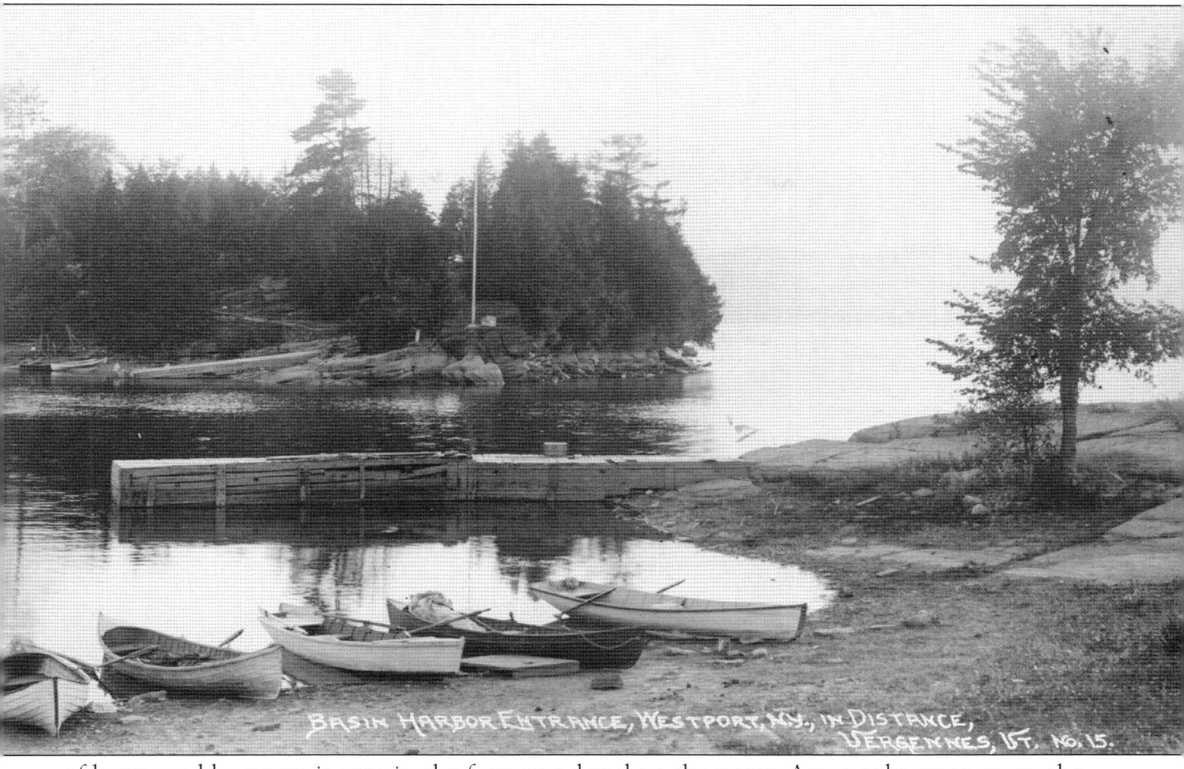

of boats used by guests is seen in the foreground and on the water. Among the trees across the small harbor stand the Lodge (left) and a barn, which is now the town hall. (BHC.)

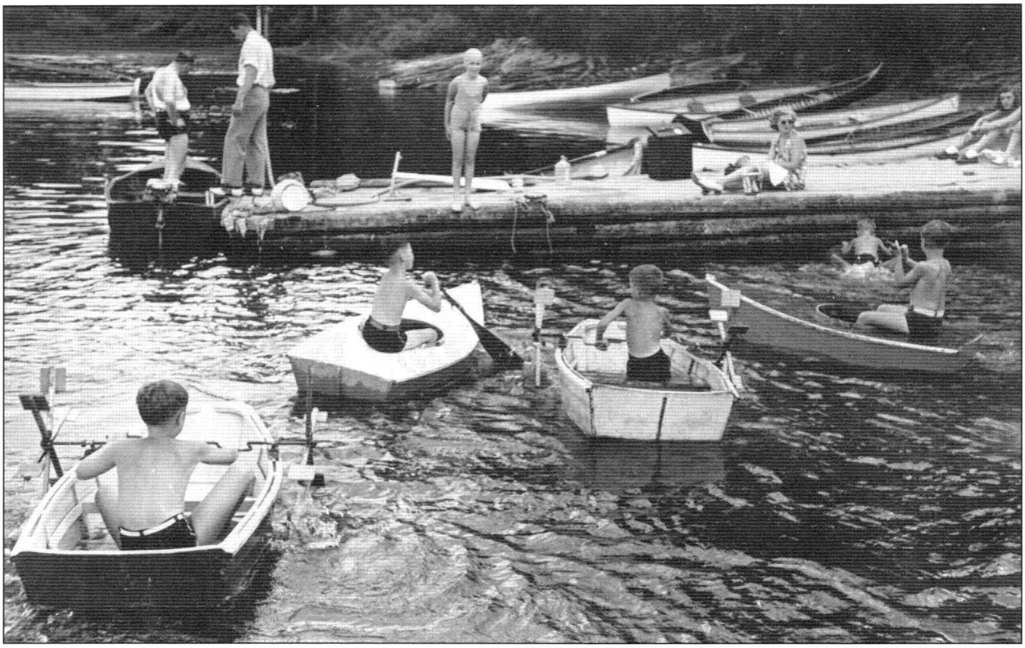

These four small, whimsical skiffs were made about 1940 to provide young guests with an introduction to boating on Lake Champlain. Two of the boats were propelled with paddles, and the other two had paddle wheels that were cranked by hand. (BHC.)

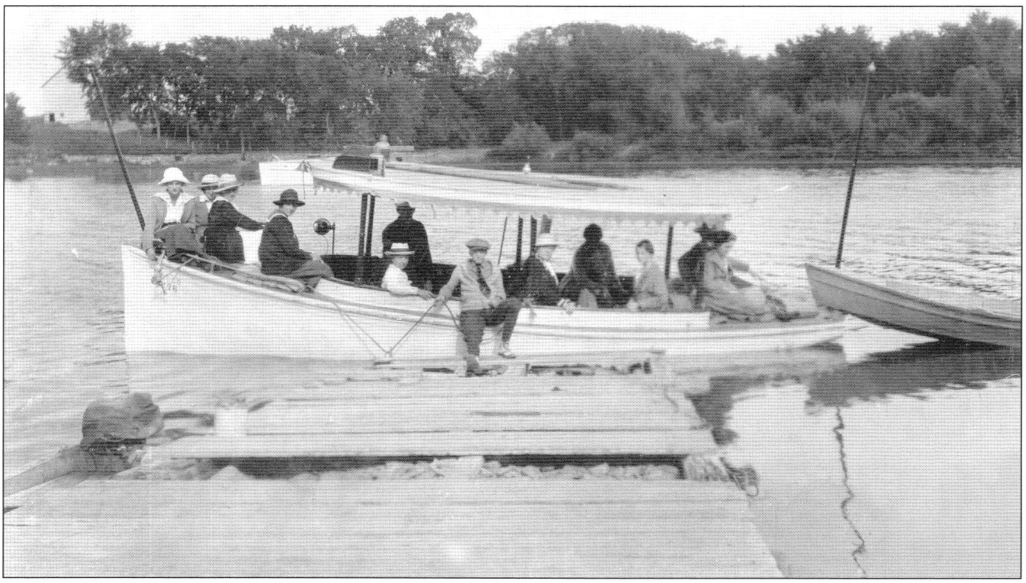

Wave was the transportation boat for the Lodge side of Basin Harbor, carrying guests to the Lake Champlain Transportation Company pickup area or providing service to Westport, New York. (BHC.)

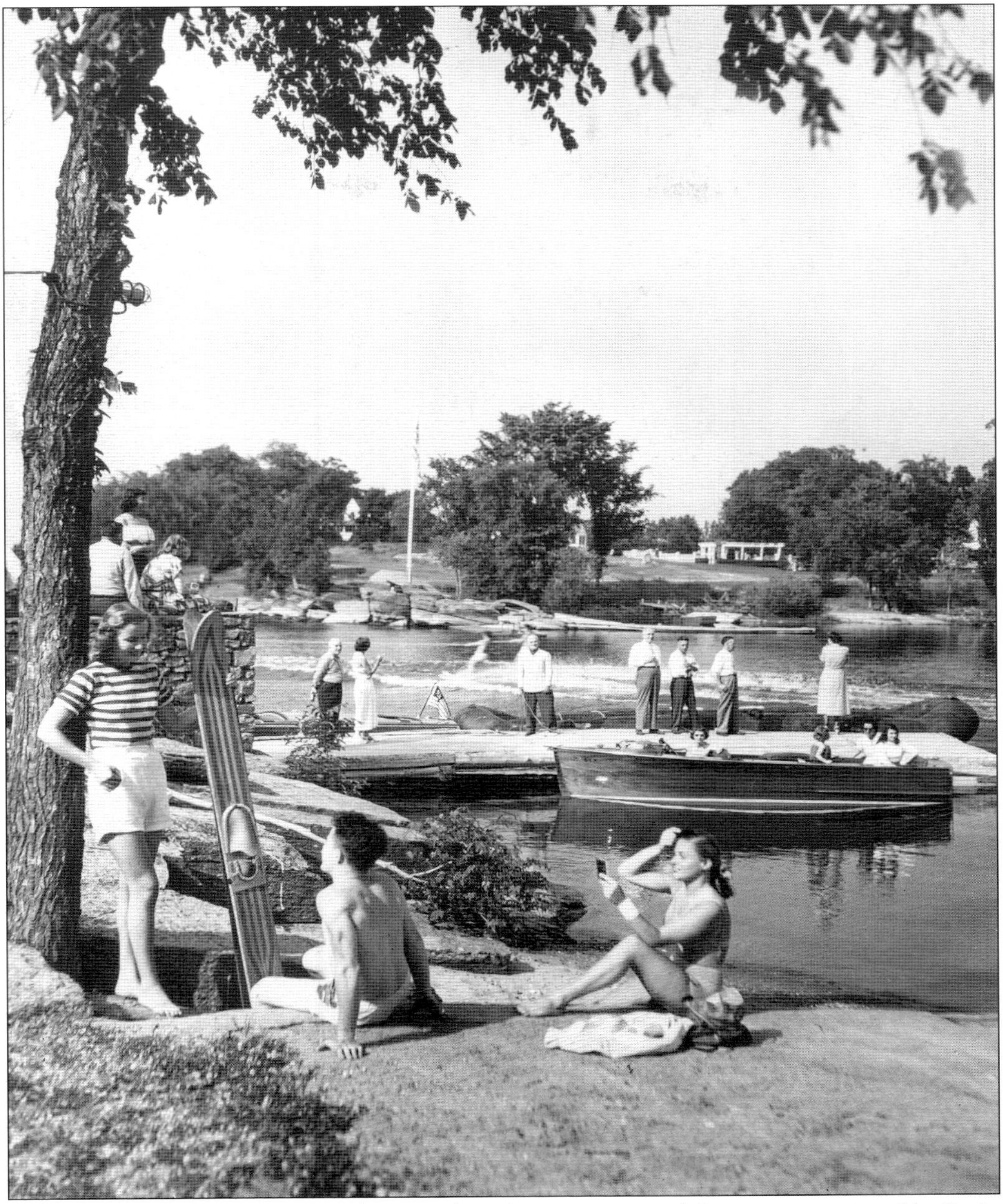

Allen Penfield Beach set up this photograph to showcase many of the pastimes enjoyed by Basin Harbor Club guests. The boat is *Frolic I*, a 1940 Chris-Craft utility. (BHC.)

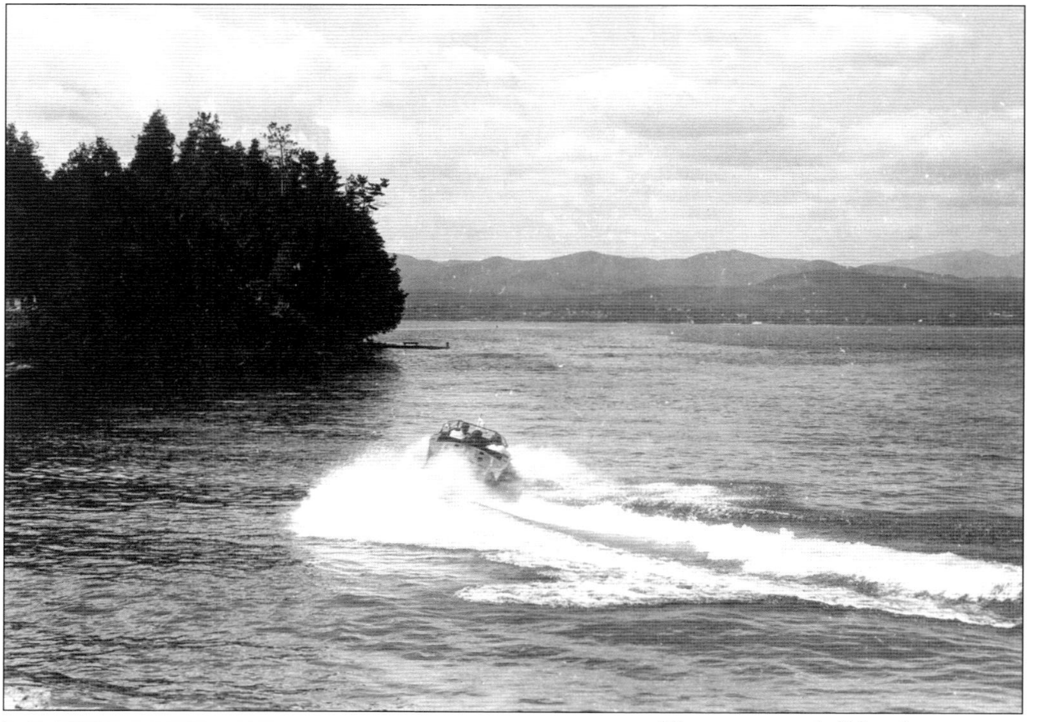

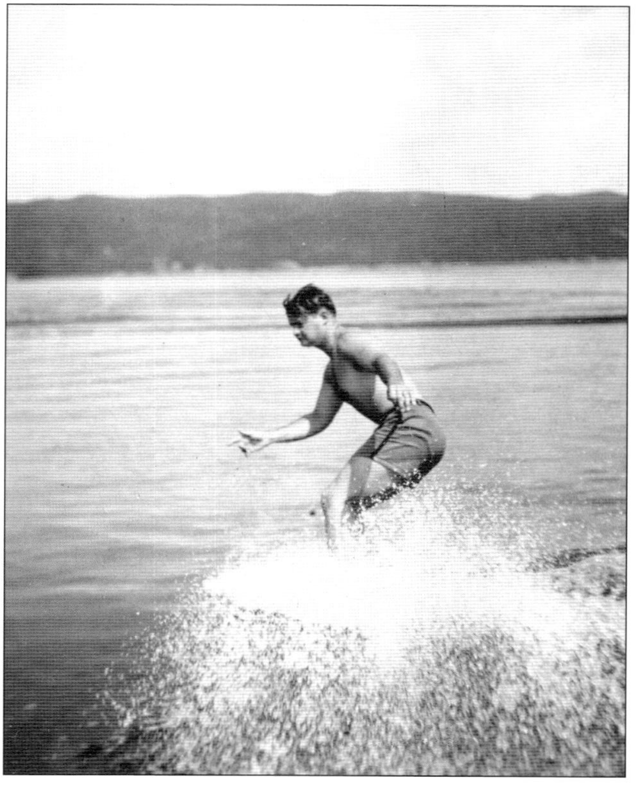

Water sports of all kinds were an important part of life at Basin Harbor. The speedboat *Princess* (above) was used in the 1940s. Ed Kurt (left) is an expert aquaplaner. (Both, BHC.)

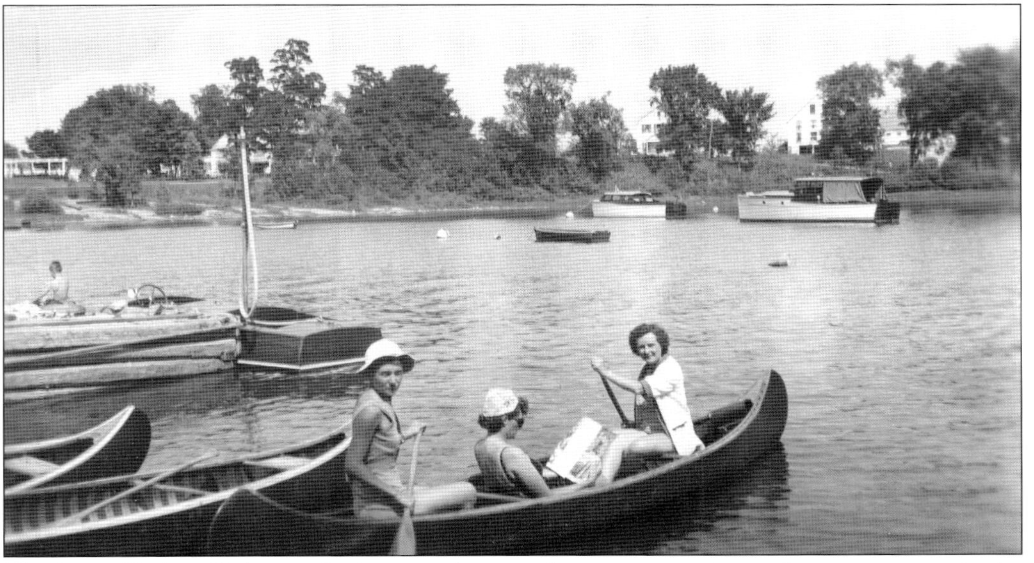

The Basin Harbor Club provides boats and canoes for guests to enjoy, and some guests arrive by boat. In the foreground, three women set off in a canoe; in the background is the cruiser *Merry May*, owned by the Melius family. (BHC.)

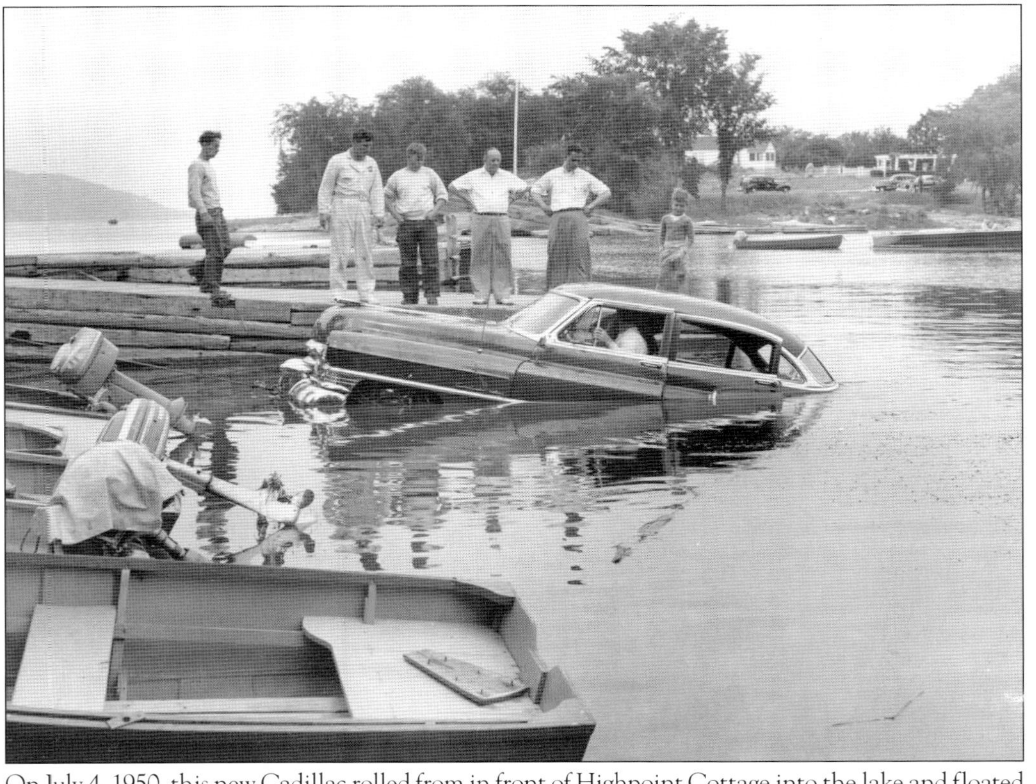

On July 4, 1950, this new Cadillac rolled from in front of Highpoint Cottage into the lake and floated halfway across the harbor before it sank. On the dock are, from left to right, unidentified, Mike Fields, Howard Miller, Paul Savoy, Bob Beach, and unidentified. John Maloney is "driving." (BHC.)

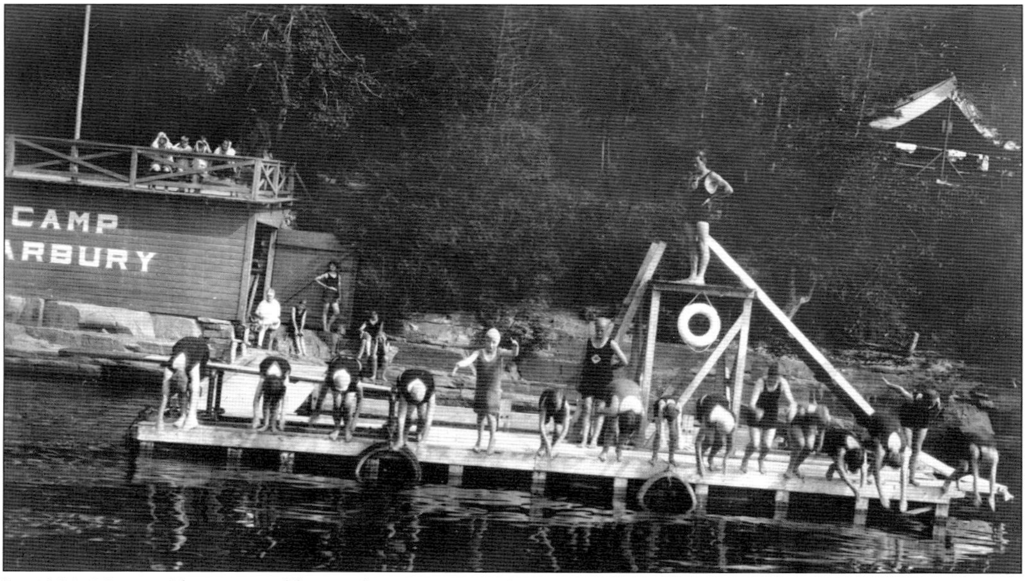

In 1921, Henry Sleeper and his wife, Mary Peet, became half-owners of Camp Marbury (above), a private girls' camp in Ferrisburgh, Vermont. The camp was named for Anne Marbury Hutchinson (1591–1643) of the Massachusetts Bay Colony, whom Henry Sleeper admired for her "ability, energy, kindness to children, interest in the welfare of women, loyalty to truth, and fearlessness in the presence of danger." Diving from the float (below) was one of many activities offered to develop strength, skill, and confidence. (Both, VHS.)

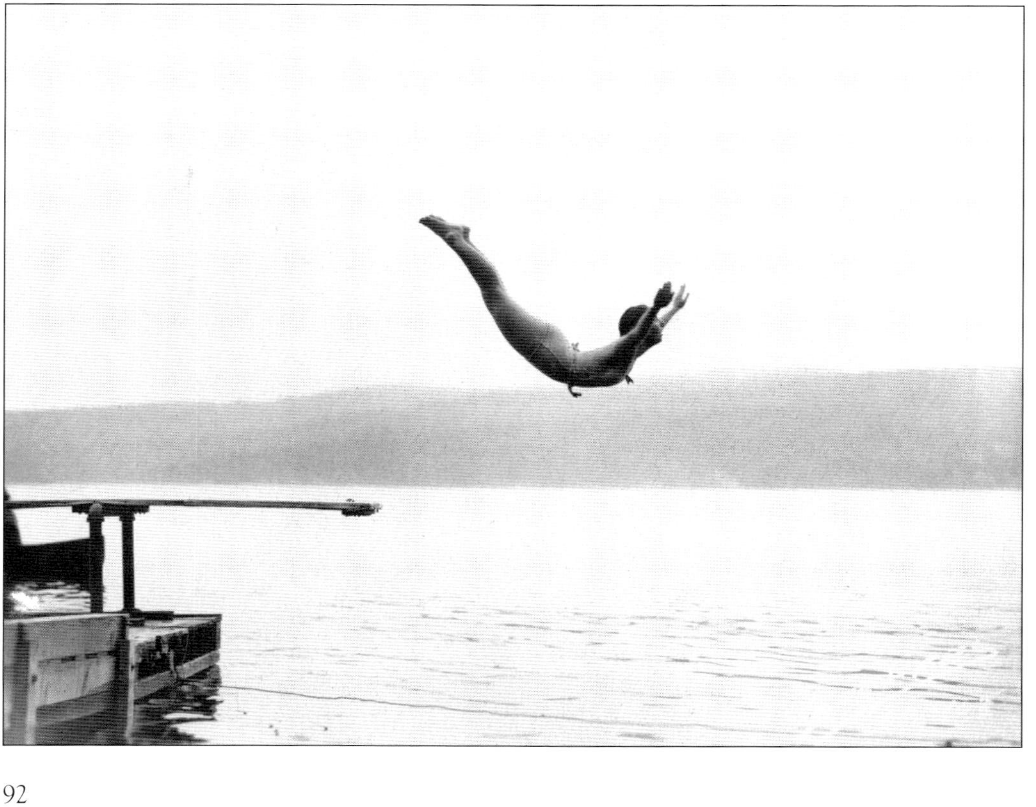

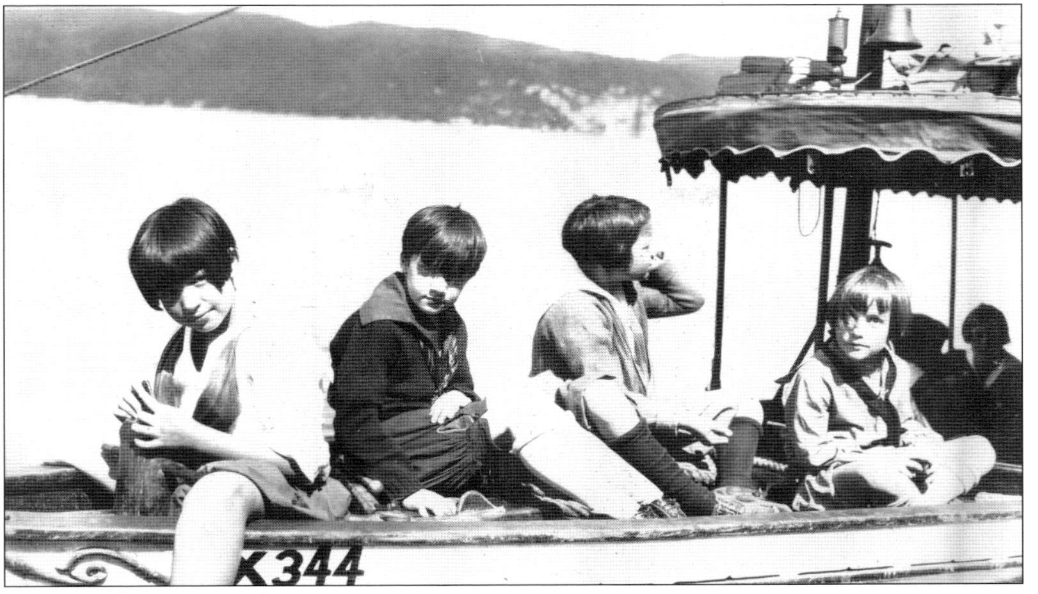

Camp Marbury operated a steam launch to take the campers on excursions like the one seen above. Note the whistle and bell on the right, just above the canopy. The workings of the steam engine (right) were all visible to fascinate the campers. (Both, VHS.)

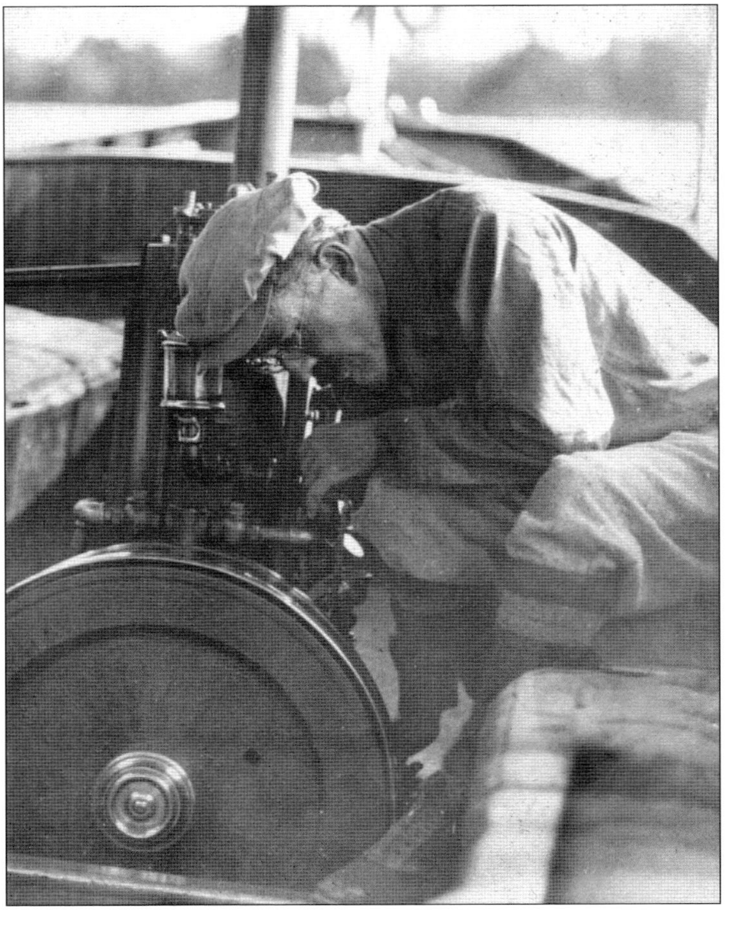

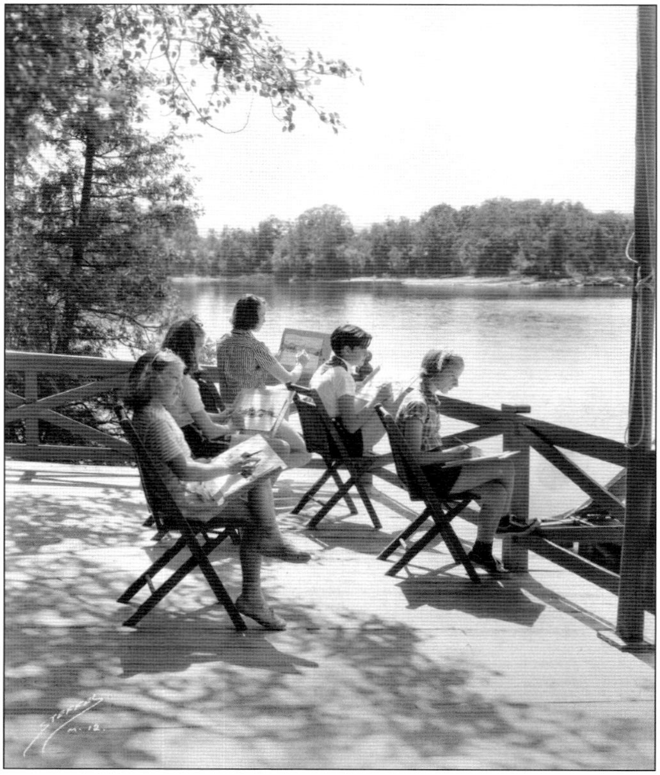

Young artists are working on views of Lake Champlain. The program at Camp Marbury also offered music, crafts, puppetry, theater, and dance. (VHS.)

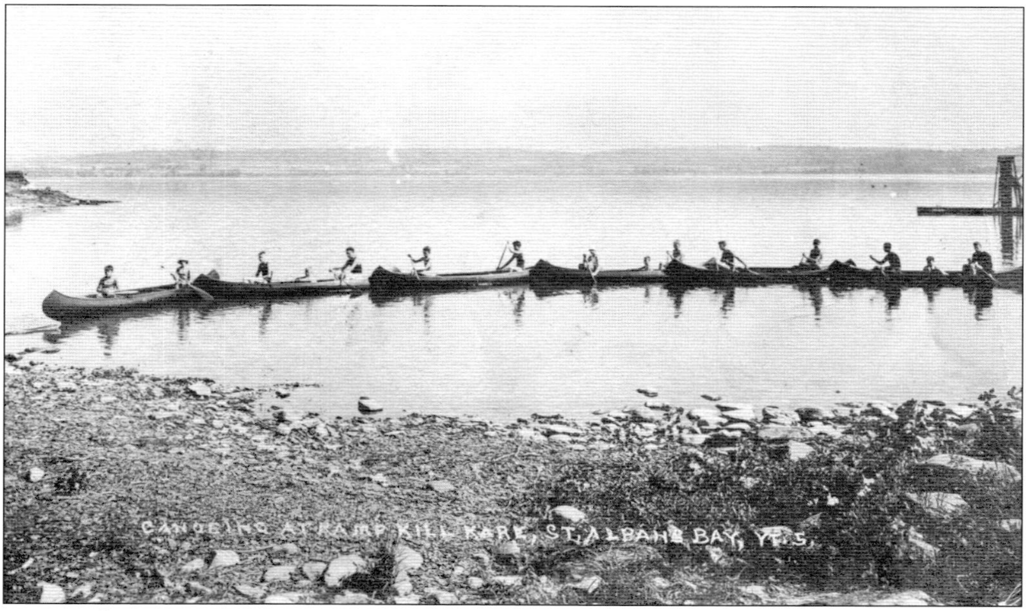

Kamp Kill Kare, a summer camp for boys, operated on St. Albans Point, Vermont, from 1912 until 1966. The main building was constructed in the 1870s as a summer resort hotel, the Rocky Point House. In 1912, the boys' camp purchased the property. The camp also included tennis courts, a baseball field, and several small cabins. The property became a state park in 1967. (UVM.)

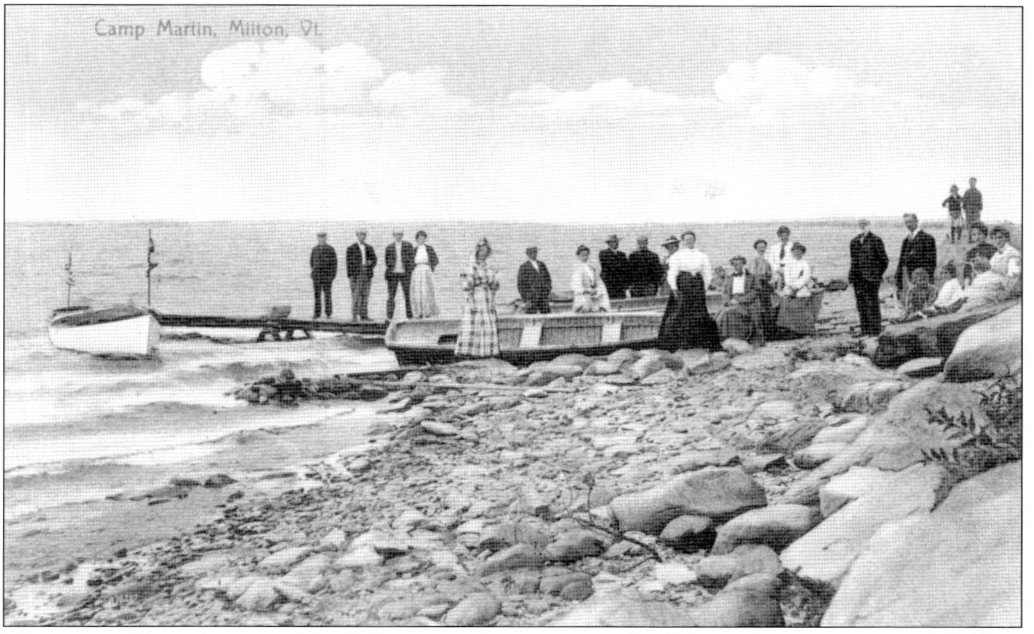

This postcard from the turn of the 20th century shows a group of well-dressed men, women, and children ready for an excursion at the waterfront at Camp Martin, in Milton, Vermont. (LCMM.)

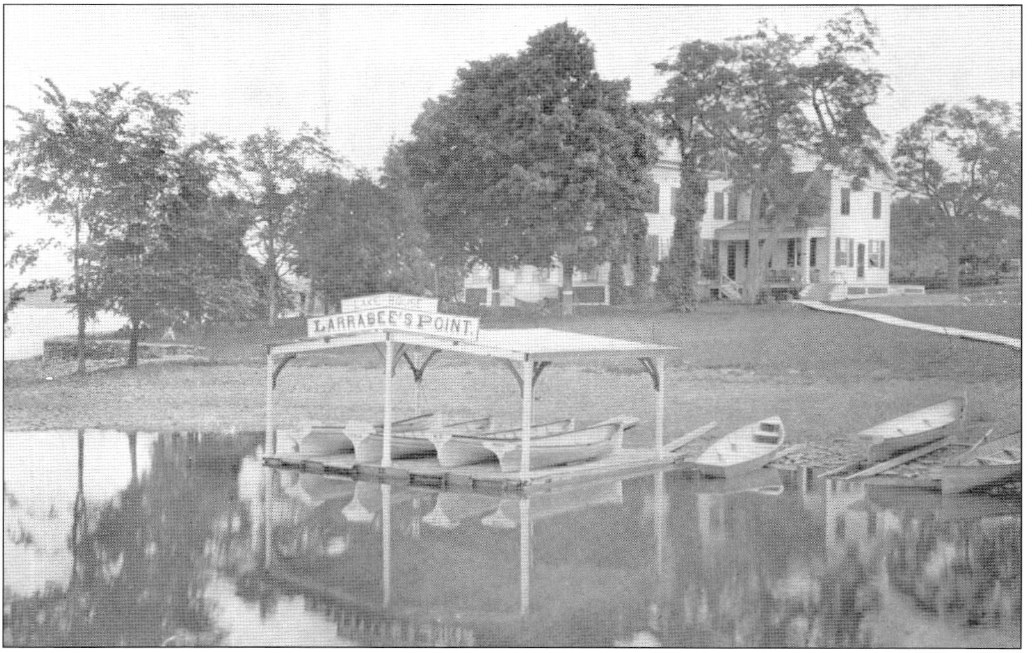

The prosperity of Lake House, at Larrabee's Point, Vermont, was due in large part to Brackett Weeks Burleigh, who built a summer home there and invested in boat docks, storage yards, and railroad tracks and trestles linked to Vermont's Addison Railroad, which crossed Lake Champlain about a mile south of Larrabee's Point. (UVM.)

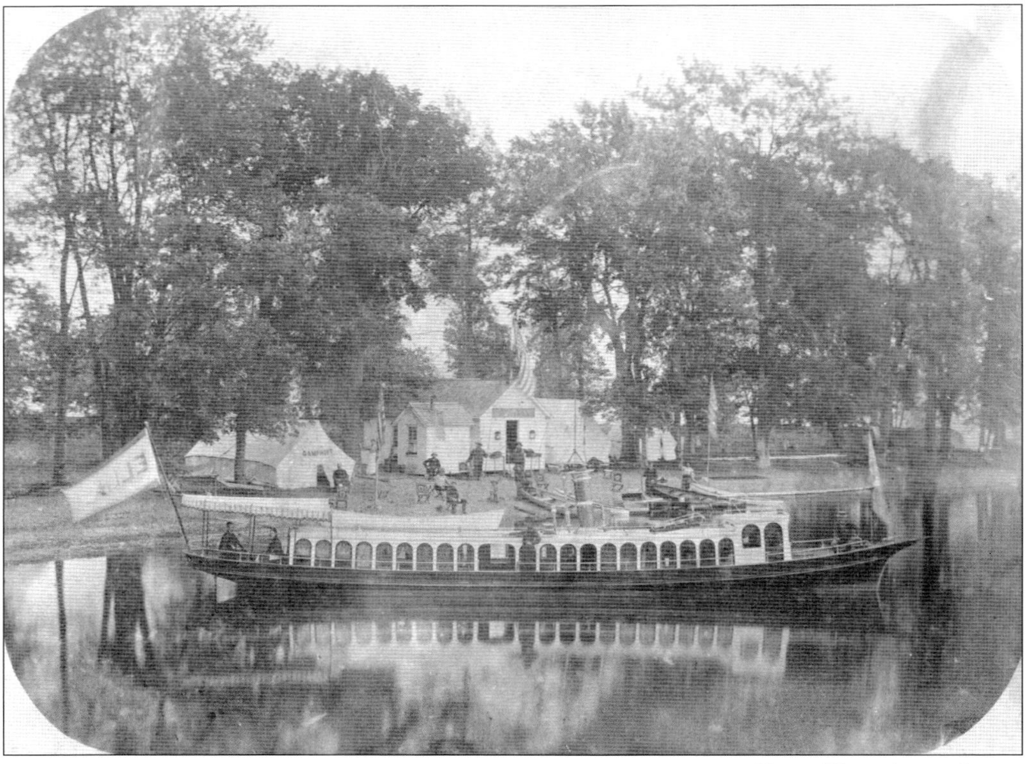

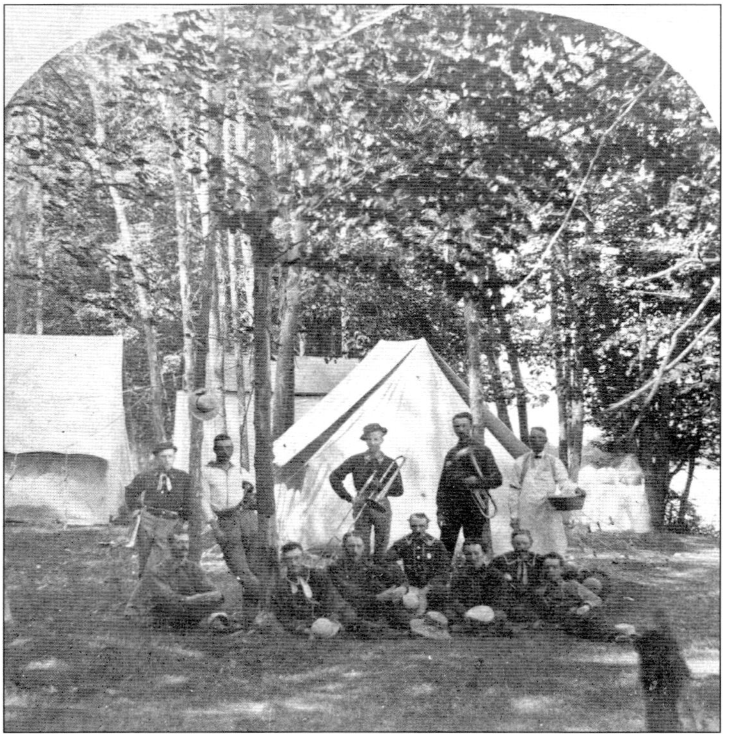

Camp Hoyt, located on Pelots Bay in North Hero, Vermont, and seen above in 1879, was probably one of the many summer camps established seasonally as a canvas tent city by the lake. In the later part of the 19th century, many traditional camps began to convert their rough canvas dwellings to wood. The term "camps," however, continued to be used, and, today, some of these summer "camps" are quite elaborate. Some of the camps had a religious affiliation, and many included music in their programs, which may be the reason for the instruments held by some of the campers at left. (Both, UVM.)

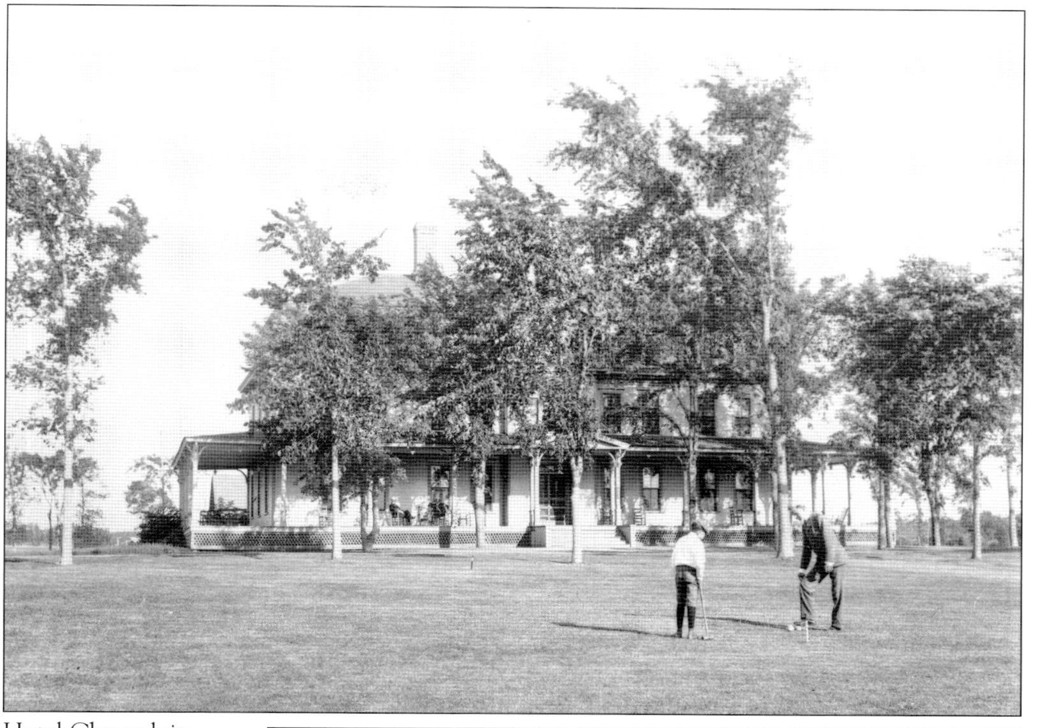

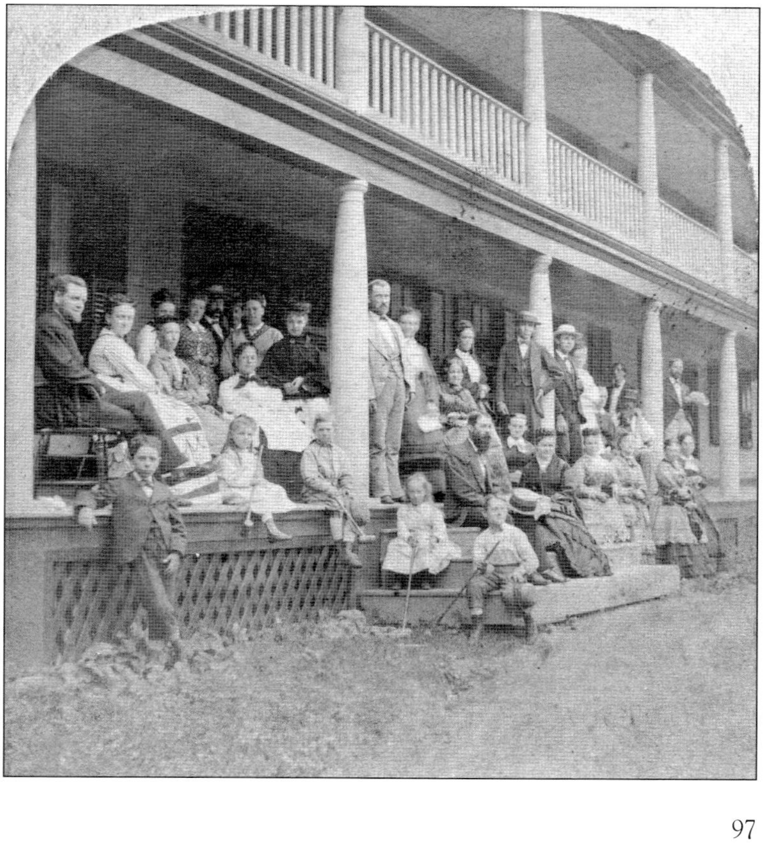

Hotel Champlain, at Maquam Bay, Vermont, is seen above in 1899 with a croquet game in progress on the lawn. It was conveniently located on a railroad excursion line. Pres. William McKinley spent a summer at the hotel, which eventually burned down in the 1920s. At right, summer boarders at Mansion House, in Alburgh Springs, Vermont, assemble on the porch for a souvenir portrait. (Both, UVM.)

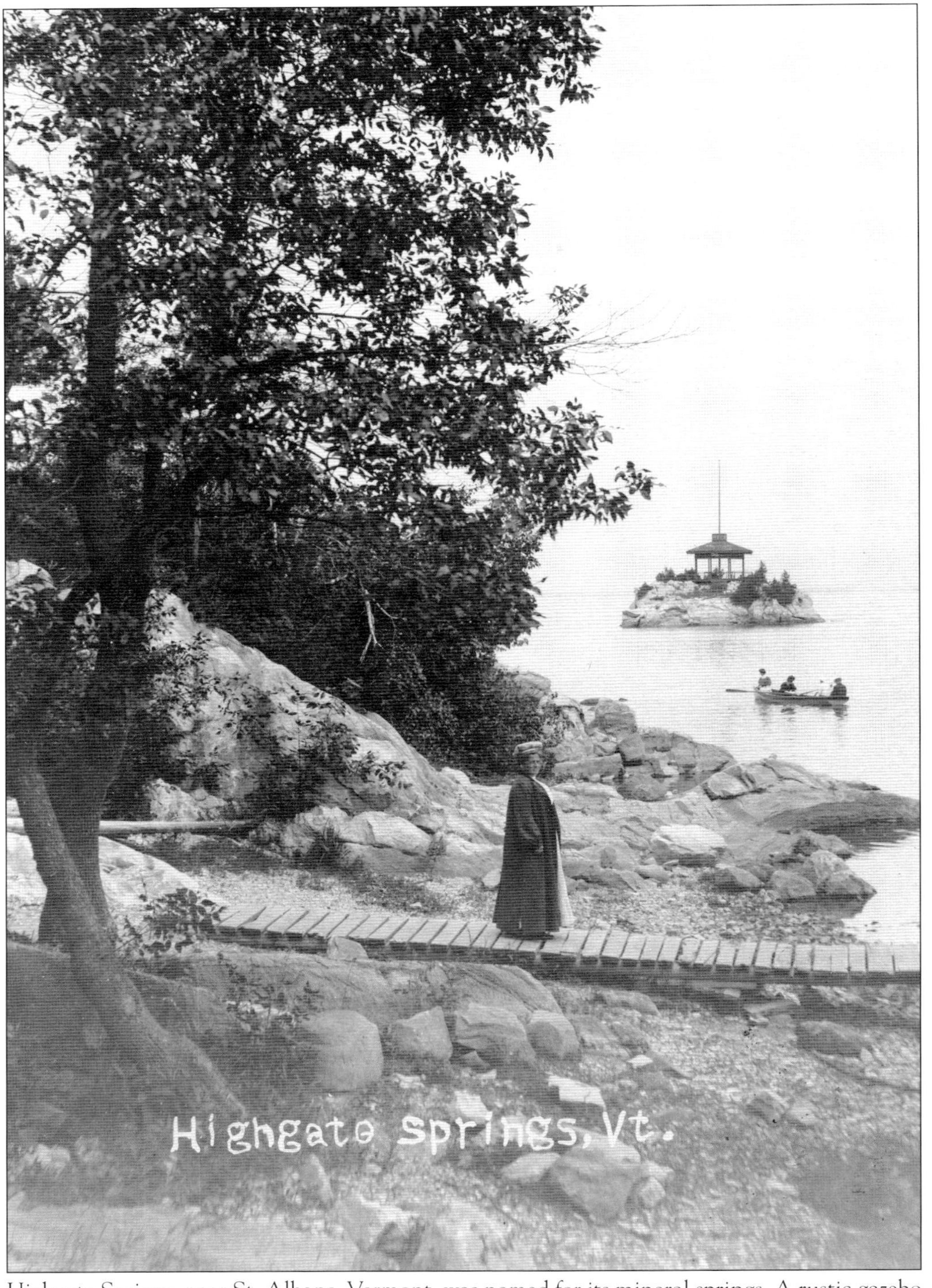

Highgate Springs, near St. Albans, Vermont, was named for its mineral springs. A rustic gazebo on the island offered a view that appealed to the popular taste for the picturesque, as well as a destination for a rowing boat. (UVM.)

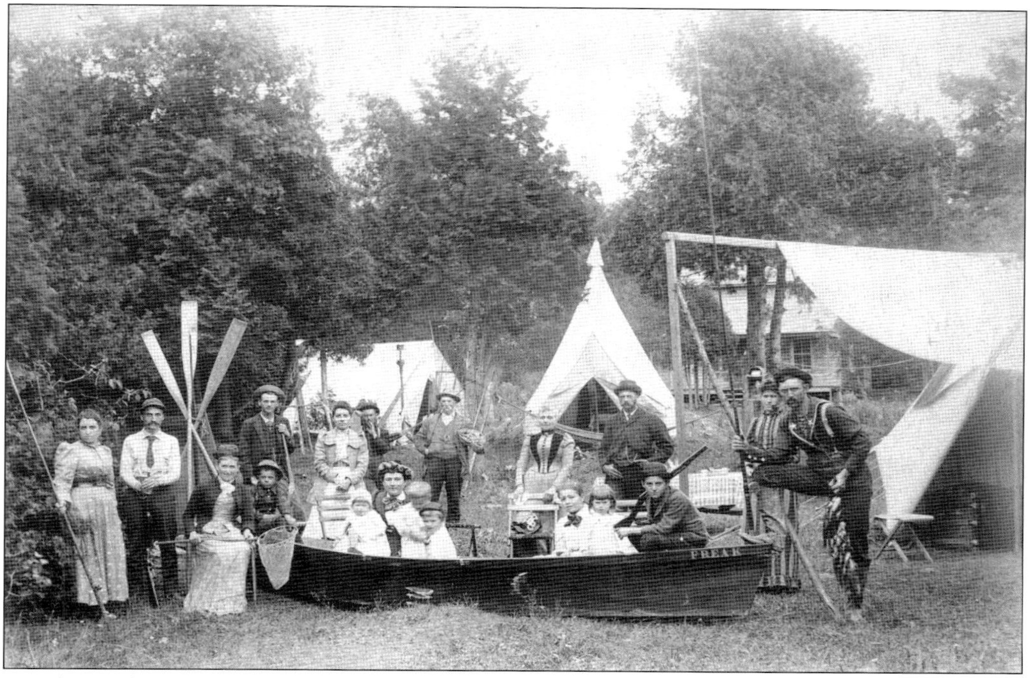

Posed in and around a skiff named *Freak*, these assembled family members have carefully composed a portrait of life at camp. From left to right, they hold a fishing pole, oars, a fishnet, a palette and brushes, a gun, and fishing rods. The raised tent flap at right reveals a camp stool and a trunk. (LCMM.)

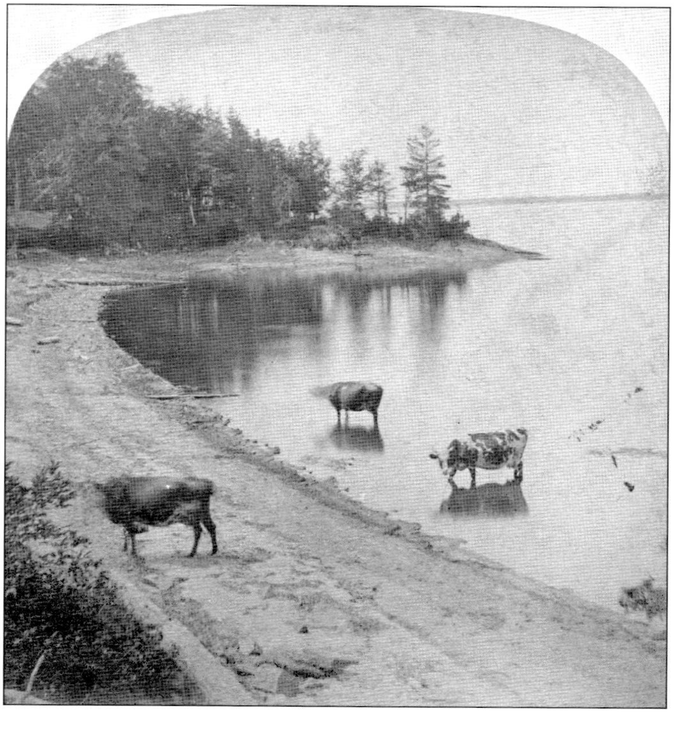

This 1889 promotional brochure for Highgate Springs extols the quality of butter and cheese produced in Franklin County. The cows represent both a pastoral ideal and economic prosperity. (UVM.)

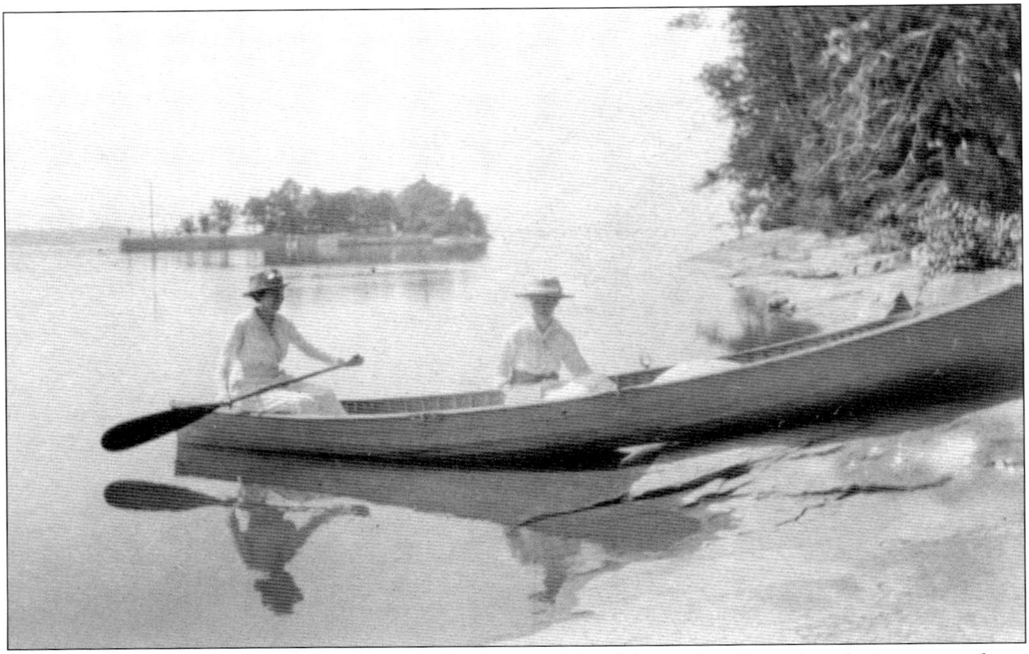

The Avery and Welcher family summered on Button Island (above) in Ferrisburgh, Vermont, from the late 1880s to the 1970s. One acre in area, the island was only 400 feet from Button Point, an easy crossing by canoe or rowboat (below) that was frequently made by the women in the family. Amy Welcher's cabin on Button Point is preserved as the Naturalist's Cabin at Button Bay State Park. (Both, LCMM.)

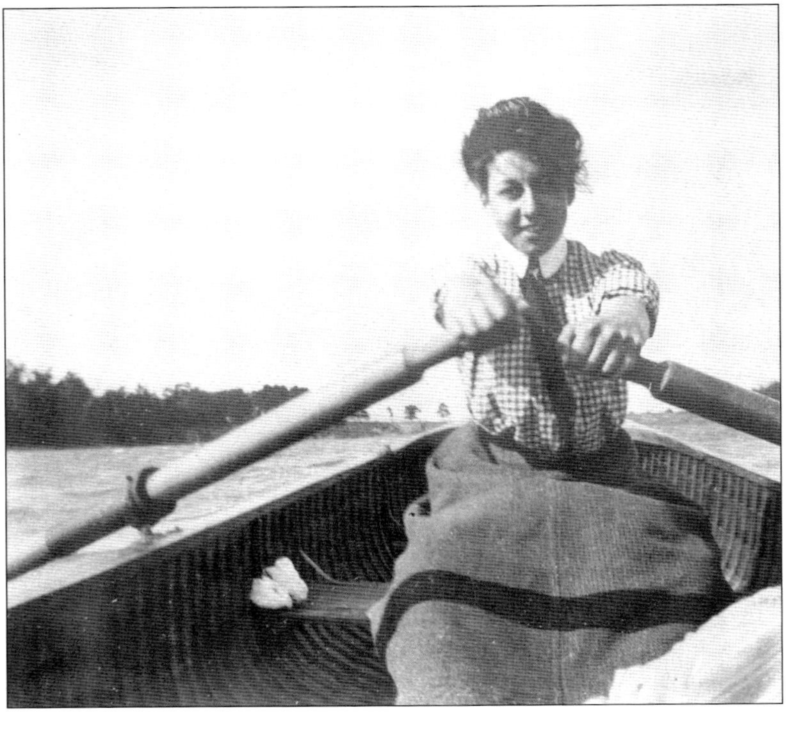

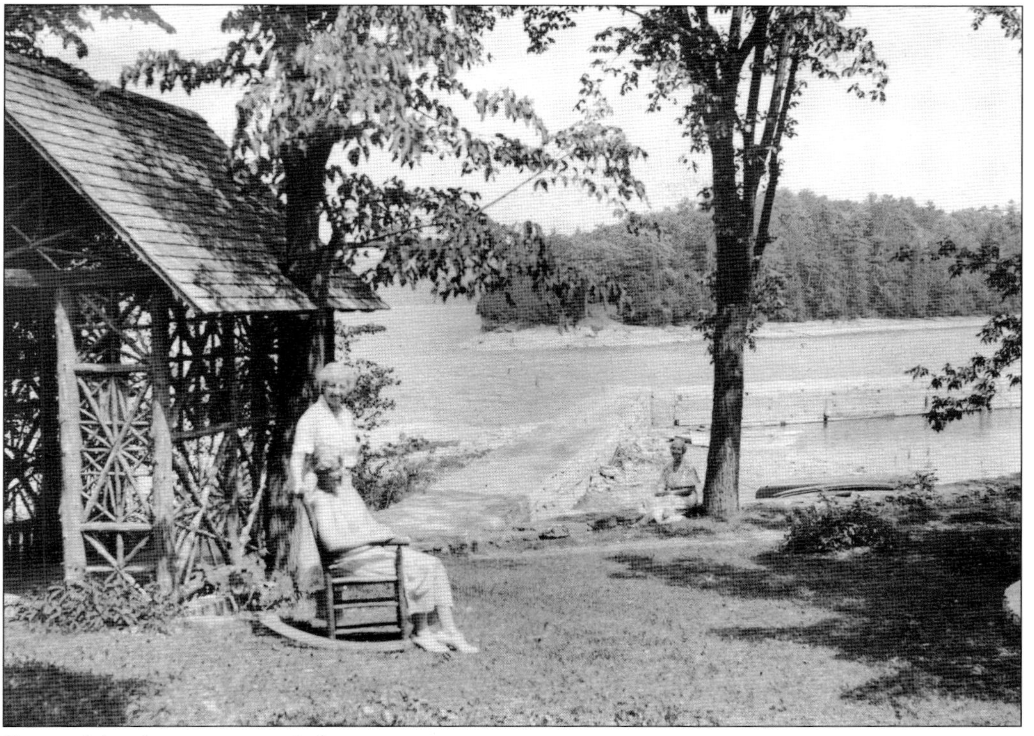

Button Island was unoccupied when it was acquired by Samuel P. Avery, who immediately constructed a summer home and several outbuildings. Over the years, the family continued to develop the property. They constructed a decorative Adirondack-style rustic shelter (above) that overlooked the lake at the head of the path to the dock, and they also raised a windmill (right). (Both, LCMM.)

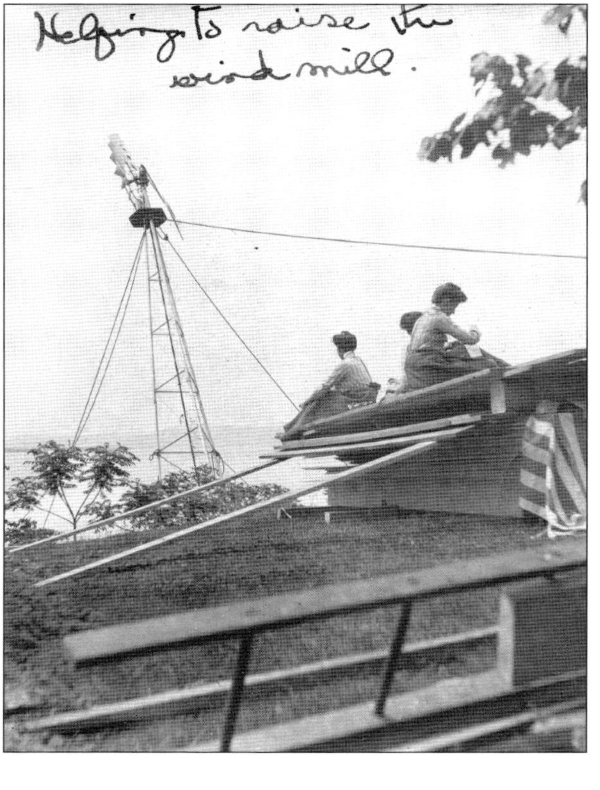

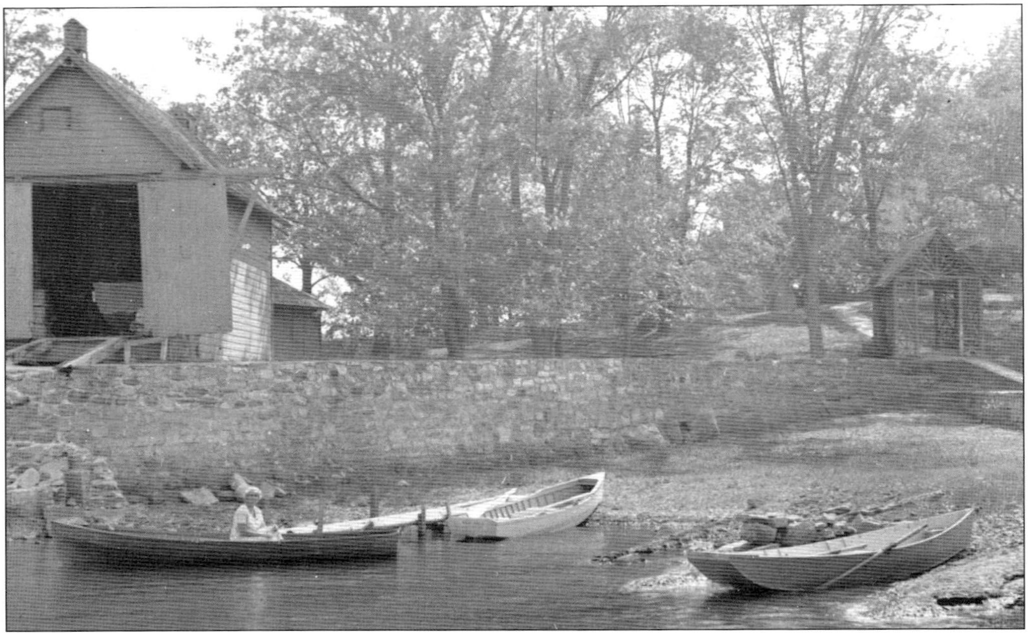

Button Island featured a breakwater and a dock 216 feet long, providing a protected harbor that Amy Welcher (seated in the pulling boat at left) jokingly referred to as "the Navy Yard." This view of the harbor in front of the boathouse also includes two flat-bottomed skiffs. The family also owned a naphtha launch, used for the four-mile trip to Westport, New York, and a variety of canoes and small boats for pleasure and work. (LCMM.)

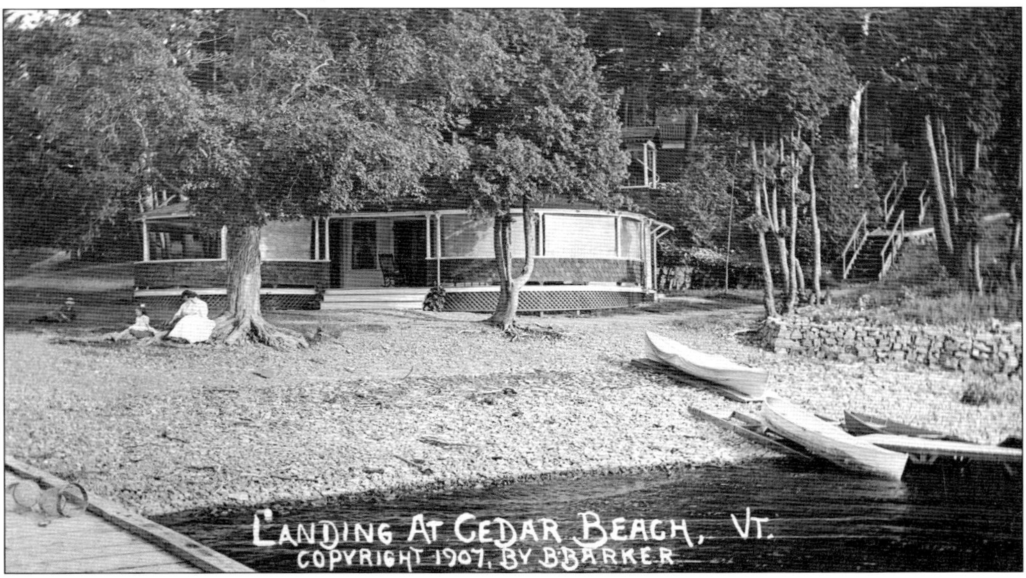

Cedar Beach overlooks Lake Champlain at Charlotte, Vermont. In 1883, a group of property owners from Burlington with summer residences along the beach established a private association to develop amenities at Cedar Beach, including a clubhouse, a post office, and ferry service to Burlington. Although the post office and ferry service are gone, descendants of the original "Jolly Club" families still cherish the community's buildings and traditions. (LCMM.)

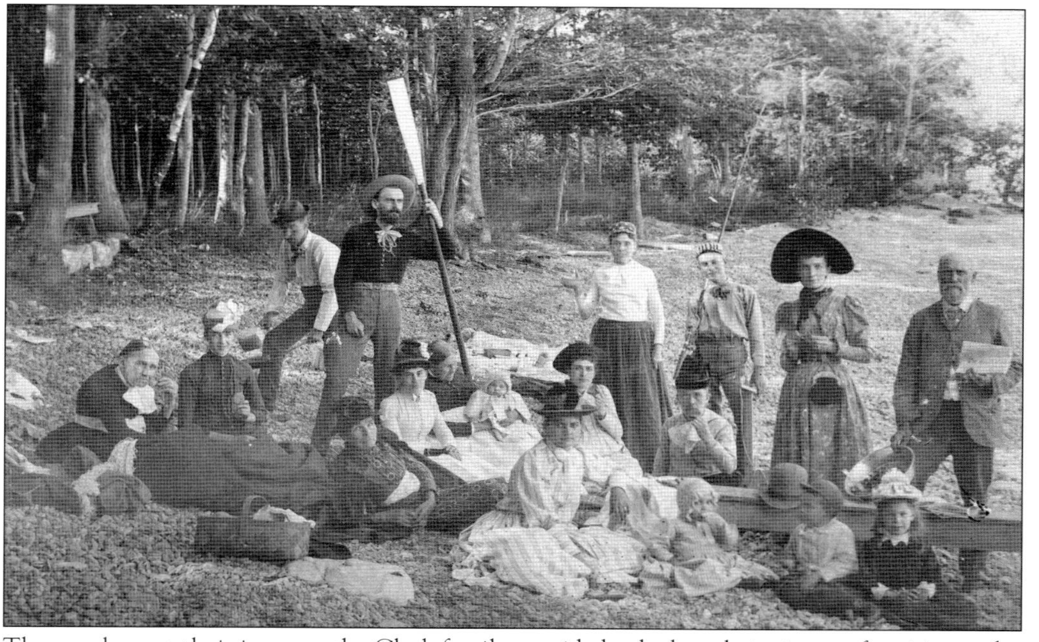

The supplement their income, the Clark family provided a dock and picnic area for visitors who stopped there while touring the lake by steamboat. Solomon and Rhoda Clark and their family wait for the steamboat *Chateaugay* to take them on an outing around 1885. (HHRF.)

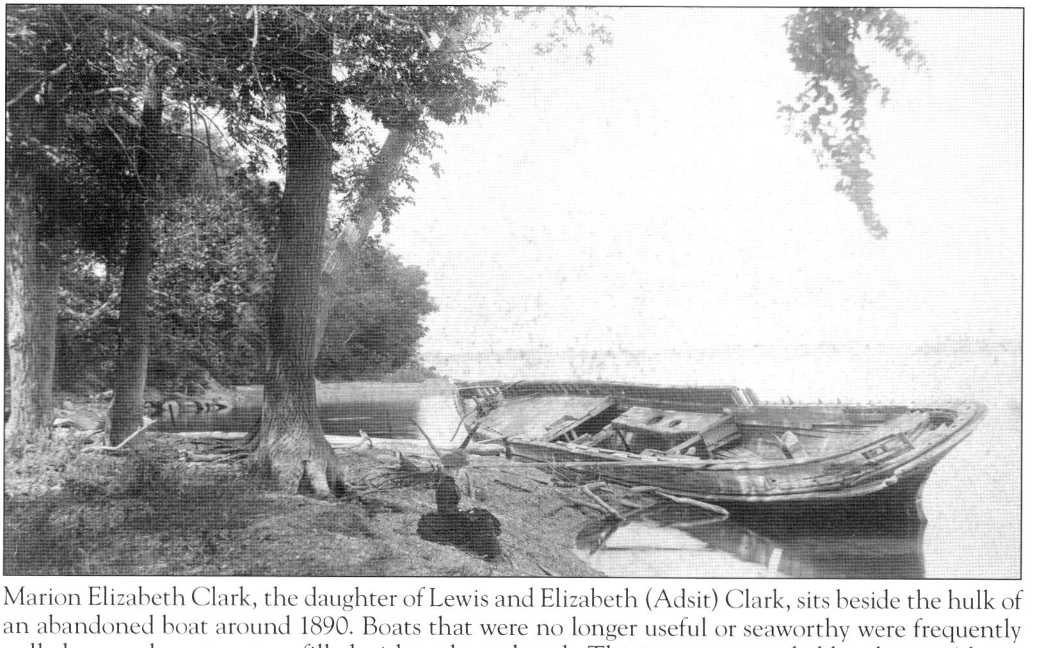

Marion Elizabeth Clark, the daughter of Lewis and Elizabeth (Adsit) Clark, sits beside the hulk of an abandoned boat around 1890. Boats that were no longer useful or seaworthy were frequently pulled up on shore to rot, or filled with rocks and sunk. This image was probably taken at Alvaro Adsit's camp on one of the Hero Islands in Vermont. (HHRF.)

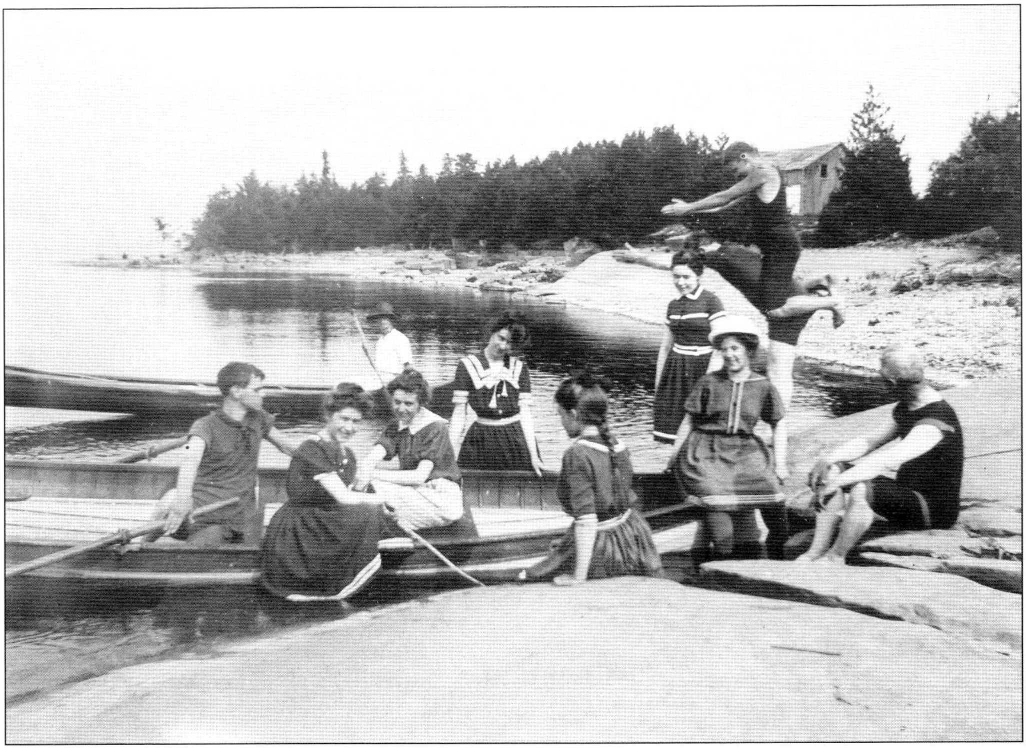

After the death of Solomon Clark in 1895, his descendants used Ligonier Point (Willsboro, New York) primarily as a summer vacation place. Above, Dorothy (Wood) Milligan entertains a group of friends on the shore around 1925. Lewis Clark's former shipyard boathouse can be seen in the background. Gathering wood for a bonfire on Ligonier Beach was also part of the day's amusement, as seen below. (Both, HHRF.)

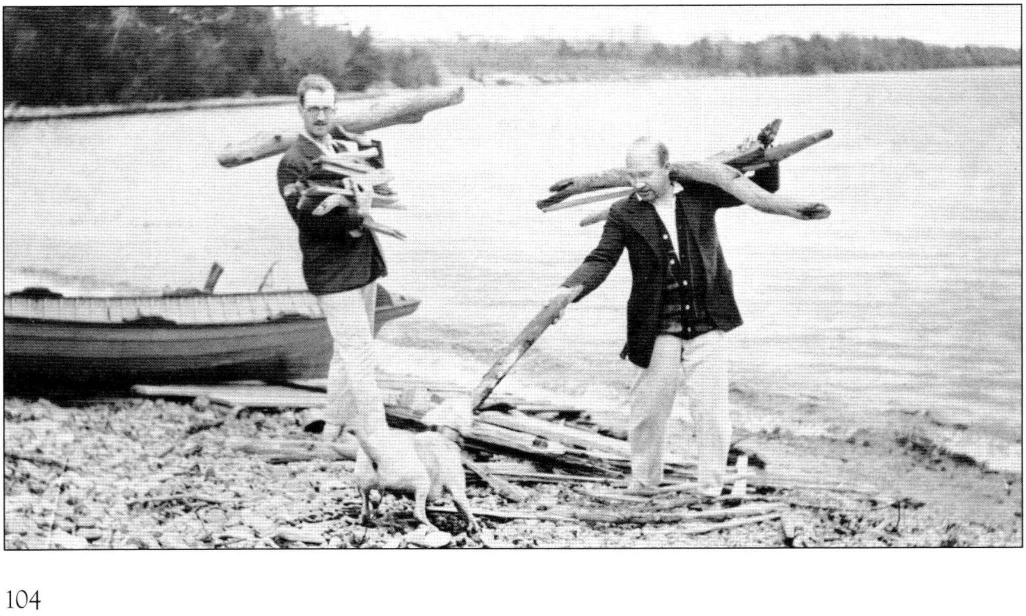

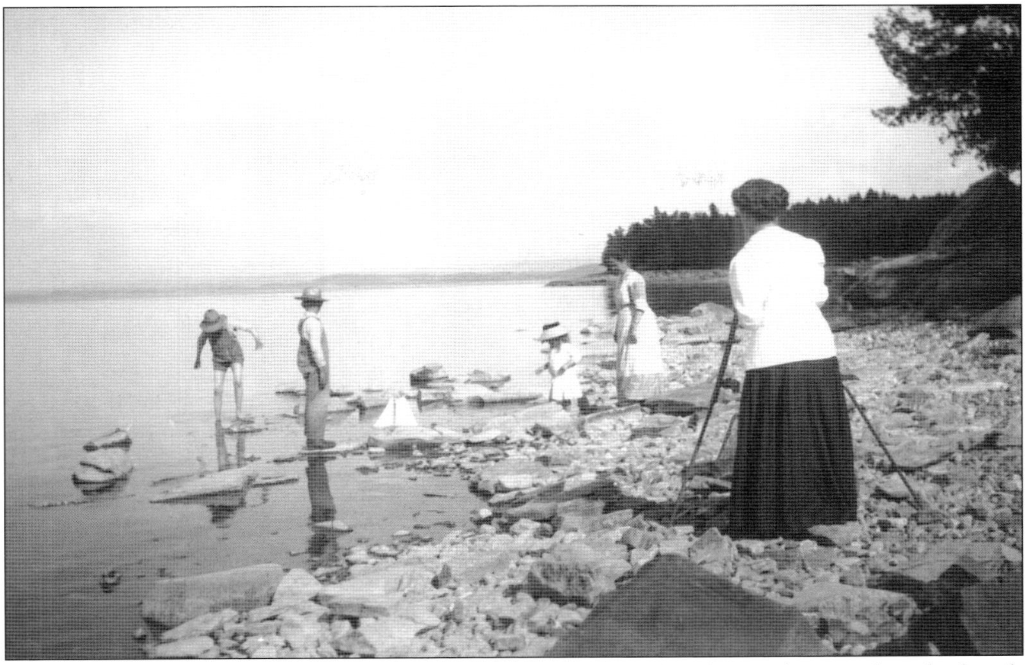

Above, around 1915, Florence Wood brings her children Carl and Dorothy Wood to the beach with their cousin Roger Clark, son of Ward Clark and grandson of Lewis Clark. Below, in the 1920s, Dorothy Wood and her friends enjoy some fashionable, modern, inflatable life jackets made of lightweight cotton canvas. The life jackets provided on board steamboats of the time were heavy affairs constructed with blocks of cork sewn into heavy sailcloth and secured with webbing straps. (Both, HHRF.)

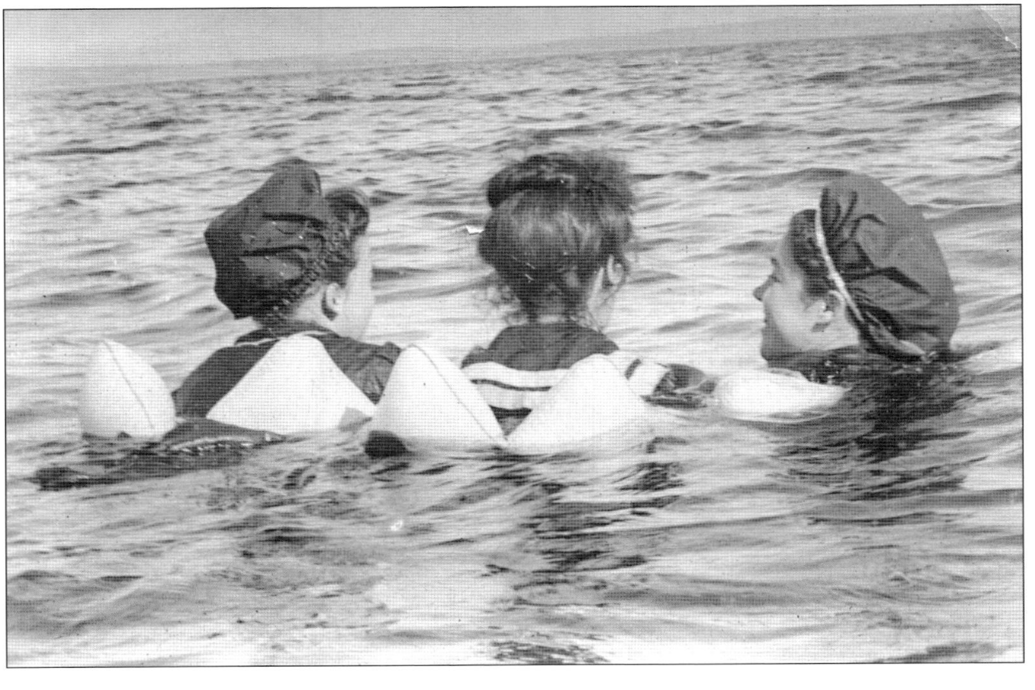

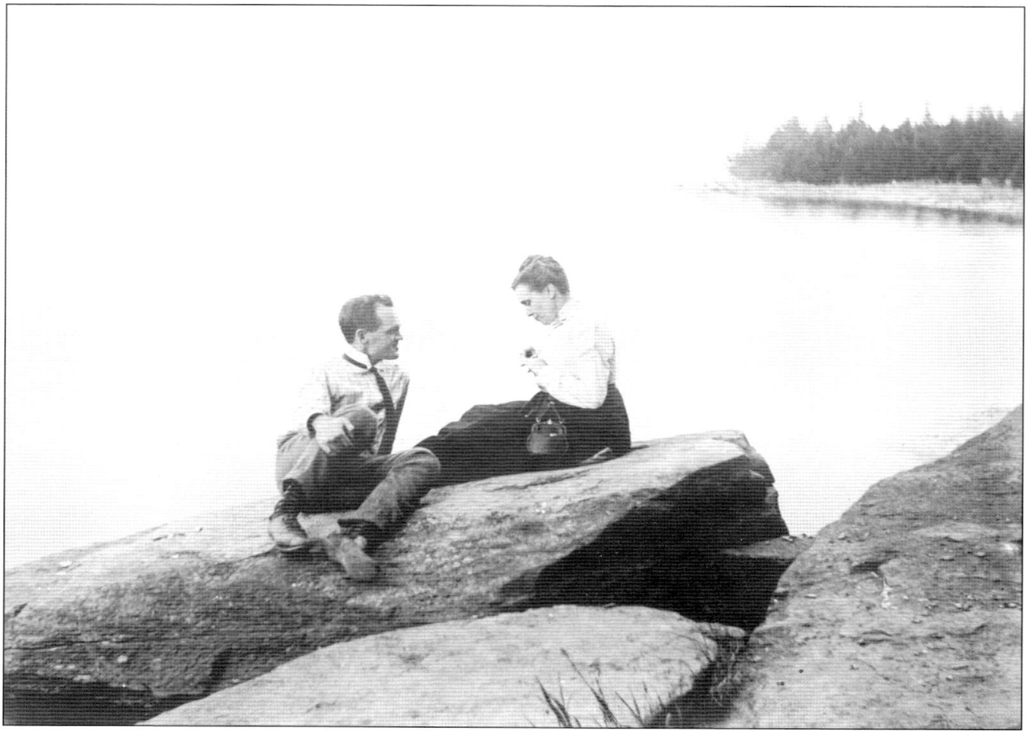

Olive G. Clark, daughter of Solomon and Rhoda Clark, and her future husband, Walter Overton, are seated on blue limestone discarded from the Clarks' quarry in the c. 1910 image above. The quarry supplied stone for the Brooklyn Bridge, Keeseville's Arch Bridge, and Lake Champlain lighthouses at Cumberland Head, Valcour, and Barber's Point. When hydraulic concrete was developed in the 1890s, most of the business for the Lake Champlain Bluestone Company disappeared. Below, a hired girl washes up the dishes after tea at Launching Rock, the former site of Lewis Clark's shipyard, around 1900. (Both, HHRF.)

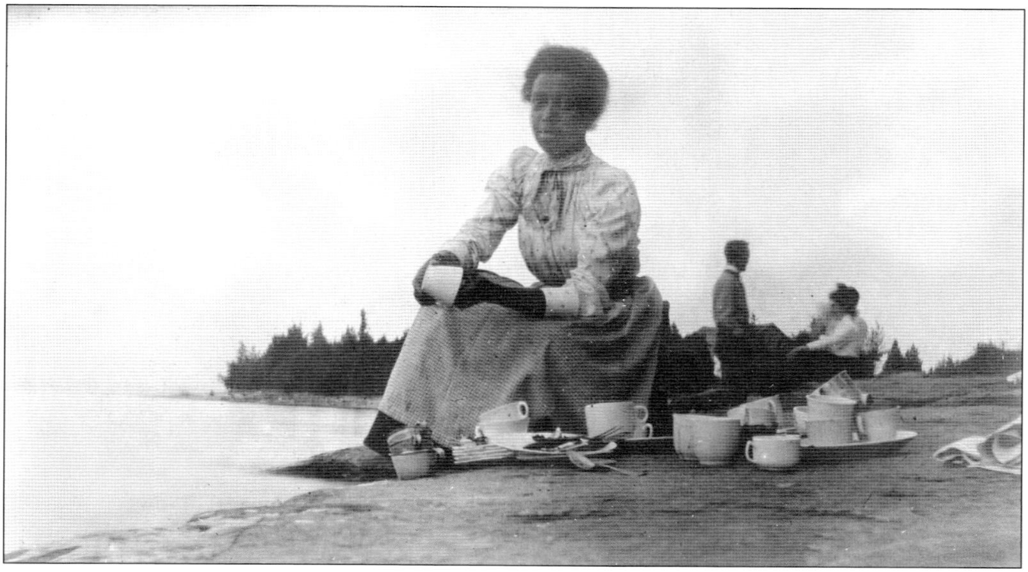

Seven

Patriotic Sites and Celebrations

The pages of history are filled with tales of Lake Champlain, from the 1609 visit by explorer Samuel de Champlain, to 17th- and 18th-century conflicts between Europeans and their native allies, to the American Revolution and the War of 1812. Romantic ruins and the remains of shipwrecks at Fort Ticonderoga and Crown Point, New York, mark sites where the naval achievements of Benedict Arnold and Thomas Macdonough took place. Throughout the 19th century, the Champlain Valley communities recalled their special association with historical events, and, as the century progressed, this historical legacy became a focus for both residents and travelers.

By the time the region was approaching the 300th anniversary of Champlain's world-changing visit, society was ready to stop, reflect, and recognize the Champlain Valley's special historical legacy through a tercentenary celebration. In one of the great coincidences of history, the 300th anniversary of Champlain's brief visit here coincided with the 1609 explorations of Henry Hudson to the river that bears his name. The two explorers were totally unknown to each another. Hudson was sailing under the authority of the Dutch, and their claim to that territory flowed from his ascent up the Hudson River. Interestingly, when New York was planning for the Hudson River tercentenary event, they added the centenary of Fulton's first steamboat, the *Clermont*. So it was that the two tercentenary celebrations took place the same year, with the Hudson being an all–New York State event and the Champlain celebration involving both New York and Vermont.

The tercentenary celebration recognized and celebrated the voyage of Samuel de Champlain as the first white man to venture onto the lake. Major events in lakeside communities, including Crown Point, Ticonderoga, Plattsburgh, Burlington, Isle La Motte, and Vergennes, highlighted that event's impact on the New World. By the 400th anniversary of Champlain's visit, in 2009, Abenaki and Mohawk people were participants and presenters in many commemorative programs and events, providing a deeper perspective on the cultural heritage of the region.

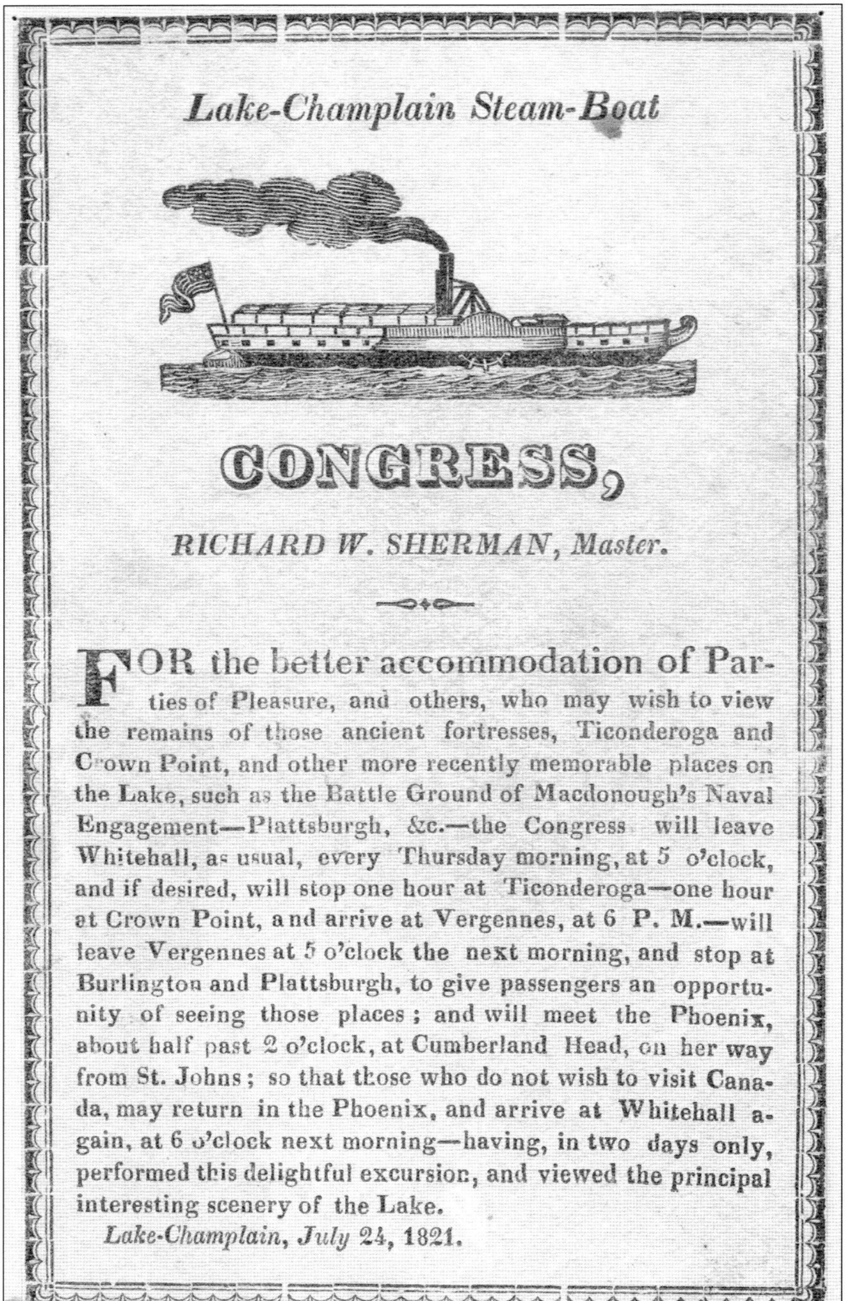

Lake-Champlain Steam-Boat

CONGRESS,

RICHARD W. SHERMAN, Master.

FOR the better accommodation of Parties of Pleasure, and others, who may wish to view the remains of those ancient fortresses, Ticonderoga and Crown Point, and other more recently memorable places on the Lake, such as the Battle Ground of Macdonough's Naval Engagement—Plattsburgh, &c.—the Congress will leave Whitehall, as usual, every Thursday morning, at 5 o'clock, and if desired, will stop one hour at Ticonderoga—one hour at Crown Point, and arrive at Vergennes, at 6 P. M.—will leave Vergennes at 5 o'clock the next morning, and stop at Burlington and Plattsburgh, to give passengers an opportunity of seeing those places; and will meet the Phoenix, about half past 2 o'clock, at Cumberland Head, on her way from St. Johns; so that those who do not wish to visit Canada, may return in the Phoenix, and arrive at Whitehall again, at 6 o'clock next morning—having, in two days only, performed this delightful excursion, and viewed the principal interesting scenery of the Lake.

Lake-Champlain, July 24, 1821.

The *Congress* (1818) was one of four steamboats built at Vergennes by the Lake Champlain Steamboat Company. This advertisement promotes recreational travel, introducing "Parties of Pleasure" to historic Ticonderoga, Crown Point, and "the Battle Ground of Macdonough's Naval Engagement." The schedule was coordinated with the steamboat *Phoenix II* (1820) to make it possible "in two days only, [to] perform this delightful excursion, and view the principal interesting scenery of the Lake." (UVM.)

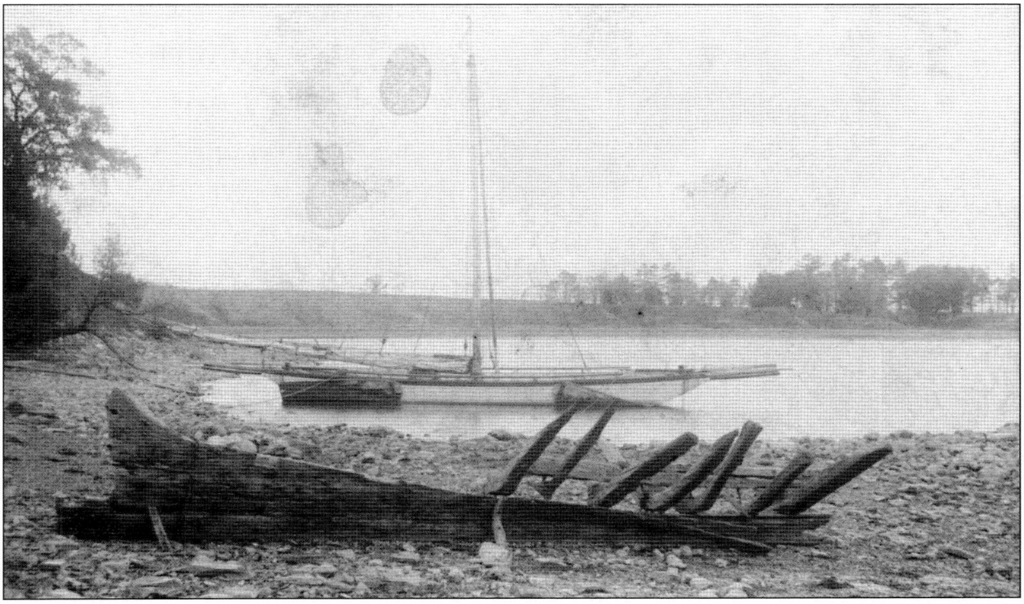

In October 1776, Revolutionary War brigadier general Benedict Arnold retreated from the Battle of Valcour Island and ran his fleet ashore in Ferris' Bay, now Arnold's Bay, in Panton, Vermont. Seen here, the lower stern portion of the row galley *Congress* was dragged out in 1891. Also pictured is Adam's Ferry, first operated by Peter Ferris in 1799 and offering service to Westport, New York. (LCMM.)

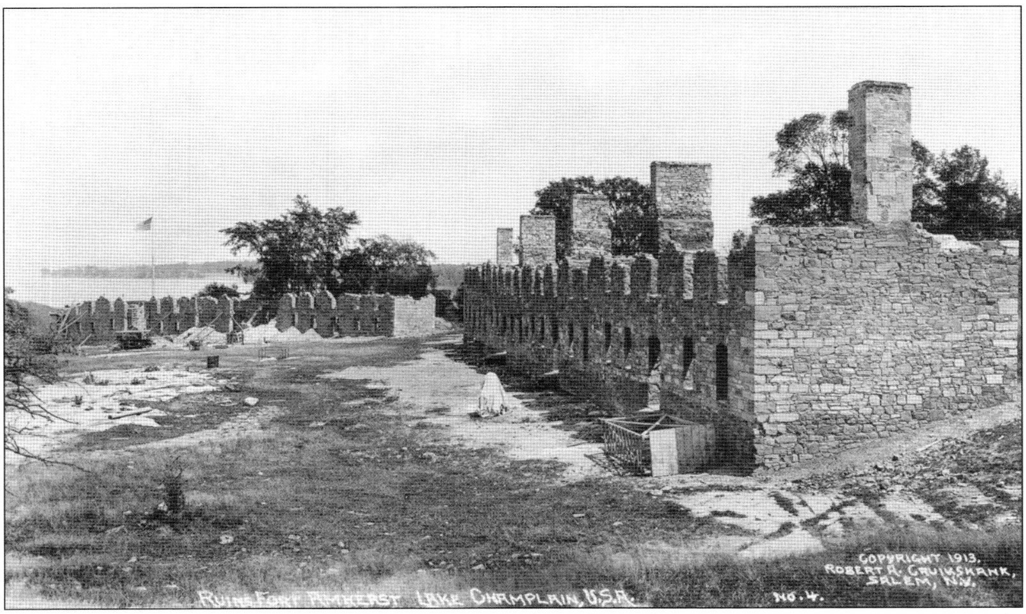

Strategically located at a narrow section of Lake Champlain, the ruins at Crown Point, New York, held the 1734–1759 French-built Fort St. Frédéric and the 1759 British-built Fort Crown Point, or Fort Amherst, which was later captured by an American militia during the Revolutionary War. This site was established in 1910 as a New York State Historic Site. It is seen here in 1913 and remains open to the public today. (LCMM.)

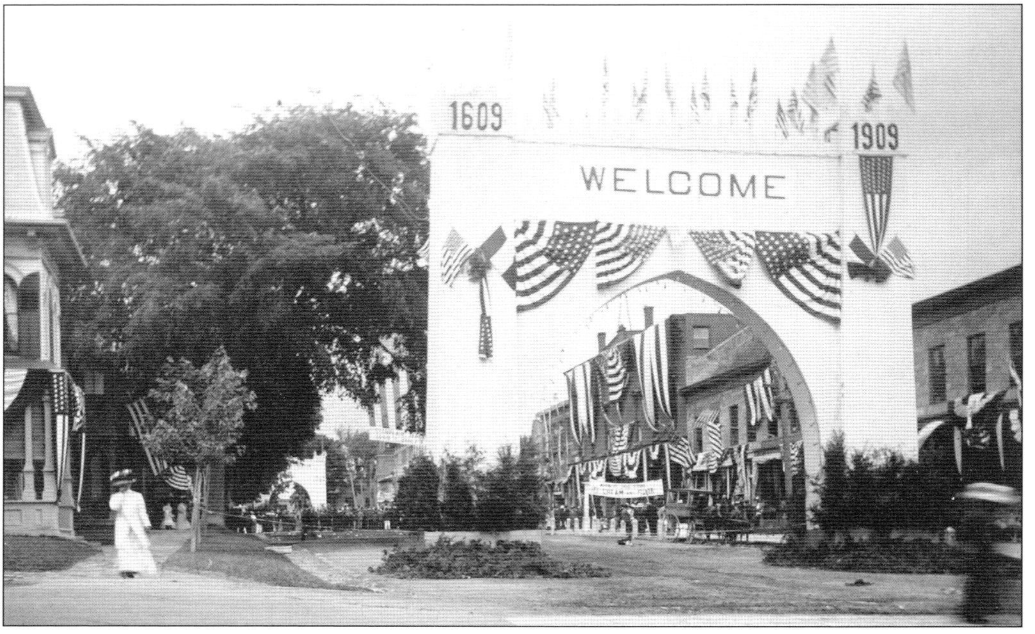

To celebrate the tercentennial of Samuel de Champlain's 1609 visit to the lake, state commissions from New York and Vermont planned an elaborate series of programs around the Champlain Valley. Vergennes, Vermont, hosted a "day of exercises" at Fort Cassin, at the mouth of Otter Creek in Ferrisburgh, and a parade through town (seen here). (UVM.)

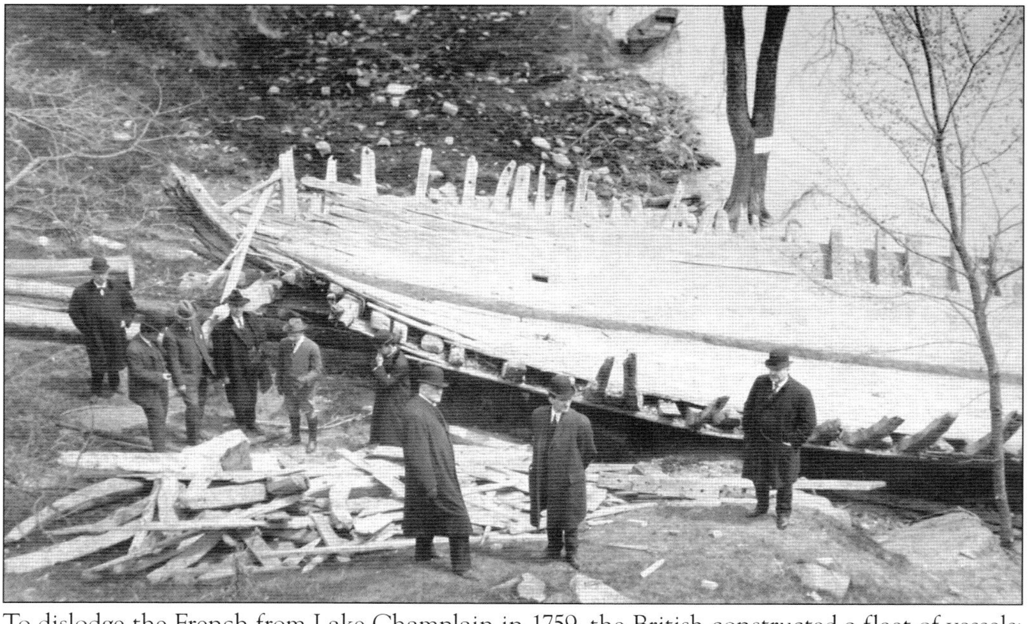

To dislodge the French from Lake Champlain in 1759, the British constructed a fleet of vessels; after the conflict, some of them sank at their moorings near Fort Ticonderoga, New York. One of these, the brig *Duke of Cumberland* was discovered and raised to share with the public in 1909. She was originally thought to be the *Revenge*. Unfortunately, conservation techniques at the time were primitive, and efforts to preserve her failed. (LCMM.)

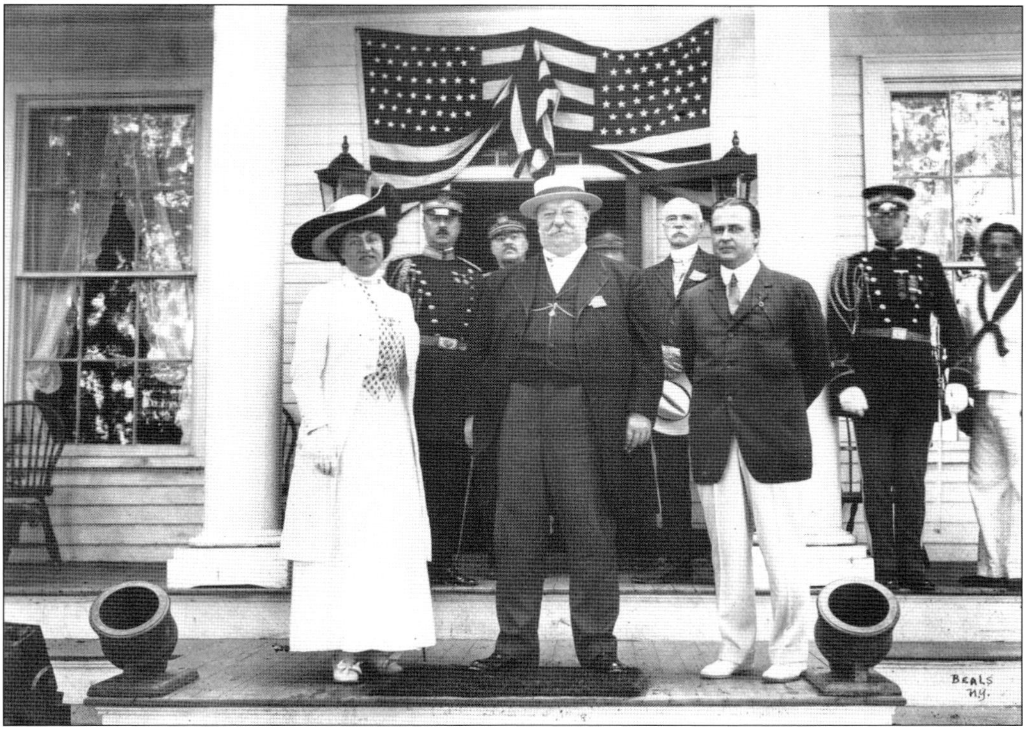

Above, Mr. and Mrs. Stephen H. Pell receive Pres. William Howard Taft and other dignitaries at Fort Ticonderoga, New York. Burlington, Vermont, was one of the five communities selected as a key venue for a bistate program. On July 8, 1909, the presidential party and foreign guests arrived, and a crowd of thousands filled College Street (below). The presidential party and guests were entertained with a historical pageant, *Hiawatha*, and fireworks. (Above, LCMM; below, UVM.)

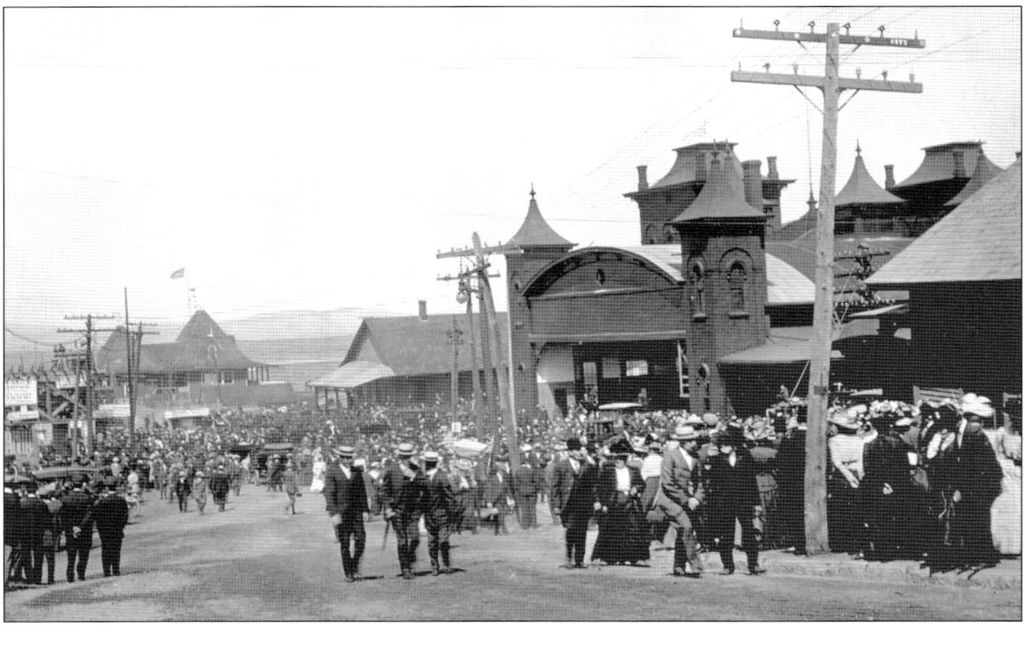

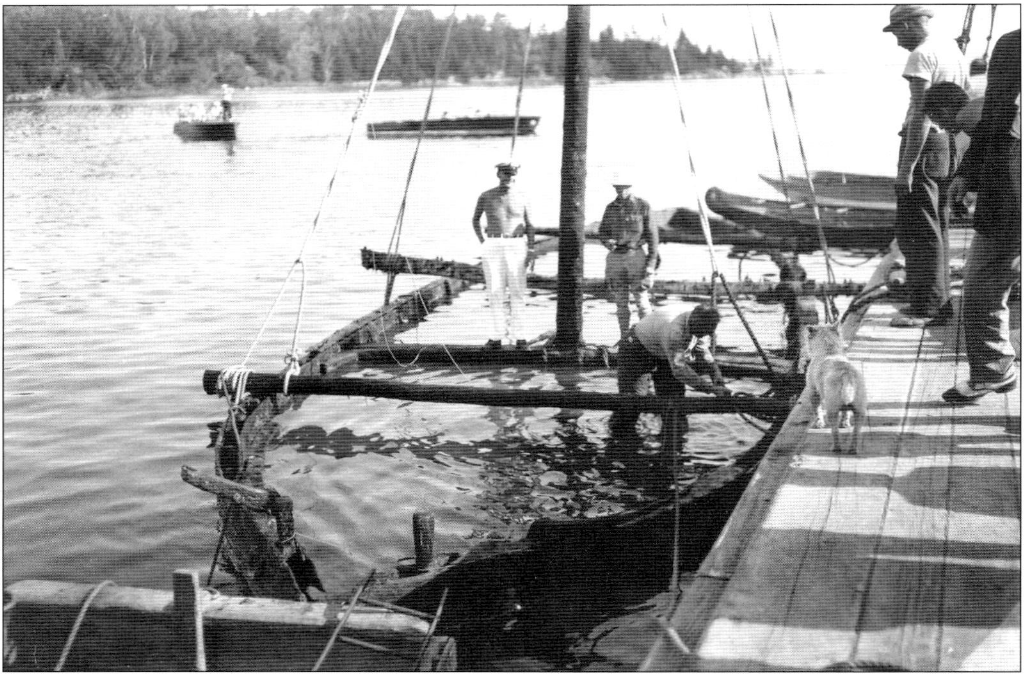

The gunboat *Philadelphia* was one of Benedict Arnold's warships. She was built in the summer of 1776 and fought the British at the Battle of Valcour Island on October 11, 1776. In a letter written the next day during the American retreat, Arnold reported to his commander, General Gates, "The *Philadelphia* was hulled in so many Places that she Sank About One Hour after the engagement was over." In 1935, salvage engineer and history buff Col. Lorenzo Hagglund located *Philadelphia* sitting upright on the lake bottom at Valcour and recovered her (above). Below, the *Philadelphia*'s salvage team in 1935 included, from left to right, J. Rupert Schalk, William Lilja, and Colonel Hagglund. (Above, LCMM; below, SI.)

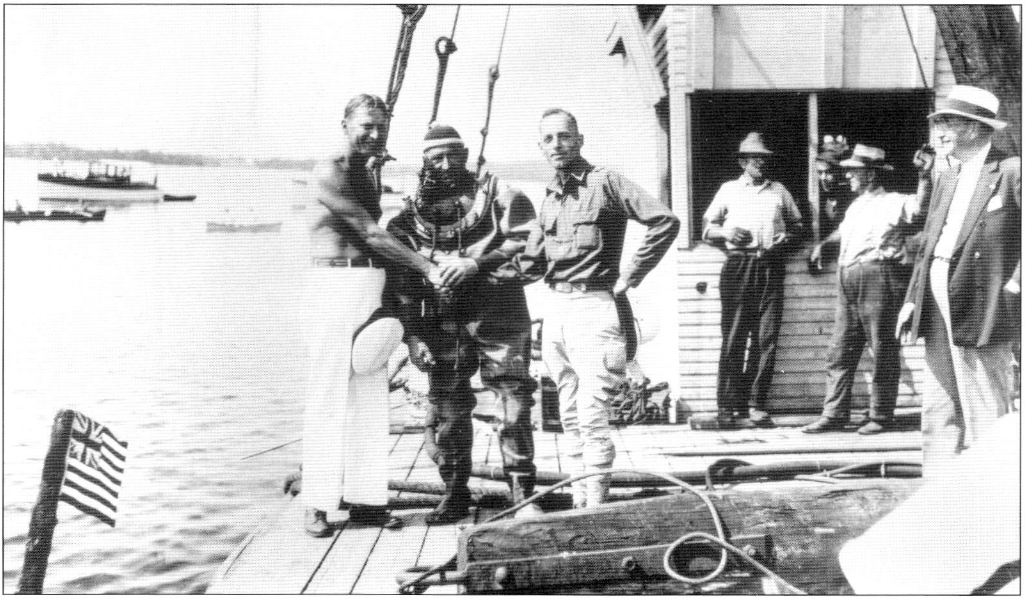

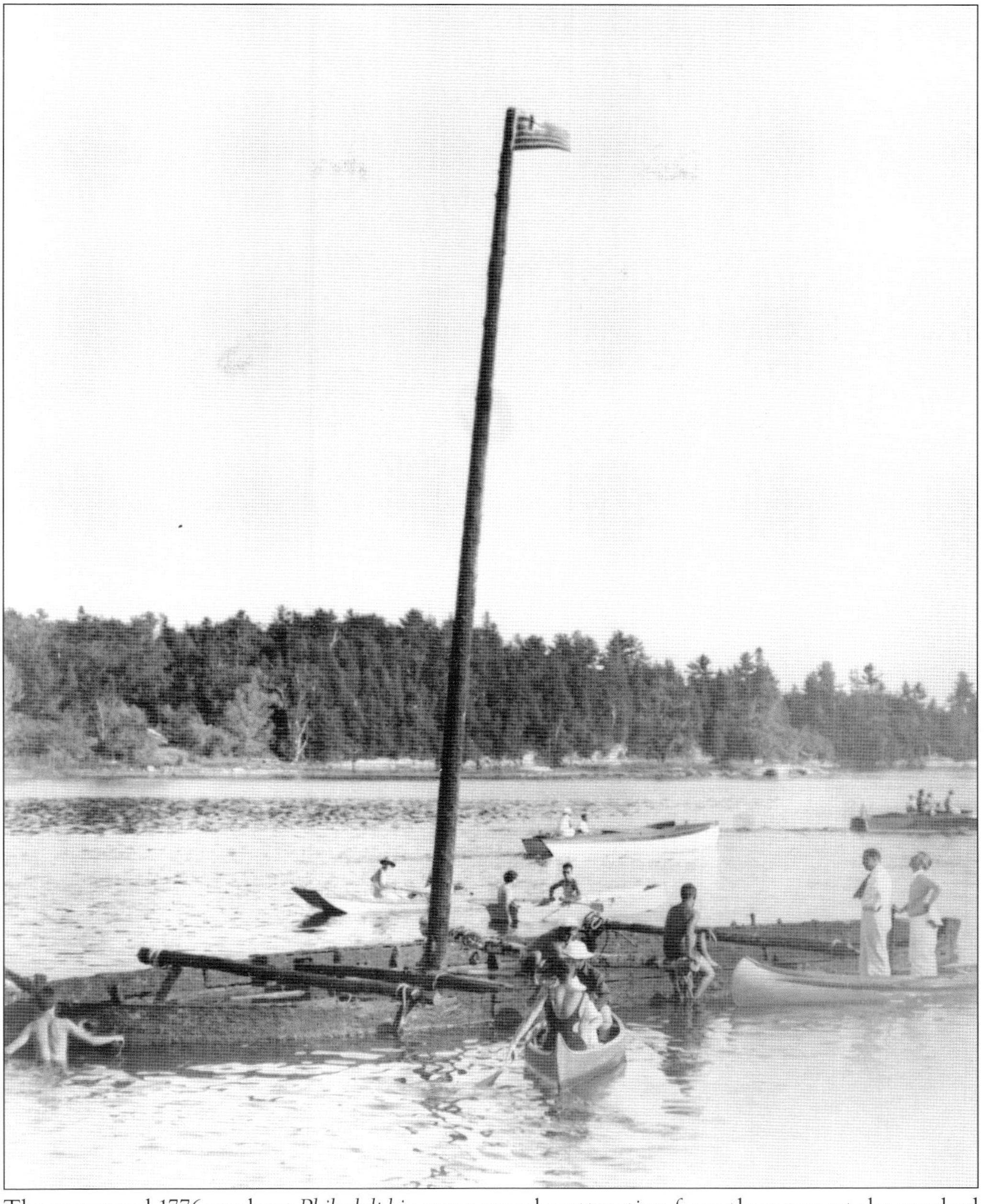

The recovered 1776 gunboat *Philadelphia* was a popular attraction from the moment she reached the water's surface. Hagglund was devoted to the history and the shipwreck, but, typical to these early recoveries, he had not made long-term provisions for her conservation and interpretation. Upon his death, *Philadelphia* was acquired by the Smithsonian Institution, where she still resides in the National Museum of American History. (LCMM.)

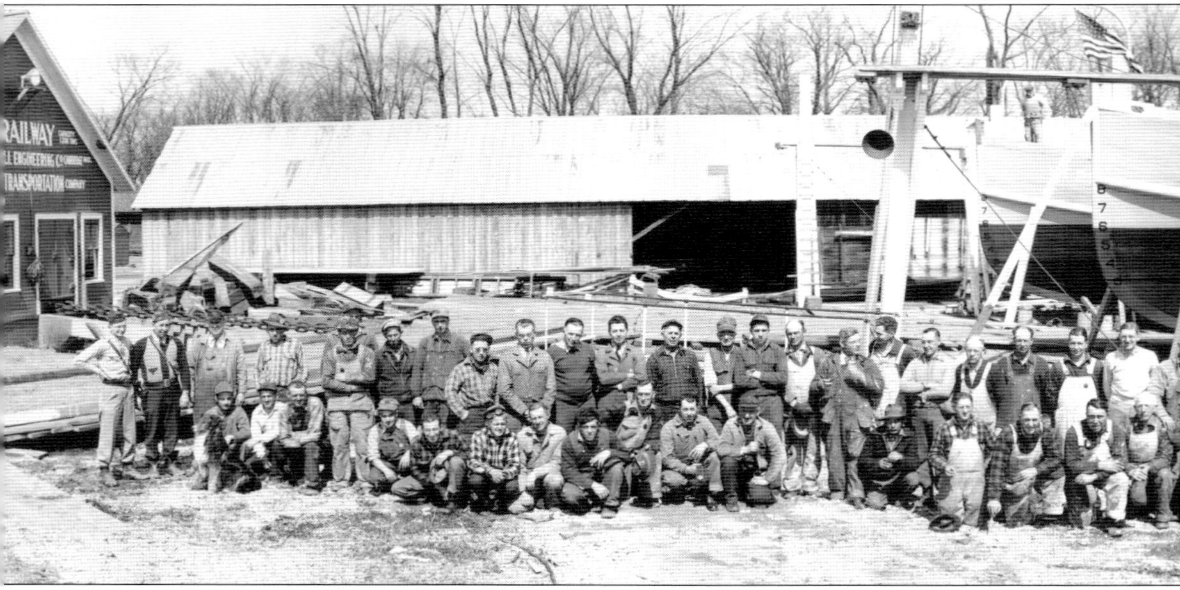

Shelburne Shipyard workers pose with yard tugs in this 1943 photograph. "The employees at the present time are all key men of the wood and steel construction industry," stated then owner Jerry Aske. "Some were born and raised at Shelburne Harbor." Some workers were involved in

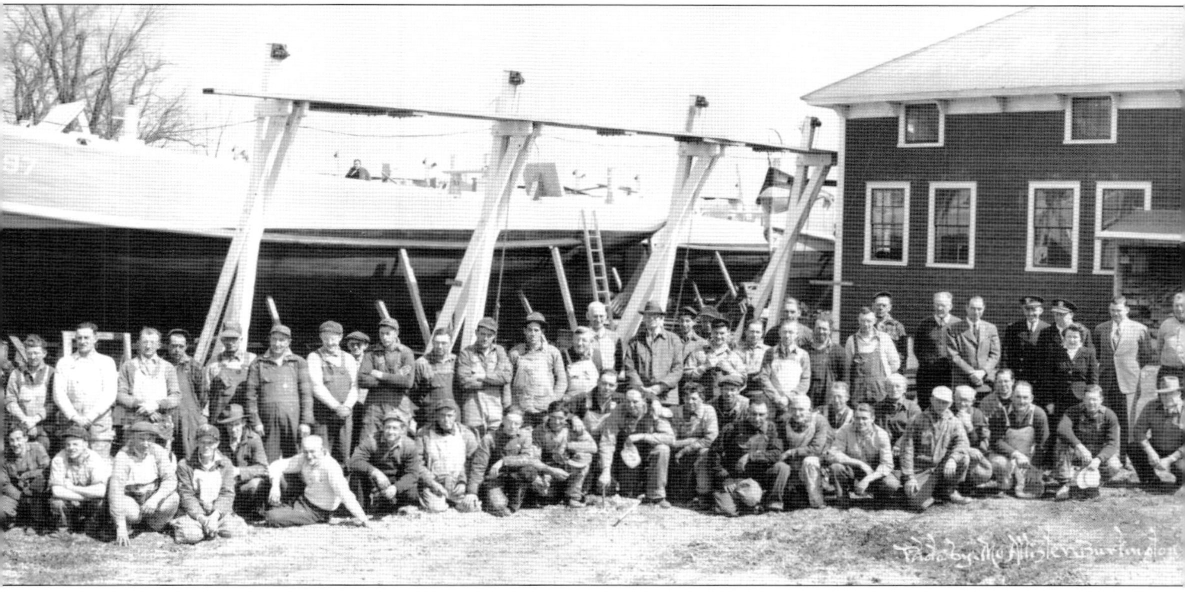

constructing ships for the Navy, while others were working to ensure that there would be ferry service at the lake's crossings. (LCMM.)

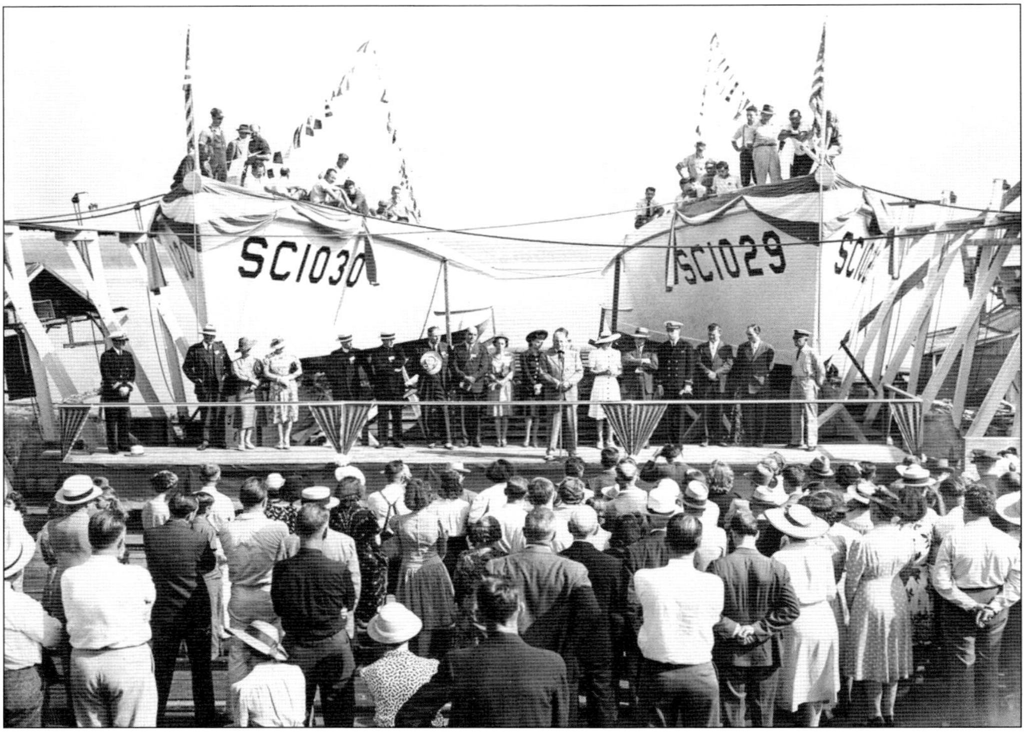

America's entry into World War II, in December 1941, rededicated the nation's patriotic energies. Shelburne Shipyard was critical to Burlington's war efforts. The Champlain Transportation Company leased the shipyard to the Donovan Construction Company of Minnesota, and they secured a contract to construct ships for the Navy. Sub Chasers SC 1029 and SC 1020 were launched on August 31, 1942 (above), followed by SC 1504 in 1944 (below). (Both, LCMM.)

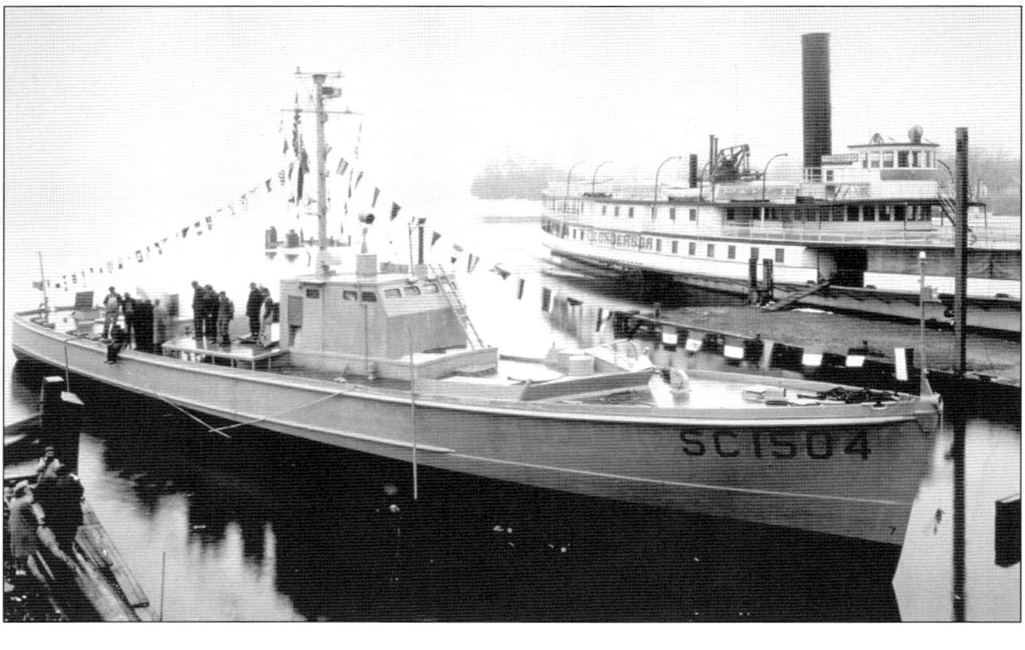

Eight

Winter

Lake Champlain's environment experiences dramatic weather changes throughout the year. The seasonal shift of the calendar is matched by seasonal changes in lifestyle on and around the lake. People have always spent much of the fair weather months acquiring provisions to last through the winter. On occasion, military activities that relied on the ice as a roadway were undertaken, although participants suffered as much from the harsh winter as from their enemies. In one historic campaign during the winter of 1776, the fledgling American Congress ordered relief forces to march over a frozen Lake Champlain to support the invasion force that had attempted to take British Canada.

The lake's merchants and mariners tried to be the first boats under way after ice-out and would extend the navigation season until the formation of ice prevented their movement. Then, they secured their vessels and moved their operations to land, working through the winter in more conventional pursuits like cutting wood. When the sun began to provide real warmth again, the land-based mariner would begin preparations for the season: boats to be repaired and painted, sails to be bent on, cabins to be cleaned, and business arrangements to be made.

People in the North Country also appreciate certain advantages that winter offers: iceboating, ice fishing, ice harvesting, iceboat racing, and snowshoeing. When the ice is thick enough, it forms a natural bridge directly across the lake, useful for calling on friends or conducting business.

Although there is now concern that ice formation has diminished under the influence of global climate change, fishing shanty camps still regularly form at traditional locations. The area under the new Champlain Bridge has become a favored spot of ice fisherman from Vermont and New York. The ice roads that used to allow vehicles to cross the lake for business and pleasure along pathways marked by evergreens have become less necessary due to bridges and year-round ferry service. The ice is less dependable than in years past. Now, every winter, the Coast Guard and town fire departments around the lake regularly respond to winter ice emergencies.

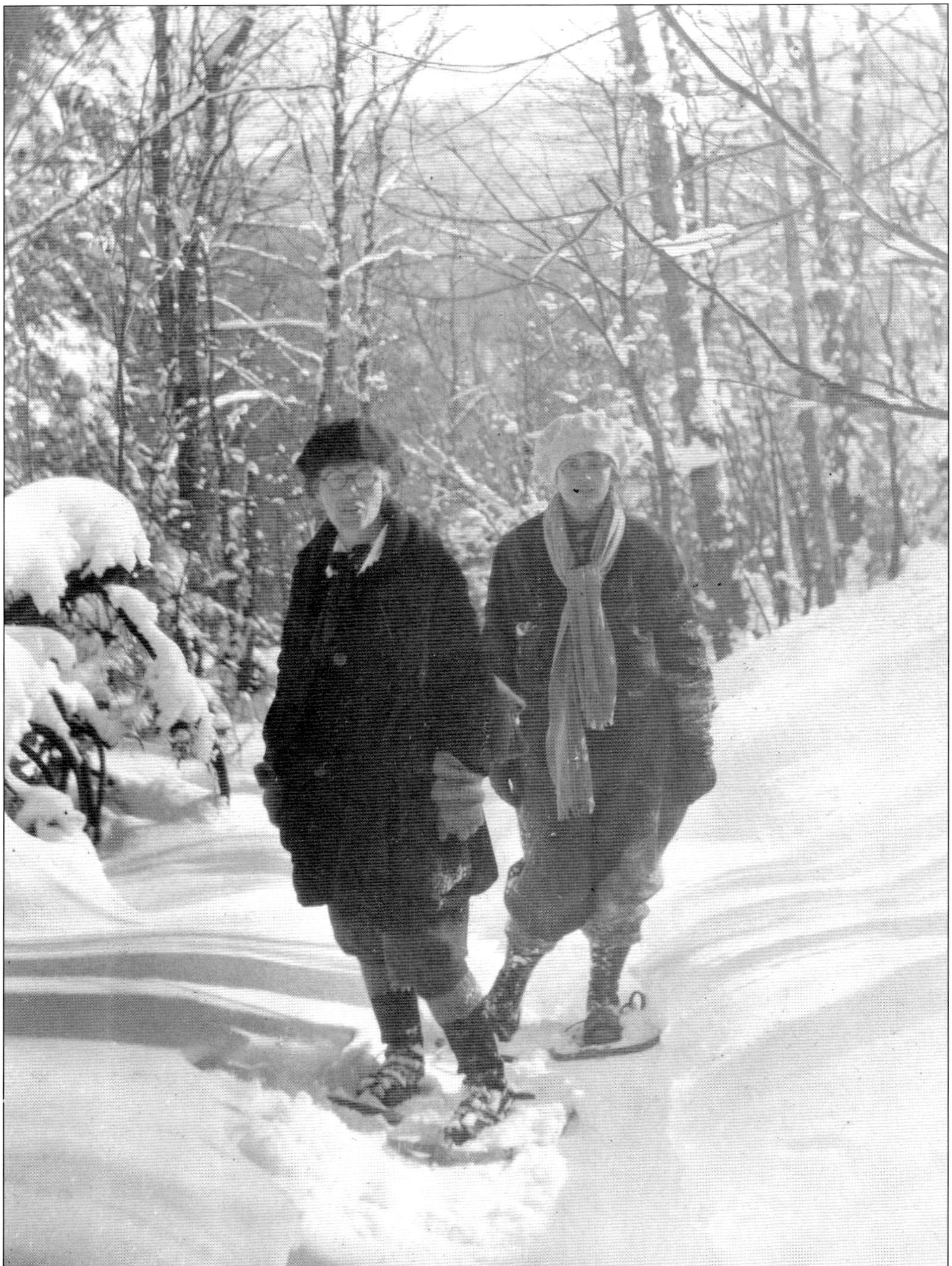

These women out for a winter walk at the Basin Harbor Club, Vermont, are wearing a heavier, wooden-board style of snowshoe, which was occasionally seen in Lake Champlain communities. (BHC.)

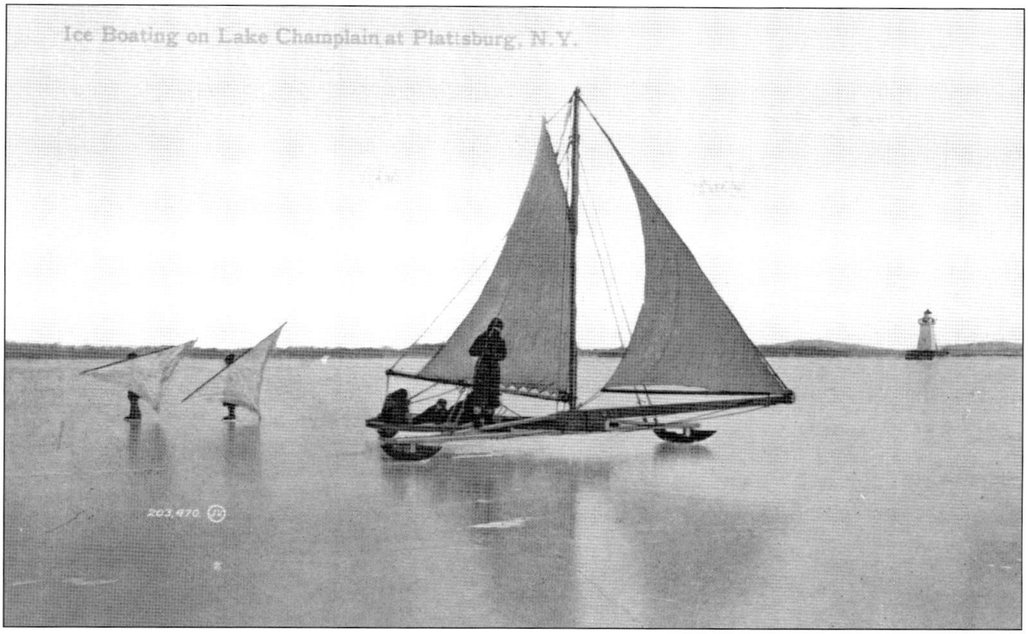

Winter's ice brought an end to traditional recreational boating and provided daring souls with opportunities for iceboating and skate sailing, as seen in these photographs at Plattsburgh, New York. Instead of a wooden hull that cuts through water, iceboats have a triangular frame that glides atop the ice with iron, skate-like runners. The lack of friction gives iceboats the ability reach speeds many times faster than traditional sailing boats. In the last half of the 19th century, iceboats set new records for speed. Iceboat regattas on Lake Champlain were very popular in the 1800s and early 1900s, even bringing participants from Canada and Europe. Iceboating is still a popular winter activity. (Both, LCMM.)

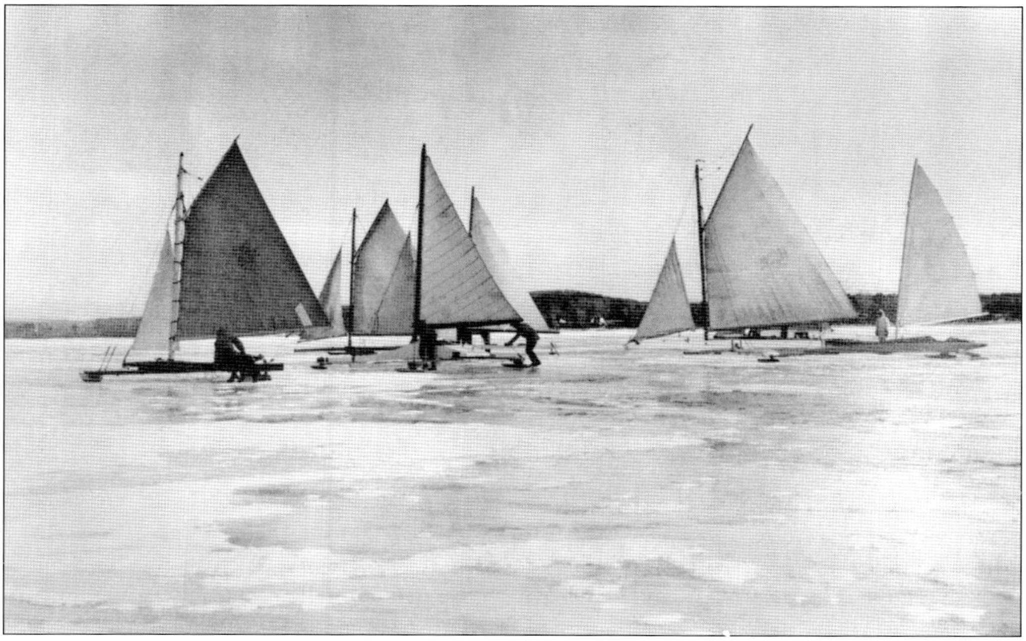

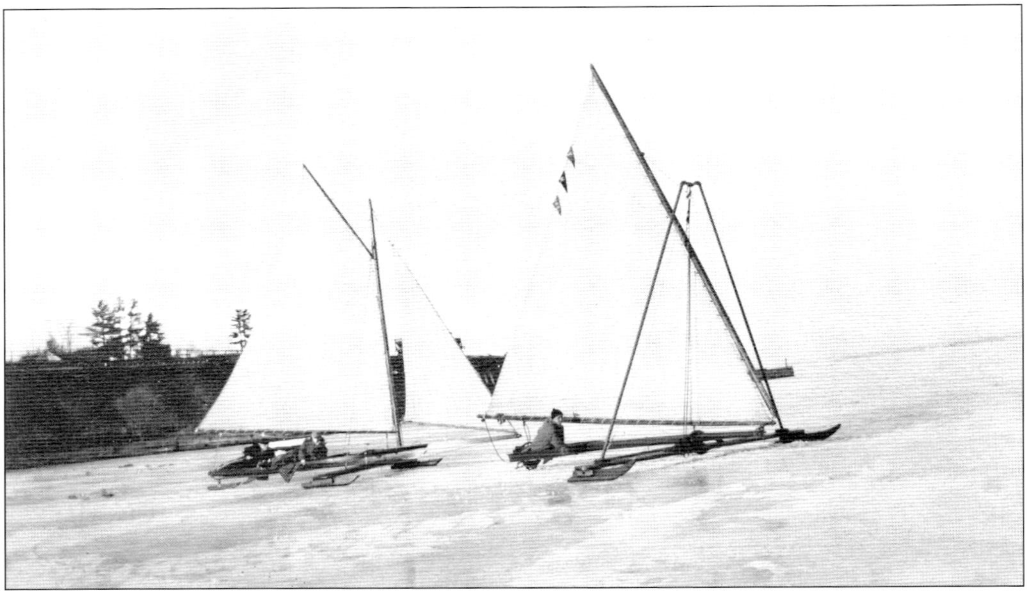

Iceboating on Lake Champlain was widespread and took many forms. Two iceboats can race each other, as seen above, testing the advantages of two riders and allowing greater traction and steering control. On the other hand, higher speeds can be reached by solo boaters like the one seen below passing Lone Rock Point. (Both, UVM.)

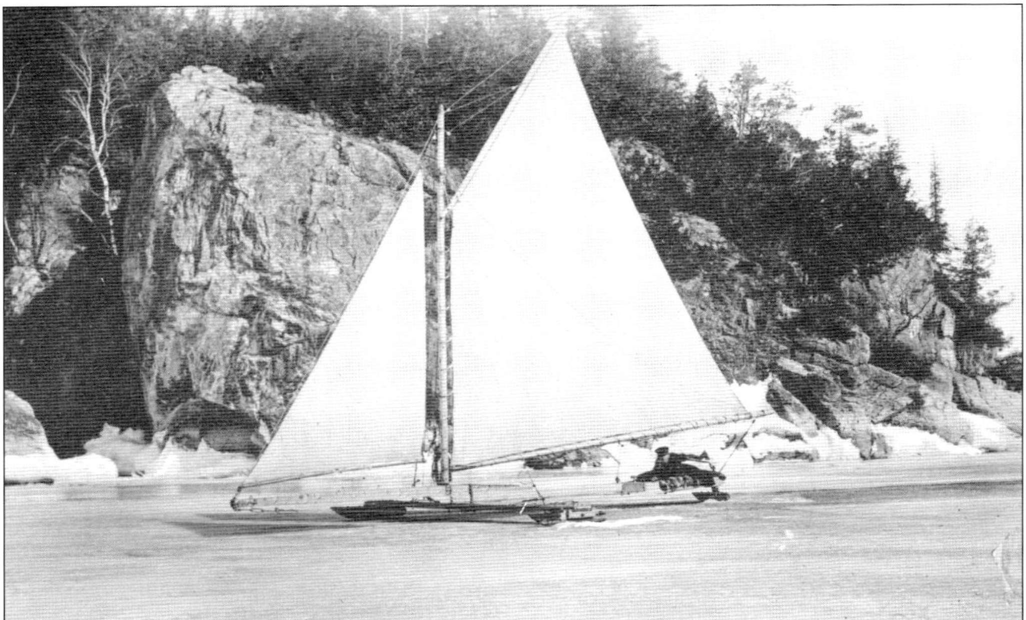

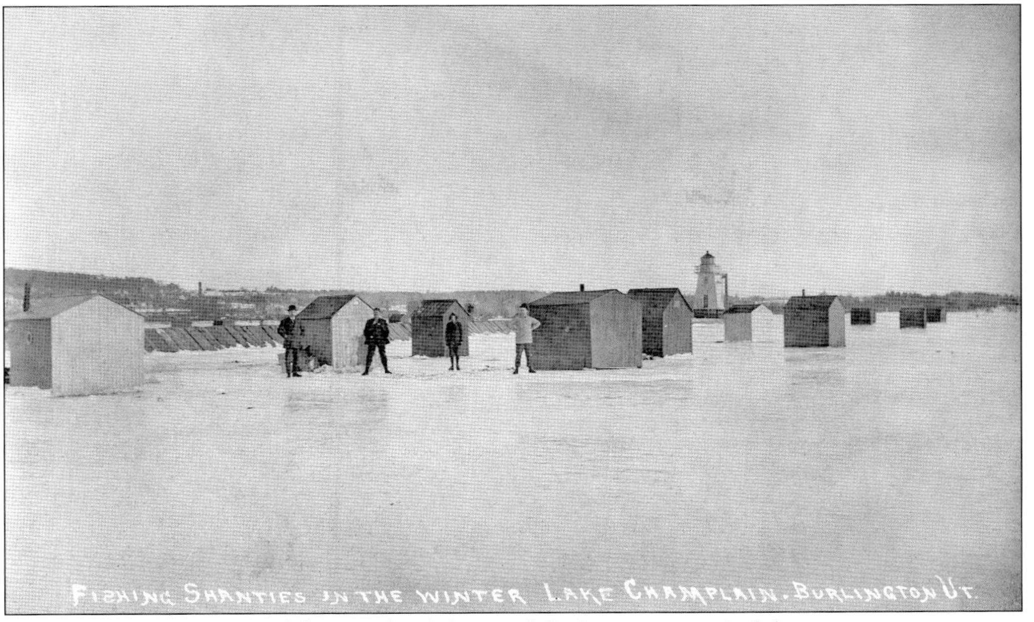

When the lake freezes, ice fishermen haul their mobile shanties onto the lake, creating a temporary village. The shanties provide a protected space where heat, food, and social interactions can take place while fishing. A network of these temporary villages often had the same group of fishermen who annually settled the same location, such as Vermont's Burlington Harbor along the breakwater. (LCMM.)

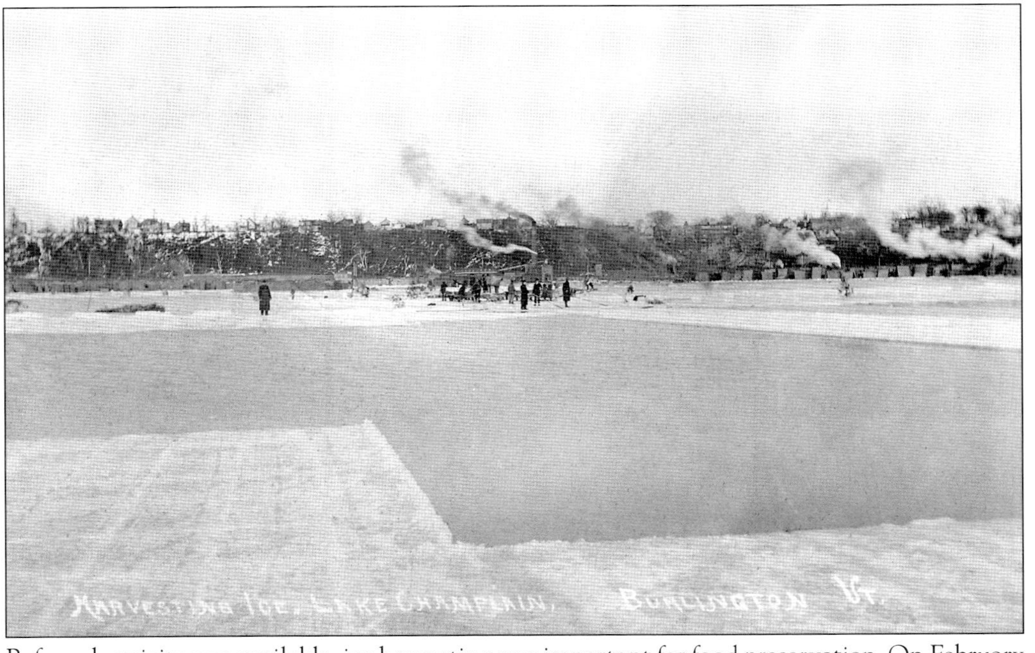

Before electricity was available, ice harvesting was important for food preservation. On February 1, 1893, the *Burlington Free Press and Times* reported that ice harvesting had begun, noting that it would take 60 men and 20 horse teams to cut the annual crop of 60,000 tons. (LCMM.)

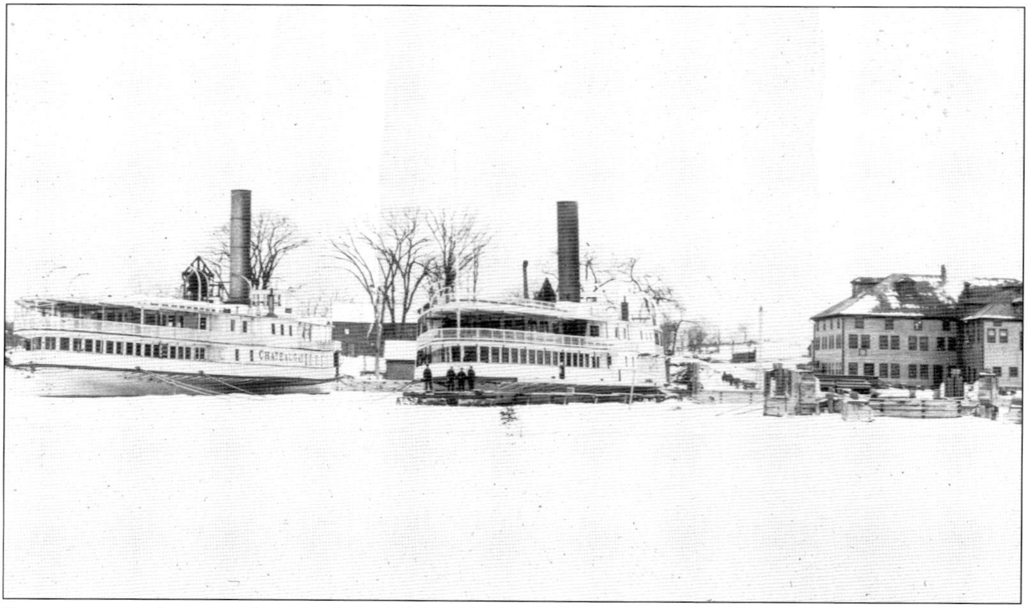

Every winter, the steamboats of the Champlain Transportation Company ended their season at Shelburne Shipyard, where a marine railway would haul them into winter berths. Burlington photographer Louis L. McAllister was renowned for his panoramic photographs, including this one. (LCMM.)

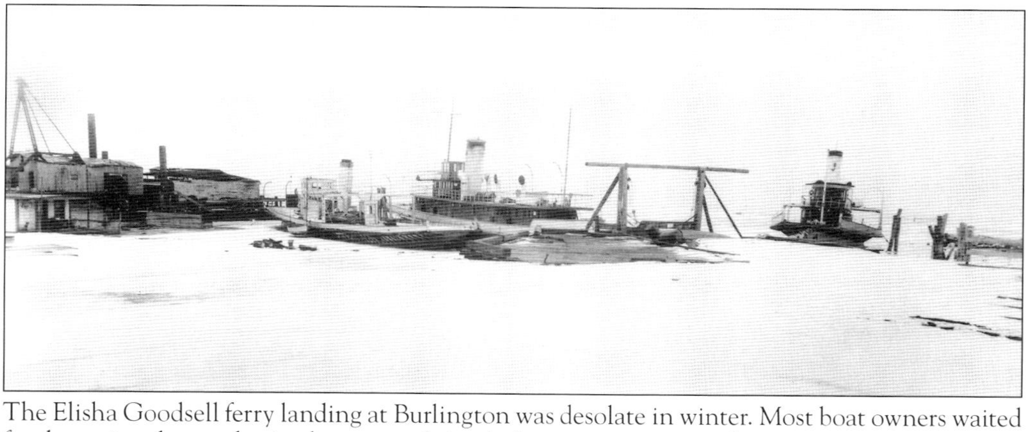

The Elisha Goodsell ferry landing at Burlington was desolate in winter. Most boat owners waited for the spring thaw to begin the seasonal ritual of repair, scraping, and painting. Some boats were hauled out on the shore to minimize potential damage caused by the ice. Goodsell's fleet of former yachts working as ferries remained in the water and suffered ice damage. (UVM.)

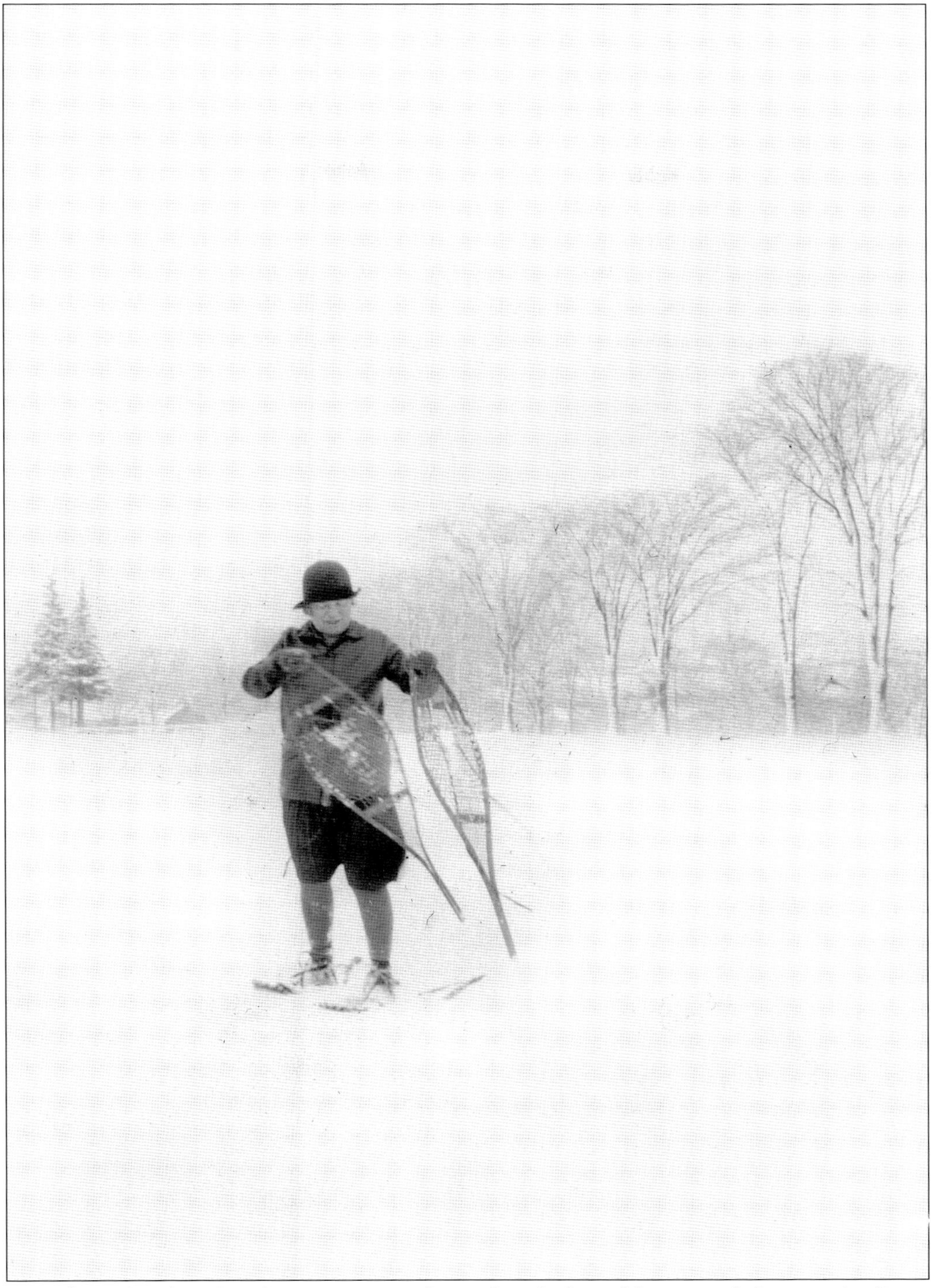

Snowshoer Caroline Beach is wearing traditional rawhide and bent wood shoes at the Basin Harbor Club, Vermont. Red decorative tassels around the rims indicated that the maker was Abenaki. (BHC.)

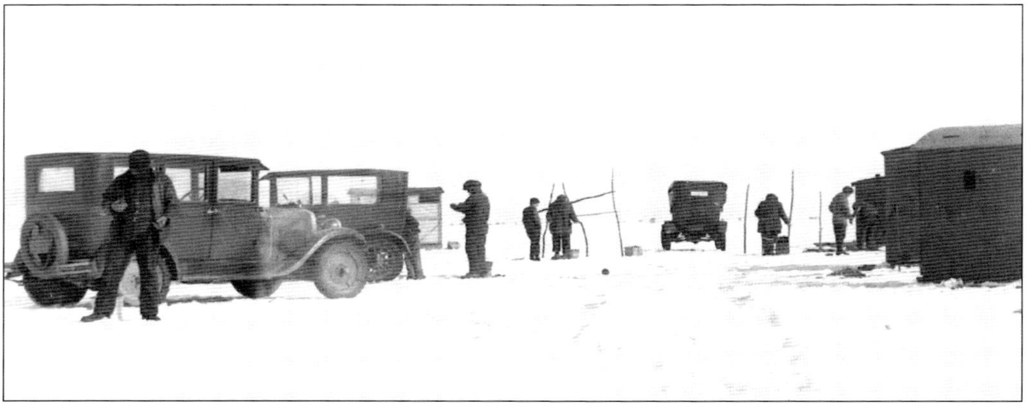

Ice shanties could be used from year to year, hauled out either by car (above) or on runners. Charlie Blow photographed the couple below, wearing fur coats and standing beside their Hupmobile on the ice at Burlington in the mid-1910s. (Both, EAB.)

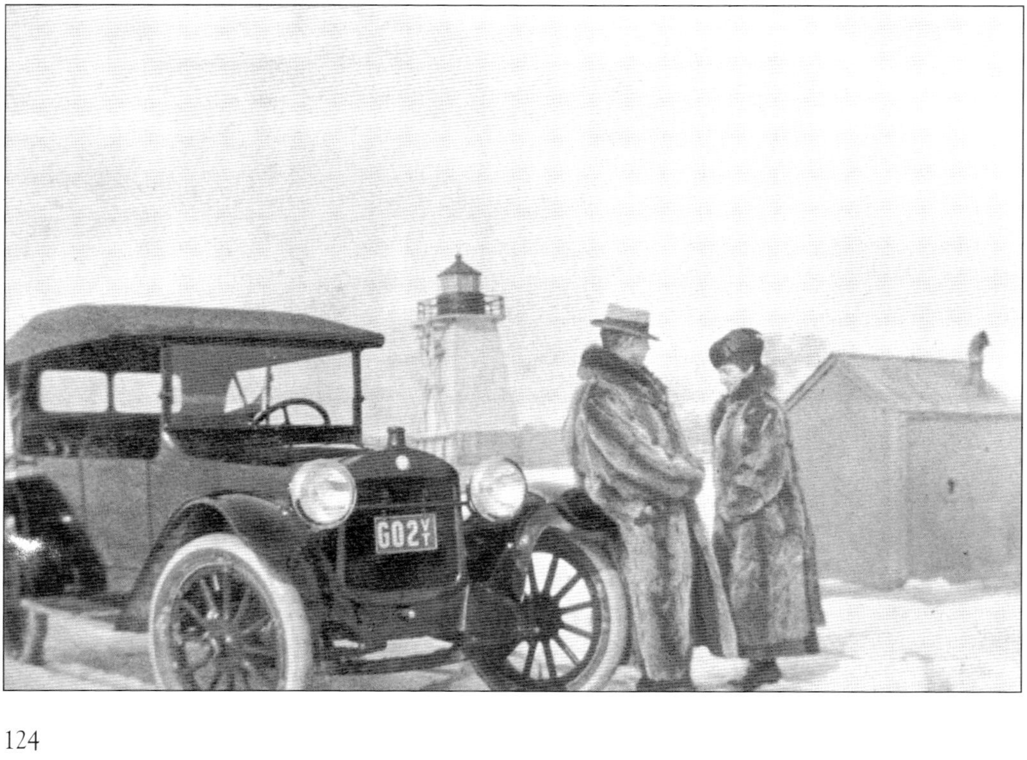

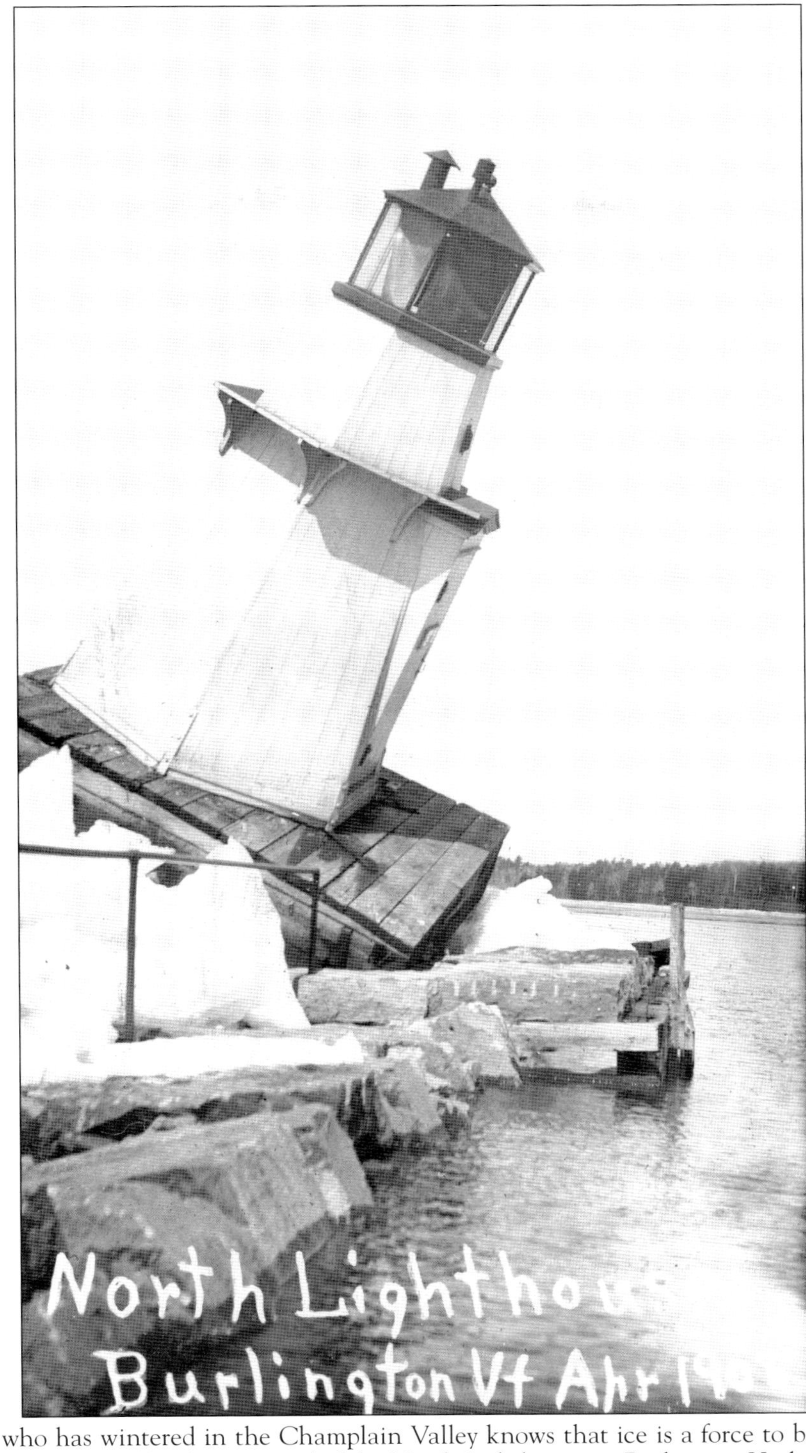

Anyone who has wintered in the Champlain Valley knows that ice is a force to be reckoned with, as demonstrated by this postcard of the North Lighthouse, in Burlington Harbor, taken in April 1908. (LCMM.)

Index

About Lake Champlain Maritime Museum

A museum that makes a difference, the Lake Champlain Maritime Museum brings underwater discoveries and lake history to the public in exciting and imaginative ways. Exhibits and programs showcase life on and around Lake Champlain, teaching maritime skills and encouraging stewardship of cultural and natural resources. Museum visitors step aboard 1776 gunboat replica *Philadelphia II*, while 1862 canal schooner replica *Lois McClure* travels to regional ports of call as a floating ambassador. LCMM's fieldwork, research, and collections document over 300 historical shipwrecks, as well as underwater cultural sites. Visitors explore 14 exhibit buildings and enjoy boat rides, special events, courses and workshops, and the museum store on a family-friendly campus beside beautiful Lake Champlain. The museum is open daily from late May through mid-October. Educational programs and archaeological research take place throughout the year. Visit www.lcmm.org.

Consistent with our mission to preserve history on a local level, this book was printed in South Carolina on American-made paper and manufactured entirely in the United States. Products carrying the accredited Forest Stewardship Council (FSC) label are printed on 100 percent FSC-certified paper.

MADE IN THE USA